Albert P Whitaker, Jr
925 Liberty Street
Rockland, Mass

11-14-58

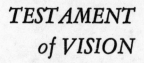

TESTAMENT
of VISION

TESTAMENT
of VISION

by
HENRY ZYLSTRA
Professor of English Literature
Calvin College

1941 - 1956

Wm. B. Eerdmans Publishing Company
Grand Rapids, Michigan

Preface

Hardly had the news of Dr. Henry Zylstra's death in Amsterdam reached these shores than the faculties of Calvin College and Seminary acted to preserve his writings and addresses in an appropriate collection. At the first meeting of interested colleagues, W. Harry Jellema, Henry J. Stob, and John J. Timmerman were requested to serve as the central committee to prepare such a volume. Subsequently, Lester R. DeKoster, George G. Harper, and Steve J. Van Der Weele were added to this committee, of which Henry Stob served as chairman. After several months of collecting and examining the extant manuscripts, we present this volume as best representing, in our opinion, the range and excellence of Dr. Zylstra's work. It is with regret that we were compelled, through limitations of space, to exclude many choice pieces which likewise begged for admission to this anthology. We have, however, included at the end of this volume a complete list of Dr. Zylstra's writings and have indicated where they may be found.

Two acknowledgements are in order. We are grateful first of all to William B. Eerdmans, Sr. for his early encouragement of this project and his willingness to act as publisher of the book. We are also deeply indebted to Mildred Zylstra for generously supplying us with a number of the manuscripts for this volume, for her cooperation during its preparation, and for reading the final proof.

It has been a pleasure for the committee to serve its colleagues and friends in preparing this volume for publication. It is the committee's hope that this book may in some way perpetuate the deeds and words of our beloved colleague, teacher, and friend.

STEVE J. VAN DER WEELE

Introduction

Henry Zylstra, the Man and His Work

Many of the late Dr. Zylstra's contributions to the Reformed and even wider evangelical community can survive only in memory and emulation. True it is that time will but slowly efface the radiance of his conversation and public address; only gradually will it erode his remembered wisdom in conference and committee. But a rarely gifted personality is primarily a visual and auditory memory and neither easily recorded nor shared. Fortunately, his pen was indefatigable. In the twenty odd years of his writing he filled many pages in learned journals like the *P.M.L.A.*, in semi-popular journals like *The Calvin Forum* and *The Reformed Journal,* and in a popular magazine like *The Banner.* These pieces together with sundry unpublished addresses have a relevance and availability which it would be immoral to neglect. To anthologize the best of them and to share them with sympathetic readers has been the aim of our Editorial Committee and the faculty group which appointed us.

Willa Cather once said that a book "is made with one's own flesh and blood of years. It is cremated youth." Henry Zylstra's writings have their roots deep in a rich texture of varied human experience. His was a full life both extensively and intensively. From a South Dakota farmhouse to the Widener Library at Harvard, from Calvin to Japan, and from Japan to Amsterdam takes in a large sweep of scenery and human experience. He knew struggle and frustration as well as conquest and honor. His boyhood was spent on the open plain of South Dakota where was fostered his permanent love for nature and growing things. He liked the feel of soil and the push and burgeoning of flower and plant. He lived in rural communities till he entered Calvin College as a sophomore in the fall of 1928. Parental piety and the nurture of his church early made him aware of "the inescapable God," to use his own phrase, who controls man and nature. The friendliness and human sympathy natural to these rural communities deepened his innate kindliness. Early aware of central realities of human experience, bound to nature, man, and God, trained in the rich Reformed tradition, he began his higher education with deep and nourishing roots that served him well.

Zylstra's formal education was impressive in its range and depth. At Calvin he majored with distinction in English, debated with brilliance, and engaged in varied and colorful extra-curricular activities. After assisting at Calvin for one year, he took his Master's degree in German at Iowa State University. Following several more years of teaching on the high school and the college level, he entered upon graduate work at Harvard where he received his Ph.D. in Comparative Literature, writing his dissertation upon "E. T. A. Hoffman in England and America." His graduate studies were pursued with outstanding diligence and rewarded with prizes and fellowships. His scholarship was wide and meticulous, illuminated with imaginative reach and mediated with the Christian faith. His voice was never the drone of the reproductive bookworm, the arid master of bibliographies and sterile literary history. He knew not only what authors had said but what they meant, not only in their special context, but for us — now. His scholarship was not cerebral but human.

He then served Calvin College from 1941-1943, when his work was interrupted by service with the Armed Forces in the South Pacific and Japan. He received the Bronze Star for "unusually meritorious service." From 1947 to 1956 he served as Professor of English at Calvin. He became Chairman of that department in 1950 and served on various important committees. During that time the calibre of his work was recognized by a Ford Foundation Fellowship and a Fulbright Professorship at the Free University in Amsterdam.

Zylstra was a rarely gifted classroom personality. Undergirded by meticulous scholarship, illuminated by imaginative reach, and mediated by Calvinistic conviction, his teaching encountered the student with an unforgettable experience. He understood books from the inside; he went *through* them with his students. The winnowing of values was done by an understanding heart, and that made the judgment humane and compelling. The apt and sparkling phrase, the sunny humor, the delicate understanding of students, the God-centered interpreting mind made his teaching indelible.

He did not confine his services to the classroom. He spent himself freely on college committees and gave himself largely to the Christian schools and the Christian Reformed Church through speeches and conference. He charmed and inspired many audiences in Christian Reformed circles from New Jersey to California. Yet during all these years he was writing, giving and sharing his educational and literary insights. This book in the opinion of the Editorial Committee comprises the best of that legacy to us. The book speaks for itself; it would be presumptuous for me to encumber the prospective reader with extended explicatory data. I may, however, make a few general comments.

The mind that is herein revealed, though devoutly and thoroughly Reformed, is in no sense provincial or ethnocentric. Zylstra was interested in truth, in healing water, and the particular conduit through which it might flow made no difference to him. He was enriched by various disciplines and brought the full gift of his critical intelligence to the duty of integration. Thus he drew heavily and impartially upon Anglo-Catholics like Eliot and Auden, upon Roman Catholics like Greene and Mauriac as well as upon Reformed writers like Kuyper, Bavinck, and Buitendyk. He found usable insights in novelists like Faulkner and Steinbeck and poets like Yeats and Bridges. He was committed to making relevant the best that had been thought and written and integrating that with the faith once delivered.

Zylstra as a critic sought for the spirit of masterpieces, the mind that informed the works of art. Not that he undervalued formal excellence, but rather that he believed form depends organically upon meaning and substance, and that ultimately literature has to be judged by theological criteria. Hence the critical essays and reviews in this volume are not in the mode of the currently fashionable formalistic critics who are preoccupied with a writer's manipulation of material, with function and organization, often to the neglect of the total worth of the formed content. The essays are concerned with basic principles. They see literature as a memorable expression of the essence of a culture, a culture to be judged by its approximation to a criterion theologically defined. They do this without annoying dogmatism because Zylstra was fully aware of the personalistic element that infiltrates criticism, the inevitability of a measure of taste and subjectivism. Literary judgment is not science.

The essays on education are a reminder of the importance of sound tradition, a recognition of the peril of disregarding cultural roots, of the immersion in the merely contemporary. They constitute an eloquent restatement of the importance of truly liberal education, of the supreme necessity of producing whole men rather than partial men professionalizing. They are conservative in the best sense, that of making relevant the best that has been thought and written to our little moment in time. What he sought in short was to make all things subservient to the mind of Christ.

These writings, it must be said, are not always easy. They rise from profound reflection and demand close attention. The prose is rich, varied, and brilliantly structured; it is a vehicle of critical intelligence rather than poetic sensibility. It is a natural, organic medium for an incisive intellect. It moves by precise and ordered statement rather than by metaphor and suggestion. It is sinewy and tough but always adequate and rewarding.

It is not possible to close this introduction on an analytical note. Henry Zylstra was through the grace of God a burning and a shining light which to our finite understanding would seem to have been prematurely darkened. His was a constantly growing spirit whose final reach seemed distant. Richly rooted in the Reformed tradition, unusually well-acquainted with Dutch culture, splendidly disciplined in English literature, widely read in German Letters, intimate through recent intensive study with contemporary English and American novelists and poets, bringing to bear upon hard study a sensitive Christian spirit and a fine critical intelligence, Zylstra seemed to be ready for a full flowering. But God had better plans for him and we can only be thankful for what he was and did. Robert Bridges, a former poet laureate of England, poured his deepest wisdom into a stately and noble poem, *The Testament of Beauty*. These writings of Henry Zylstra we also regard as a testament, as a legacy of his finest, always forward-looking insights, as, indeed, a testament of vision.

JOHN TIMMERMAN

Contents

Part One

LITERATURE AND LIFE

1

Literature and Dogma

If you really want to get at the spirit of an age and the soul of a time you can hardly do better than to consult the literature of that age and that time. In the novels and stories and poems and plays of a period you have a good indication of what, deep down, that period was about. I am thinking now, of course, of the real literature, the honest and soul-searching literature, the valid and undissimulating literature. I am not thinking of the quantities of drug store fiction, sure-fire Broadway hits, "slick" magazine stories, or of the tons of synthetic entertainment and pastime books in which people in our time seem determined to hide from themselves and their problems.

But of that significant literature of any period it can certainly be said that it is as a face on which the soul of the time is written. Thus, if you want to know the very quality of the Western mind when the Middle Ages had broken up but the new world of the Baconian science had not yet defined itself, you do well to look to the plays of Shakespeare. Or, more specifically, if you would like to know whether the Reformation sense of sin and guilt did not sometimes break through that Renaissance sense of the goodness of man and the world, you do well to study the *Hamlet*.

And so it is of the literature of other times and places. That exuberant hope, for example, which the romanticists entertained, namely, that things would change and the revolution would come if only an intuitive *Vernunft* were substituted for a rationalistic *Verstand,* is it not written plain and large in the book of Goethe's *Faust,* Carlyle's *Sartor Resartus,* Shelley's *Prometheus Unbound,* and Emerson's *Essays?* Or, again, if you want to see, a little later in the nineteenth century, what becomes of both the *Verstand, i.e.,* the Enlightenment, and the *Vernunft, i.e.,* the roman-

tic idealism, you can again turn to literature as the barometer for
gauging the spiritual weather. Arnold, for instance, who had
hoped that the spirit and values of Christianity could be maintained after its dogmatic supports had been destroyed, is very
pessimistic in his "Dover Beach":

> The Sea of Faith
> Was once, too, at the full, and round earth's shore
> Lay like the folds of a bright girdle furled.
> But now I only hear
> Its melancholy long withdrawing roar....

Tennyson, too, felt the old certainties faltering as Strauss and
Renan and Feuerbach came in the wake of Voltaire and substituted something called science for faith. Tennyson tried to cling
to both but he had his troubles:

> We have but faith: we cannot know,
>   For knowledge is of things we see;
> And yet we trust....

A generation later these fading certainties of Arnold and Tennyson, of Fitzgerald and James Thomson, become the total disillusionment of and despondency of Hardy and Houseman. The
century that had come in so bouyantly with Wordsworth saying
"Bliss was it in that dawn to be alive" goes out with God saying
in Hardy's poem "A Plaint to Man":

> ... I dwindle day by day
> Beneath the deicide eye of seers
> In a light that will not let me stay.

Not only did God for Hardy thus pine away under the glaring
scrutiny of science: He died while under examination, and Hardy
buried Him in his poem called "God's Funeral."

This same Thomas Hardy, deeply despondent, wrote his poem
"The Darkling Thrush" on the eve of the 1900s. On a disagree-
ably dank day and in a dismally bleak surrounding, symbolic both
of them of the spiritual morale at century's end, the doughty little
bird with its "blast beruffled plume" hurls its gay song upon the
air. Hardy heard it, and wrote:

> So little cause for carolings
>   Of such ecstatic sound
> Was written on terrestrial things
>   Afar or nigh around,

That I could think there trembled through
His happy good-night air
Some blessed hope, whereof he knew
And I was unaware.

Such was the culmination of the scientific liberalism and the romantic liberalism of the nineteenth century: such was the end of the Rationalistic and Idealistic efforts. Both of these offshoots of Renaissance humanism — the Enlightenment, *die Aufklarung*, on the hand, and the Idealism, *die Romantik,* on the other — continue green and alive in our own time, it is true. But it cannot be said that they are thriving. Both of them flourished in a climate of humanism; both of them came up out of the dogma of the natural goodness of man. And it is precisely on this fundamental level of religious assumption that our century is beginning to change from its predecessors.

If the witness of a large and important segment of the contemporary literature is to be trusted at all, we can say that the dogmatic change now being realized in our western world is a bigger change than took place when the *Verstand* of the age of Voltaire became the *Vernunft* of the age of Goethe. The difference is bigger than the difference between Rationalism and Romanticism. Those two differed significantly from each other, for they were not identical twins. But in the end the common parentage of Renaissance humanism and the family trait of the natural goodness of man outweigh the individual differences in the scale of importance. We can call the two by the common name of Liberalism. And in speaking now of an important spiritual change from it, we can call it a change from Liberalism to Religion.

To say that the contemporary literature indicates a change in basic assumptions so fundamental as that expressed by the difference between Liberal Man and Religious Man is to put forward a big claim about an important matter, and some warrant for it must be given. There follows, accordingly, some account of a few of the more representative literary witnesses to the changing dogmatic climate in our twentieth-century world.

One of the first men of letters of our age to distinguish between what he called the religious attitude and the humanist attitude was Mr. T. E. Hulme. The work of this influential young Englishman, consisting for the most part of literary and general philosophical criticism, and also of some Imagist poems, was, after his death in battle during World War I, collected and published in a book called *Speculations*. As early as 1912 he addressed a group at Cambridge, England, on the subject "Anti-Romanticism and Original Sin." He felt that a shift in attitude from Romantic pride to Classical humility was overdue.

Hulme discriminated but two periods in the history of our West:

> The first . . . is that of the Middle Ages in Europe — from Augustine, say, to the Renaissance; the second from the Renaissance to now. The ideology of the first period is religious; of the second, humanist.

By the religious attitude he meant the humility proper to radical human imperfection; and by the humanist attitude he meant the pride of disposing of absolute standards and accepting life as the measure of all values. The modern mind for him was essentially one mind from its beginnings in the humanist or "natural goodness" attitude:

> In spite of its extreme diversity, all philosophy since the Renaissance is at bottom the same philosophy. . . . The obvious diversity is only that of the various species of the same genius. . . . It all rests on the same conception of the nature of man, and exhibits the same inability to realize the meaning of the dogma of Original Sin.

What is particularly interesting in Hulme is the way in which he struggled with the problem of destroying in the mind of the humanist "the conviction that his own attitude is the inevitable attitude of the emancipated and instructed man." He recommended for this what he called the historical method. Since this method comes pretty close to defining what we all mean when we say that Christian higher education is necessary for disenthralling ourselves from the modern mind, we educators in all kinds may care to take special note of it:

> I think that history is necessary in order to *emancipate* the individual from certain *pseudo-categories*. We are all of us under the influence of a number of abstract ideas, of which we are as a matter of fact unconscious. We do not see them, but see other things *through* them. . . . Just as a knowledge of the colours extended and separated in the spectrum enables us to distinguish the feebler

colours confused together in the shadows, so a knowledge of these ideas, as it were *objectified,* and *extended* in history enables us to perceive them hidden in our own minds. Once they have been brought to the surface of the mind, they lose their *inevitable* character. They are no longer categories. We have lost our *naivete.*

A writer of much greater scope than Hulme, who has taken Hulme's cue, and who talks what is almost Hulme's language, is Mr. Wystan H. Auden. This distinguished poet-critic, English by birth and breeding, but American now by citizenship, has put a good deal of his prose and some of his lyrical and dramatic poetry into the exposure of the Liberal mind. He had himself explored several of the avenues of this mind, for example, the Freudian, the Marxian, and the aesthetic, before entering upon the religious way. In 1941, however, he wrote in *The Intent of the Critic:*

> ... we are all agreed on one thing: that the times through which we are now living mark the end of a period which, for convenience, we can say began with the Renaissance ... The statement, "Man is a fallen creature, with a natural bias to do evil," and the statement, "Men are good by nature and made bad by society," are both presuppositions ... If, as I do, you assent to the first, your art and politics will be very different from what they will be if you assent, like Rousseau or Whitman, to the second.

Considerably influenced by the Danish Kierkegaard, Auden in 1944 wrote the Christmas oratorio *For the Time Being* in which there is a fine contrast between the positivistic, rationalistic, and presumably modern mind of Herod and the Christian realism of Simeon. In 1947, still moving in the wake of Kierkegaard, he wrote his play *The Age of Anxiety.* This title is sometimes taken in newspaper editorials and the popular press generally to refer to the fear in which people of our day live because of the atom and hydrogen bombs. It was not any such natural fear, of course, that Auden was thinking of, but a religious fear such as can hardly be generated within the compass of the liberal mind. And in that former work Auden wrote: "Because of His visitation, we may no longer desire God as if He were lacking: our redemption is no longer a question of pursuit but of surrender to Him ... Therefore at every moment we pray that, following Him, we may depart from our anxiety into His peace."

[19]

The literary testament of Thomas Stearns Eliot is an even more formidable foe to the modern mind than is the word of Auden. It should be safe to say that, outside of Roman Catholic circles at least, Eliot's voice is the strongest lay voice that has been heard against Liberalism in our century. He has steadily affirmed the religious as distinguished from the humanist attitude, and he has effectively brought the post-Enlightenment and post-Romantic mentality to bay. Ever since giving out his *Ash Wednesday,* composed in the late twenties, he has, particularly in the poem sequence called *Four Quartets,* and in his successive dramas, borne in upon the modern man the inescapability of religious choice.

In this achievement, it would seem that Dante and Pascal have influenced Eliot most, but there is in him something also of the newer existentialist religious awareness. Eliot thinks of the people of our late-Renaissance world as lost, Laodicean souls, evasive, hollow, undone, because they refuse to work out their redemption by a conscious choice of the will:

> Our age is an age of moderate virtue
> And of moderate vice
> When men will not lay down the Cross
> Because they will not assume it.
> Yet nothing is impossible, nothing,
> To men of faith and conviction.
> Let us therefore make perfect our will.
> O God, help us.

Eliot's sense of the moral innocuousness and grey neutrality of people in what Auden calls "the late age" is confirmed also by such a literary critic as the English Mr. Derek S. Savage. In his book *The Withered Branch,* which is interesting in itself as an estimate of modern literature viewed from a dogmatic vantage point, Mr. Savage delineates the liberal mind as

> a *medium* mind, a mind which fears extremes and which therefore is predisposed towards compromise . . . The compromising tendency of liberalism causes it to give mental hostages both to the realm of ideals and to the world of affairs, but it is rooted in the latter and in a crisis it is the latter which proves the stronger. Liberalism is a half-hearted creed . . . making a gesture of more or less sincerity toward spiritual values . . . Those spiritual values, however, tend to become something rather less than the

ultimate and therefore terrifying ones. The absolute is carefully excluded from the liberal way of life.

It is this kind of mentality, stopping well short of the ultimate and terrifying values, that Mr. Eliot has tried to reach and disturb. He speaks of the people who have it as unable to bear very much reality, and he tells us that such people

> ...constantly try to escape
> From the darkness outside and within
> By dreaming of systems so perfect
> that no one will need to be good.

Auden and Eliot are by no means alone in this reassertion of the role of faith in life and literature. Their younger successors such as Anne Ridler, Sidney Keyes, John Heath-Stubbs, David Gascoyne, Norman Nicholson, and others, are also writers whose work comes from an acknowledged Christian belief. And what is one to say, in this quick account of the changing dogmatic temper of our time, of the massive Catholic literary witness in these decades of our century? The quality and scope of the work is staggering; a mere catalogue of the bigger names is itself impressive: Leon Bloy, Charles Peguy, St. John Perse, George Bernanos, Ernst Psichari, Paul Claudel, Francois Mauriac, Ignazio Silone, Gerard Manley Hopkins, Graham Greene, Evelyn Waugh, and many besides. Their work is nothing if it is not a spiritual protest to the fundamental bearings of the Renaissance mentality, that is, to the Baconian-Rousseauist moral world.

No, the names are not enough. A token paragraph at least must go to fleshing the skeleton of this powerful Catholic body of writing. Take Leon Bloy, for instance, whose life spanned the second half of the last and about two decades of our own century, and who has powerfully influenced so many contemporaries, Jacques and Raissa Maritain among them. If T. S. Eliot is right in saying that "the greatest proof for Christianity for others, is not how far a man can logically analyze his reasons for believing, but how far in practice he will stake his life on his belief," then Leon Bloy was a great soul winner for the Catholic faith. He was radically thoroughgoing about his conviction.

Deeply disillusioned by what his biographer, Emmanuela Polimeni, calls the spiritual dearth at the end of the nineteenth century and the inadequacy of the Balzacian conception of life, Bloy nevertheless before his death felt the "slight breeze" of a new spiritual discontent stirring in the twentieth century air:

> A new current is at work among us... The intellectuals are in search of God, and many no longer fear to ask publicly and openly to know our Lord Jesus Christ... Pharisaism cannot continue to hold sway over men's minds, for the day is approaching when God will vomit from his mouth merely respectable Catholicism.

The fact is that one gets from the modern novels of Bernanos, Mauriac, and Graham Greene an exploration of moral evil and of good far beyond the ability of a liberal Hardy, Wells, or Huxley to delineate, and far beyond the range also of a naturalistic Ernest Hemingway or D. H. Lawrence.

Those, it will be understood, are but a representative few of the writers of our period who signalize unmistakably that in a considerable segment of the literary world a spiritual change is in progress. In fact, things have reached the point at which a person would hesitate to profess modern literature except he have a fairly good knowledge of theology. Hardly a book of criticism appears without its chapter or two on the knotty problem of literature and belief. Such terms as Natural Goodness, Original Sin, the Fall of Man, Creation, Grace, the Pelagian Heresy, and the like, weave in and out of literary discussion as familiarly as they did in the older theological treatises. Amos N. Wilder is right when he says in his book *Modern Poetry and the Christian Tradition:* "much of the literary criticism of our time inevitably passes over into what can be called a theological level."

The fact is that one goes nowadays for some of the best accounts of poetry and fiction, not to the literary journals, but to *The Hibbert Journal,* to *Theology Today,* and to *The Journal of Bible and Religion.* This is a sort of acknowledgement on the part of theologians and churchmen that there is a high religious vitality in modern literature and something also of a prophetic dimension. Professor Wilder goes so far as to suggest that the strongest Christian testimony of our years is coming from the laymen, not from the clergy. Such a man as C. S. Lewis, for instance, who writes those many arresting books of Christian apology, is professionally a literary historian, and by avocation a writer of religious romances. His friend, the late Mr. Charles Williams, was also a lay theologian. He wrote books on church history and doctrine, and produced, in addition to his poetry, a good half-dozen novels of religious phantasy.

So considerable and so effective has this anti-liberalism in modern letters become that it is already eliciting a reaction from those who want to continue in the way of scientific or romantic humanism. Thus, the American critical weekly, *The Saturday Review,* is in its editorial position always either tacitly or expressively opposed to the returning dogmatic bases of life and literature. Thus, too, the English paper called *The Literary Outlook* vindicates its existence mainly by its opposition to the "new" religious attitude. One of the writers for the *Outlook* last year published a book called *The Emperor's Clothes,* the whole burden of which was that the new attitude posed the threat of "medieval" authoritarianism and benightedness. What bothered the author, Miss Kathleen Nott, was this:

> ... the writers whom I discuss and whom I call neo-scholastic ... are reverting at various speeds and from various directions to a pre-scientific philosophy ... Chief among the doctrines which they try to import into our intellectual outlook is the dogma of original sin, which is certainly the psychological foundation of Christian orthodoxy.

If it be granted, then, as Professor Wilder said, that "the creative, imaginative expressions are often our best clues to the diagnosis of men's hearts and the deeper movements of an age," we can perhaps be allowed the conclusion that interesting things are happening to the modern mind. Writers are no longer saying, as the novelist E. M. Forster said in *I Believe* a few years back: "I do not believe in Belief." And he added: "My motto is 'Lord, I disbelieve — help thou my unbelief.'" In fairness to him it must be said that he was thinking of irrational totalitarianisms when he said it. But that is the spirit of the Enlightenment and not the spirit of Religion.

The new spirit, as it comes out in this large segment of the modern literature, is another spirit. Ignazio Silone speaks of it thus: "The rediscovery of a Christian heritage in the revolution of our time remains the most important gain that has been made in these last years for the conscience of our generations." It may be that after four hundred years we are due, not just for a change of thought, but for a change of attitude, not just for a change of mind, but for a change of faith. Even Stephen Spender, a poet of Auden's generation, who does not share in the changing convictions, admits in his book, *The Creative Element*, that the remarkable thing about modern literature is precisely this: "Today there is a reaction towards orthodoxy, and the most vital movement in literature in the West is religious."

The Reformed Journal, March, 1955.

2

The Role of Literature in Our Time

What I have to say in this paper is that literature is important and that we should maintain and enhance its importance in the schools. I submit for your consideration this idea, that we teachers of English on the several levels of school and college will do best if in our interpretation of literature we look upon it as humane letters, as one of the humanities. My suggestion is that we should regard literature as humane letters rather than as *belles lettres,* that we think of it as one of the humanities rather than as one of the fine arts. My idea is that unless we think of literature in this way, literature will lose importance for us, and will lose status and dignity in the schools. And by way of applying this principle of interpretation, I shall try to make these points: (1) that in our teaching of literature we make it an exacting discipline; (2) that we teach it intensively rather than in historical survey; (3) that in the selections of literature which we teach intensively, we should nevertheless honor the historical sequence; (4) that we make our students achieve the personal experience of literature; and (5) that we try to give literature more time in the schools than we are currently giving it.

Just a little look backwards should be enough to remind us that in an important way literature has lost status in the schools. Consider it historically. In the Christian medieval and humanistic renaissance periods the schoolboy was put through the paces of his *literae humaniores,* that is, through his humane letters, or literature, by way of Latin. He got his letters by way of the horn-book, committed Lilly's or some other Latin Grammar to what was called the "ventricle of the memory" and then worked his way up through seven or more forms of the tower of learn-

ing to the Greek and Roman and Christian classics of literature.
In the schools as well as at the universities, literature in the form
of humane letters was the main course of his diet, the meat of his
meal, the core of his education. A schooled man was a lettered
man, one who knew his letters, his literature. It was as a man
of letters that he counted; he had to count that way or he did not
count.

Humane letters thus continued to be the core of school and
college education until pretty well into the last century. Such an
education was an aristocratic education, an education intended
for the privileged few. It was an education which was not seriously challenged until that disintegration which began in the renaissance culminated in the democracy, the science, and the industrialism of the nineteenth century. You know what evolved.
Out of democracy this evolved, that everybody came to school.
Out of the new science this evolved, that the natural sciences,
which had theretofore hovered over the boundary of the province
of knowledge, now became the principal landholder within it.
And out of the industrialism this evolved, that there was a demand for the practical and vocational. In the second half of the
century, Matthew Arnold and Thomas Huxley fought out the
issues between the values of a general education in literature and
a specialized education in applied science. We know now that
Huxley won the battle, not, be it said, because he was the abler
contender, but because he had the momentum of the time behind
him. When Arnold saw that the traditional education in literature was at bay, he did his heroic best to indicate why a literary
general education was indispensable in a democratic and industrial society. But Arnold could not, of course, with his single
hand, stem the onrushing tide of science and utility.

It was so, roughly sketched, that the attention of the student
in the school and college got dispersed over more and more subjects. New arts and sciences began emerging and pressing their
plausible claims for a share of attention, and they got it. It is in
this sense I meant it when I said that it seemed to me literature
has lost status in the schools.

Nevertheless, I am convinced that we, as teachers of English,
ought occasionally to take a full look at that old traditional education and at what it was about with its tradition-sanctioned emphasis upon literature as the core of a student's general education. For it is from the role and function of literature in that

older education that, it seems to me, we ought to learn its role and function in our time.

For it was then thought that literature was important, literally full of import. You remember, perhaps, how Arnold, in defense of the tradition, argued: "We should," he said, "conceive of poetry [by poetry he means literature in the broad sense of the German *Dichtung*] more worthily and more highly than it has been the custom of conceiving of it .... More and more mankind will discover that we have to turn to poetry to interpret life for us ... to sustain us. Without poetry, our science will appear incomplete." And, in another place, Arnold goes on to say that "the great men of culture [he means men of letters in this present broad sense] have labored to divest knowledge of all that was harsh, uncouth, difficult, abstract, professional, exclusive, to humanize it, to make it efficient outside of the clique of the cultivated and learned, and yet still remaining the best knowledge and thought of the time." It is precisely in this spirit of Arnold's account of what literature is that Wordsworth before him maintained this: that poetry is the breath and finer spirit of all knowledge. "If the labor of the men of science," he added, "should ever create any material revolution, direct or indirect, in our condition . . . the poet will be ready to follow the footsteps of the man of science. . . . The remotest discoveries of the chemist, the botanist, of mineralogist, will be as proper objects of the poet's art as any upon which it can be employed, if (and mark the condition) the time should ever come when these things shall be familiar to us." Well, there, then, you have the old familiar ideas: that the area of literature is the great central area of human concern; that the man of letters cares not for knowledge that is harsh, uncouth, difficult, abstract, professional, and exclusive; that the man of letters is unperturbed by the knowledge which is not humanly significant, familiar and real, but that when knowledge is that, he takes it and transmutes it into vital form. Knowledge thus transmuted is literature, is humane letters, and should be the principal means to education.

So conceived literature is greatly important. It is full of all kinds of import — religious, philosophical, social, practical, and other. Meanwhile it remains literature, does not become something else. Literature is not philosophy, but is full of philosophical importance. What would Kant's influence have been without the Goethes, Schillers, Schlegels, Carlyles, and Emersons and Coleridges to humanize it and make it familiar? Literature is not history, but history when it is made real and familiar and is felt upon the pulses and in the heart is humanly significant history, is history in vital form, and that is literature. Literature is not natural science, but natural science is not humanly significant until it is seen in relation to all other human concerns, and when it is thus seen in relation to all other concerns and is captured in living form, it is literature, and is important. For literature, whatever else it is, is never specialized. It is forever and essentially the foe of specialization. It is committed to seeing life steadily and seeing it whole. That is why it can be of such indispensable service as an integrating influence in society. Literature, finally, to return to Arnold's series, is knowledge which is not harsh but mellow, not uncouth but shapely, not abstract but concrete, not professional but real, and not exclusive but common. So, said Wordsworth, the poet (the man of letters) binds together by passion and knowledge the vast empire of human society, as it is spread over the whole earth and over all time. This literature, this criticism of life, this wisdom of life, given us by gifted men alive and active with extraordinary power at an unusual number of points, touching, as Arnold used to say, on life at more points, and more powerfully at more points than other knowledges, this deserves recognition, continuing recognition in the schools and in the colleges.

Now this view of the importance of literature as humane letters was once, I say, and for a very, very long time the common view. It was most common and most effectively operative, of course, even before a Wordsworth or an Arnold, men who saw disintegration and discreteness undermining the common sense, the spiritual community, the continuing tradition of man, ever felt it was necessary to go to the defense of it. But this view of the importance of literature is not common now, and if we teachers of English are not to lose our nerve, and are to think better of ourselves than as being useful to throw a little coloring of what we call "culture" over a course of study made definite, substantial, and durable by other courses, we ought to return to something like this older view. For you know what the situation is. The whole body of literature, of humane letters, has fallen to the departments of English. There we are now: when we can afford to take time off from grammar, rhetoric, and composition, we try to get a smattering of human significance in the vital form of literature sneaked edgewise into the overburdened curricula of students impatient to get on to practical success.

Literature has lost status, and this is in part how that came about. Literature and the status of literature, both in real life, and in the schools, became the victim of those same disintegrating influences which make the body of human knowledge so discrete as it is in our time. When as a result, I think, though I have not time to demonstrate it now, as a result of the disappearance of a common religion and a common philosophy, scientific method began to make itself fruitfully felt, then each of the several provinces of knowledge, greatly increased as a result of the method, declared its independence from every other, staked out a claim of inquiry for itself, and made impressive autonomous progress within the compass of itself. The result was that the presses began pouring out millions of books and studies not literature but very certainly conforming to Arnold's description: harsh, uncouth, difficult, abstract, professional, and exclusive. Some of these now constitute the principal textbooks and subject matters of our pupils and students, these instead of literature. So it happened that after each of these provinces of knowledge pressed its busy and fruitful specializations for a while, literature found itself in a province of its own also. It was all its own but it was little. Literature found itself with the humane knocked off the letters and *belles* substituted for it. Literature found itself in the ivory tower.

At first that seemed to be all gain. Now for the first time literature seemed to the writers, the critics, and the teachers, to be free; it seemed to have divested itself of religious, and moral, and philosophical burdens. Now it could operate independently, tend to its own business, cultivate the aesthetic, aim at beauty, be art. Out with its philosophical import. A poem should not mean but be, MacLeish said. Out with its moral content; what was wrong with Arnold anyhow, and with his new humanist disciples, in insisting that literature, because it deals with life deals with morals, because morals are three-fourths of life? Out with morals: "There is no such thing," said Oscar Wilde, "as a moral or an immoral book; books are only badly or well written." Out with those other concerns, those extraneous concerns, let the poet, let the writer, let the artist cultivate beauty. Literature, it was now stressed, is a fine art, a very fine one, so fine it is precious, fine rather than liberal, a fine art rather than one of the humanities in vital form. The man of letters, so far from being alive and active with extraordinary power at an unusual number of points, is an artist, an artiste, a connoisseur of the beautiful, the beautiful independent of the true and the good, the beautiful anything, the beautiful thing. Men of letters, critics, and teachers concentrated their attention upon that in which literature differed from everything else, rather than upon that which it had in common with everything else. Criticism was no longer literary criticism; it was form criticism, technical criticism. In literature as in science the favorite word became technique. Of course, this was not all loss. The aesthetic movements in the several countries of the Western world, the art for art's sake movement, gained something, and to ignore the gain is to impoverish ourselves. But all the same literature lost importance.

It lost importance, and the men of letters, the writers, and critics, and the teachers noticed that it had lost it. They noticed that literature had lost status. They noticed that literature had lost dignity. The teachers noticed that the term Literary Department was dropping out of the nomenclature of the schools. Those at the universities noticed that the so-called Lit-School, still housed for tradition's sake in the oldest building on the campus where the rest of the relics of a humanistic past, such as Greek and philosophy, were also kept, was getting to have a pretty thin connotation. It began to be the common opinion on the campus that the substance of the university, that what mattered most to most students, that what impressed the constituency and therefore the President, and the Senate, and the Deans, was going on elsewhere at the University, namely, among the natural and the social sciences. Indeed, the only surprising thing was that the Lit-School was not put in the same building with Divinity, also thin, tenuous, and defunct, and that the teachers of literature did not put their collars on backwards like the clerics, they too being so singular and disoriented in this practical and scientific world.

Now a strange thing happened. When literature forfeited its importance by allowing humane letters to become *belles lettres,* and so lost status, it pleaded for re-admittance to serious consideration on another ground. It took another tack: it claimed to be scientific. Now when you went up to the university to study, you had to have a look around you, for there were various camps in the literature departments. There was still the aesthetic camp, consisting usually of gifted, brilliant young men, busy with their form studies, with what they called "poetry as poetry and not some other thing," ruling Milton out of the tradition because he

was crude in comparison with Donne, their envious eyes on La-
forgue and Pound and Hopkins. Dante gained new life, not because the teachers had got a new respect for Aquinas and Augustine, or appreciated Dante's giving vital form to the medieval system of thought and way of life, but because he was skillful in
metrics. There was also the linguistic, the philological camp. Its
devotees were scientific with a vengeance; they held that literary
achievement, judgment, taste, and value were conditioned by
linguistic studies scientifically pursued. In their hands Hamlet
became an episode in the development of grammar. There were
the social scientists seeking in literature for an illustration and a
demonstration of the sociological or economic or political conditioning of man in society. And there were also the psychologists:
in their hands the poems, the novels, the essays, the dramas, were
neglected. Instead the mothers, the nurses, the sweethearts, the
lives of the authors were scrutinized. Biography flourished. Poe
and Byron got a new lease on life because they made such interesting clinical specimens.

Happily both the aesthetic and scientific extremes in the interpretation of literature are being modified in late years. If I
read the most recent trend aright, something of the older view of
literature as humane letters, of literature as one of the humanities, is returning to the writers and to the schools and colleges.
One indication of this return to the broadly cultural role of literature is the attention that is being given to "cultural orientation
courses" in the colleges, to what is called "basic education programs." Others are the senior high school and junior college
program at Chicago, the St. John's experiment in the hundred
great books (most of which are, of course, literature), and the
ambitious adult education programs in cultural reading emanating
out of Chancellor Hutchins' office.

This new shift from the narrowly aesthetic and the merely
scientific approaches to literature can also be accounted for.
Western civilization is somewhat alarmed. That neutrality of
mind which accompanied the ripening of scientific method
in the nineteenth century has for some time now proved
wanting. It was the totalitarian spectre that frightened
us into an acknowledgment of the limitations of scientific
discreteness and atomism. Accordingly, over against Nazism,
Fascism, and Communism it seemed best, particularly in

the absence of religion and of any philosophy but the philosophy of scientism, to foster democracy by teaching the traditions of democracy. And those traditions are, of course, embodied in literature. Hence there is now hardly a collection of readings, anthology of prose pieces, or textbook in literature but has some such title as Pathways to Freedom, The Democratic Way, or Earning our Heritage. Clearly, this betokens an interest in the importance of the content as well as in the form of literature, and is cultural rather than scientific in its emphasis. The new trend to this extent seems to me a return to good sense. Only, when literature must do its work without the benefit of religion and philosophy, it becomes (as for Arnold it became) the only thing that can integrate life and make of it a culture and a civilization. In fact, our need for literature is so desperate now that we are likely to force it into something like propaganda for freedom or democracy. This role literature should refuse, for if it yields and becomes propaganda it will cease to be literature.

And this I say, that need for literature as an integrating influence is almost desperate in our time. I mean this in somewhat of Wordsworth's sense. Our contemporary situation is, after all, simply Wordsworth's contemporary situation greatly multiplied. Hear him: "For a multitude of causes unknown to former times are now acting with a combined force to blunt the discriminating powers of the mind, and unfitting it for all voluntary exertion, to reduce it to a state of almost savage torpor." That was Wordsworth. Now among the causes which thus blunt the discriminating power of the mind in our time two are prominent: the one is government and the other is economic propaganda. The import of both, what with the mass media of distributing propaganda on radio, press, and screen, is alarming enough. The best antidote to propaganda is truth, and truth in vital form is literature.

If, then, we go to the older view of literature as humane letters for our sense of its importance and function, we teachers of English will not feel that we have to be either "arty" or scientific in the modern sense to justify our place in the schools or colleges. If we come to look upon literature as nothing less than the most perfect speech of man, that in which he comes nearest to being able to utter the truth, we shall be able to maintain and enhance the importance and dignity of our subject. By keeping literature at least as closely allied to religion and philosophy as to music and painting we can contribute to keeping the word *cultural* from becoming as thin as even for Arnold it tended to become. For Arnold, poetry was an only stay. He had only tradition as embodied in letters to rely on for the continuity of civilization. Hence his need for literature as an integrating influence in society was quite desperate. "The civilized world," he argued, "is to be regarded as now being, for intellectual and spiritual purposes, one great confederation, bound to a joint action and working to a common result." For Arnold, literature alone was going to achieve this. And from our present vantage point, with our present hindsight, Arnold's "civilized world being for intellectual and spiritual purposes one great confederation, bound to a joint action" sounds as superficial and tinny as UNESCO propaganda. Certainly, literature cannot hang suspended in a philosophical and religious vacuum, and remain literature, that is, and not become propaganda. Arnold did not know this. We who know it will keep literature, as I say, closely allied with religion and philosophy, and so keep it from becoming merely aesthetic, merely scientific, and even merely cultural.

Perhaps you say, But is this indeed a refurbishing of the older view of the role and function of literature so necessary in what we call our circles? I think it is. I think that among us also, perhaps even among us teachers, something of this attenuation and perversion of the significance of literature has been operative. We too can be zealously scientific and practical sometimes and so develop a weak regard for the achievements of the literary departments of our school. For example, permit me to let you in on a peep behind the scenes at the college. We teachers there sometimes review the standings of weak students, and follow that by recommending a change in the student's program. Of one it is then said by those interested, "He can never make the Seminary." And of another, "We can't recommend him for graduate work in Engineering." And of a third, "He can't make the Med School." Well and good. It is true that this evolved from democracy that everybody comes to college. But what then? Dismiss him from school because his grades are not high enough? Why, no. Send him into the literary department. I suspect something in this kind occurs also in the high schools. Parents tell their children to get this in and that in at school, and, yes, finally, if there is time for it, a little English, poetry and such . . . it's cultural and they ought to have a little of it. This puts English in the same class as pink handkerchiefs and tea. Now frankly, are not the connotations of that pretty characteristic present even in what we call our circles? They are, and I suggest that we teachers of literature take a full look at its role and function as humane letters, as one of the humanities, before we allow ourselves to be pushed around that way. We should take our stand on the tradition-sanctioned reputation of literature as the heart and center of the general education of the student.

This brings me to a point or two in application. First, I suggest that in our teaching of literature we make the subject an exacting discipline. I sometimes ask myself whether there is not something to it, that as compared with the challenging disciplines of the foreign languages, as compared with the definite and measurable learning of the natural sciences, and as compared with the systematically pursued and factually informative social sciences, we teachers of English are not really sometimes pretty general, vague, and indefinite. Our subject seems to lend itself to interest more than to effort. The subject matter is so appealing that it is a delight. And in consequence of this, I think, we have been too willing to accept any student's first and careless reading of a piece of literature as good enough. But surely the competent and right reading of a piece of literature, the full appreciation, and the sound judgment of it, is as exacting and as challenging a discipline as anything in science. It requires calibre of mind, gift of imagination, and power of thought. The best are not too good for it, and some cannot achieve it. There is no real reason why language work should be easy, why English should be a snap, and why the flunk-lists should run higher in foreign languages, mathematics, and the natural sciences than in English. Mark now . . . I am not saying that we had better make English hard and disagreeable to keep it important. I say only that the doctrine of interest ought not to supplant but only to supplement the doctrine of effort in this subject quite as well as in others. I think we have been too easy.

I suggest by way of making our teaching of literature an exacting discipline, that in interpreting a poem or story or drama we assume first that the spirit killeth but the letter giveth life. Our students must learn that literature is more important than other forms of material in print precisely because it has vital form. It is in literature that details matter, and it is in the best literature that they matter most. The more severe the literary form, as in a sonnet, say, the more important the details. Now the attention to these details must be discriminating. Matters of structure, and style, and diction, and even punctuation are of great formal importance and require thorough and competent attention. I once asked a class of thirty freshmen to read Longfellow's simple little sonnet called *Nature* and beginning "As a fond mother when the day is done, Leads by the hand her little child to bed" and to state its theme. I discovered that fewer than half of them had any inkling that it was about death. Now if that sort of reading of a piece of literature is accepted as good enough, we shall never succeed in giving literature the dignity, even among our students, of an exacting discipline. And if that kind of full-ness of the appreciation of literature were to continue, we should report at faculty meetings that Johnny had better go into Pre-Med, or Pre-Sem, or Pre-Engineering. He hasn't wits enough to take English.

And, of course, after the critical analysis, after the word study and phrase study, after attention to denotation and connotation, after following out the figures of speech, the rhymes and the rhythms, and the elements that go into style, we should again re-verse the dictum and say it is the spirit that giveth life. But only afterwards: and the letter in order to get at the spirit, the letter because it is the only way to get at the spirit, the letter because if we get at the spirit in some other way, we get a different spirit, namely our own, and then we learn nothing. But all the same: the letter only to get at the spirit, at the full being and meaning of the literature, and to have that spirit fully then and influentially.

For it will not do, as I fear we sometimes do, to make the by-product the main product, or the means the end. We vindi-cate literature on such odd grounds sometimes. So we say it is good for a student because it improves his diction. But the end of the study of literature is not of course the improvement of dic-tion; the end of improved diction is the appreciation of literature. Why don't you give them Adler, I am sometimes told, on how to read a book. That will teach your students how to read a lot faster than all that literature. Well, I do sometimes give them Adler. But Adler ministers to literature, not literature to Adler. The object of literature is not word study: the object of word study is literature, the competent experience of it. This is so true that I am not ready to make a special course, or even a spe-cial part of a course, what is called word study. Words in con-text is the only place words mean anything specific and definite. Words in the context of literature mean most. Word study, very necessary, is impossible except in literature, and is incidental to it. Who that looks up words in a dictionary knows what they mean? No, the right understanding of literature as literature should be the motive of word study. And literature is the best form of it.

Enough for the moment of making literature an exacting discipline. I want to contend next that we maintain and enhance the importance of literature best by teaching it intensively. It has long seemed to me that of all subjects, literature lends itself least to a survey method. There is no substitute for literature. A textbook description of the history of literature, for instance, a textbook account of its origins, a characterization of its movements, a sketch of its principal monuments, and a survey of factual data about authors and their works, appealing as these are to the curriculum-crowded schools as a way "to cover the ground," seem to me to miss everything literature has to give. The history of literature is history and not literature. This kind of thing, it is true, makes testing easy; we can call for data, we can call for information, as if to say, see it is history really, or again, see, it is as definite as science. But this method begs the larger question, for literature is not data, is not information, and is always more than the sum of its parts. A teacher can stand up there before his class and trace origins and influences, describe environmental milieus, and survey critical opinion, and there is a limited use in this if only it aims at the heart of literature and does not move farther and farther away from it.

But a better method than this of historical survey, I feel altogether convinced, is the intensive one, the time-honored and time-tried one of what in the middle ages was called "glossing the text" and in France is still called *explication de texte*. It is a method which has this fine defense for itself: it always keeps the student's attention centered upon the first-rate. On this matter of intensive teaching I once wrote and now repeat, that teachers, especially teachers of literature, are likely to substitute secondary or tertiary matters for primary matters. Teachers of literature are likely to teach a novel or poem or play as representing this or that, the romantic movement, say, or as illustrating this or that, Greek influence, say, and to present poets and novelists and essayists as being the exponents of some school or other which only the meddling intellect of the historian can define. So the poem, the novel, the essay, tends to get lost in the science of classification, background is substituted for foreground, and the first-rate in literature is supplanted by the third rate in teacher or textbook. Instead of the breath and finer spirit of knowledge which is literature, we thus get a method of derivation, matters of influence and style and types — whether of classic, romantic, realistic, naturalistic, expressionistic, or what not and on down to as many adjectival examples of labeling as we can dig out of our inkwells or typewriters. And if with a show of reason it can be argued that the intensive method must be very selective in its concern for the best, and is therefore pursued at the cost of comprehensiveness, I ask, What of it? Can it not be plausibly argued that a full sense of the import of the *Iliad,* of Dante's vision, or a few of Shakespeare's plays, of the *Paradise Lost,* of some of the poetry of Wordsworth and Keats, and of *The Waste Land* can give a student as much of the tradition of the Western world, can enable him to earn his heritage, can cover the ground as well for him as an historical survey of all the writers and periods? Anyhow, in fourteen years of English teaching we should be able to do a little better than that.

May I emphasize next that we should insist that our students really achieve the personal experience of a body of literature. Our students should have some common knowledge, some knowledge in common with each other. This is, may I say, a condition of education, and also of a culture, a civilization. I confess that I find it extremely difficult nowadays to refer to a piece of literature for illustrative purposes in the classroom which all the students know. Only lately, while making a point about plot, I tried *Tom Sawyer, The Legend of Sleepy Hollow, The Gold Bug,* and *The Gift of the Magi,* and discovered that for each of these a considerable number of the class could not say that he knew it. How, I wonder, can language, can thought, can any community of interest, and culture develop in such an atomistic state of affairs? On this point, I believe in minimum reading lists which ought to be made the condition of graduation on the several levels of school and college. I wish we could come to the point at which we could say of all our junior high graduates that they "knew" such and such pieces of literature, and that the high school could assume this to be so. I wish we could go on then to say that all our senior high students knew such and such pieces of literature, and that the college could assume this was so. And I wish that on the college level also we could say, not only of every English major, but of all students who graduate bachelor of arts, that they had the competent personal experience of all the literature on a prescribed list. In this connection I fear that our book reports are not what is needed. A comprehensive examination is better. We must make sure the personal experience of literature is really operative. And it may be necessary, in order to achieve this, that we stock our libraries with quantities of duplicate volumes. These, besides an insistence on something towards a common education in classics, would make reliable testing possible.

Another point, and it can be briefly made, is this. If in the granular condition of knowledge in our time, the work of literature as an integrating influence is to be accomplished, we should, in our selection, honor the past as well as the present, and pay some attention to historical continuity and to the tradition. The selections we choose for intensive work in literature, ought, even in high school, and perhaps also on lower levels, to reflect the whole tradition of letters. It will not do to say that so long as the student is studying fiction or poetry, it does not matter what fiction or poetry it is, or of what period it is. I should like to see the whole tradition of man embodied in these selections, to give tradition a chance, and to offset the contemporaneity of life in our time. This seems to me the more desirable in our Christian system, particularly because in matters of thought and conduct we are nearer to the values of the older literature than we are to the modern.

There remains, and I shall deal with it very briefly again, the consideration that if we could spare some time from our other English work, namely the grammar, rhetoric, and composition with which we are preoccupied most of the time, we would have more time to let literature do its work. When I consider that little body of grammar, for instance, and the fact that students apparently cannot achieve it in twelve years, no, nor in thirteen, I wonder what is wrong with us anyhow. We on the college level, as you can guess, greatly wish that we could substitute for Freshman English, now a course in grammar, rhetoric, and composition, a first course in the tradition of English letters. But we cannot do it. The students do not know their grammar and their rhetorical principles. I suppose that the chief cause of this is not bad English teaching but democratic educational practices in which all who go to school must graduate on every level. Even so, I present it as an ideal, that the better and the quicker we dispatch the work in grammar, the more time we will have for the work of literature.

Address, Teachers Conference, October, 1948.

3

Poet and Public

So far as the people, the mass of the people, are concerned, contemporary poetry hardly exists. Even you, *mon cher lecteur,* if you are still with me after reading my title, will probably admit that you read no modern poetry and that you suppose you can neglect it without missing anything of importance. You have heard of the difficulty and of the daring of modern verse, and have about concluded that poetic sensibility as it manifests itself nowadays is either a singularly private or a dangerous thing. Though you cannot say that you have encountered the lines, you perhaps agree with William Butler Yeats:

> The ceremony of innocence is drowned;
> The best lack all conviction, while the worst
> Are full of passionate intensity.

What you saw of contemporary poetry you did not understand, and having by resolution once or twice undertaken to puzzle out a page or two, you felt that the poet was not being very cooperative, and in the end you left him to his own devices.

If this be true, your attitude is that of the average American. My guess is that the average American — and I mean the average tutored American — can at best manage one short quotation from Millay and Frost and Sandburg, something, it may be, about a candle burning at both ends, a boy swinging on birches, and fog that comes on cat feet. But confront him with a list of modern poets, drawn up at random, like this one: William Butler Yeats, Siegfried Sassoon, Walter de la Mare, Leonie Adams, Elinor Wylie, Robert Lowell, Edith Sitwell, Robinson Jeffers, Marianne Moore, E. E. Cummings, Wallace Stevens, Dylan Thomas, Stephen Spender, Karl Shapiro, Peter Viereck, Michael Roberts, Muriel Rukeyser, William Carlos Williams, Louis MacNeice, Richard Eberhart, and C. Day Lewis. Show him such a list, and ask him from how many of them he can visualize a single complete poem. My guess is that except to a limited group of poetry fanciers, people who collect poetry as others collect French dolls or Australian postage stamps, and except to a group of practising literary people — writers, professors, and English majors at college — those names are as meaningless as a similar list of active archaeologists or lieutenant colonels in the Army.

What am I saying? Merely this, that in these days the poet and the public do not meet. The poet says that he cannot abide a mass culture or cater to it. He says that he cannot produce greatly or communicate significantly in a texture of language and dogma shaped by a strident commercial press, a noisy *cliche*-ridden radio, a popular taste formed by interested business and expressed by Hollywood and Video, and a sense of life compounded often of sentimentality bent to the uses of propaganda. To the poet, consequently, the success of popular education seems a myth, and his evidence for thinking so is the public indifference to poetry. To the public, poetry seems a game played by a malcontent *elite* for the amusement of its members. Snob, says the public to the poet; beast, says the poet to the public. And the two do not meet, at least not in that frame of mind.

The tokens of this breach between artist and society, between the poet and the people, are many. Sometimes the poet, in protest against a standardized culture, moves into what he thinks is a better climate of values. This may take the form of an expatriate movement, such as that which Henry James started and which gained momentum from the departure of Ezra Pound, T. S. Eliot, Richard Aldington, and so many others. In much the same way the romantics of an earlier era had been exiles too. Three of England's best romantic poets died out of England, at least two of them, Byron and Shelley, because they could not tolerate the public mind, nor the public mind them. They assembled in knots on the continent, thrown upon each other for community, just as Wordsworth and Coleridge were in their Cotswold island of retreat, or the members of the Schlegel circle at Jena, or the transcendentalists at Brook Farm. Thus, also, in the interbellum years, the poets sought out their kind, sometimes deliberately flouting *bourgeois* mentality, establishing islands of sensibility in worlds of moralism, whether on the Parisian Left Bank or at Greenwich Village. Quite aware of what Wordsworth said of the poet, that he is a man "of more than usual sensibility," they gave only lip-service to the rest of what Wordsworth said, namely, that "he is a man speaking to men." They began speaking to each other. Little magazines flourished: *Blast, Hound and Horn, The Egoist, Transition,* and others. Thus the poet lost contact with life, cut himself off from communication, and talked to himself about himself in lines hardly ordered by an obfuscating technique. And even as the poet moved into an eccentric privacy of feeling and statement, the public lost the modifying influence of the poet's sensibility, and became better prey than ever to the forces making for a mass mentality.

An appalling symptom of this cultural schizophrenia was an event of the summer of 1949. The poet Ezra Pound, looking for a villain in the general disintegration, and driven half-mad by his problem, had in time of war taken to Radio Rome and blurted out phrases bristling with invective against what he construed as a Jew-dictated and dollar-fomented war. He praised Mussolini and Hitler, condemned America and Roosevelt, and at war's end was summoned home to stand trial for high treason. He was saved from sentence, it is supposed, only by an intervening declaration of insanity. A group of literary people, meanwhile, acting as a Committee of Fellows in American Letters for the Library of Congress, voted his *Pisan Cantos* (1948) "the highest achievement in American poetry in 1948." His bitter anti-democratic and anti-Semitic sentiments thus crowned with the laurel by an officially national institution, the public was aroused. A Congressional Committee took note and told Mr. Luther H. Evans, Librarian, to stop all awards. The Committee explained: "We think it's bad policy for the government . . . to be giving prizes and awards, particularly in matters of taste." This surely is a dramatic demonstration of the rift between poet and public, and, though the Committee must be diplomatic, the "matter" is one of dogma rather than of "taste."

Say that the rift between artist and society is more or less present in every time. Say that such a man as Milton, republican as he was in his sympathies, nevertheless addressed his *Paradise Lost* to an audience which was select but few. Point out that the metaphysical poets of the English seventeenth century, struggling also with the disintegration of the old faith and traditional thought, wrote verse which was forbidding in its technique and limited in its appeal. Show that Wordsworth, whose *Lyrical Bal-*

lads had met with no response in 1798, undertook in 1800 to explain his failure: " . . . a multitude of causes, unknown to former times, are now acting with a combined force to blunt the discriminating powers of the mind . . . ." Maintain that Browning and Blake were not luminously self-evident to all who ran and read in their day. Conclude even that fine things are for fine sensibilities, that poetry is at bottom an aristocratic affair, and that when the call comes for the music of verse, the beast, Public, like Bottom in Shakespeare, is likely to demand the tongs and bones.

All this is true, of course, and in a way it is true also that the history of poetry is a sort of tacking and veering between poetry which by definition almost is popular and poetry which by definition almost is learned. The poet, if he be poet and not poetaster, if he be genius and not talent, is always superior in sight and insight to the average man, Shakespeare to his groundlings quite as much as T. S. Eliot to the modern many. But the point is that Shakespeare despite his individual superiority had infinitely more in common with all sorts and conditions of men, whether above or below him in the social hierarchy of his time, than Eliot has with the many of whom he says,

> Here were decent godless people,
> Their only monument the asphalt road
> And a thousand lost golf balls.

Those "causes . . . blunting the discriminating powers of the mind," of which Wordsworth with prophetic inspiration spoke, have gone on apace, and the public's indifference to poetry now is greater and more widespread than it ever was before.

All the earmarks of the contemporary poetry, inevitably expressive though they are of communal disintegration, are well calculated to widen the breach. These are some of them: extreme subjectivity, pre-occupation with self, self-consciousness; erudition, sophistication, refinement upon refinement of sense and statement; technical experimentation and virtuosity; radical sociopolitical feeling accompanied, in the poets, by conversions to Marxism, Catholicism, Conservatism, Mysticism, Classicism, and the like; schools, coteries, and cliques; and general "difficulty." Such earmarks would seem to be enough to make the poets themselves responsible for their obscurity. But they are not alone responsible. As Pound once said, "When something is wrong with the arts, it is not wrong with the arts only." The best historians of recent verse, Elizabeth Drew and John L. Sweeney, in their *Directions in Modern Poetry,* point to the real cause of the difficulty, the real cause also, I think, of the gap now separating poet and public: "The great nineteenth century writers were the last who appealed to all social grades, who could feel that they were addressing a homogeneous society which shared the cultural tradition of which they were themselves the embodiment, and to whom they could speak in the language of common human experience." The contemporary poet, in short, finds it hard to be eloquent in Babel.

Concerning the "difficulty" of contemporary verse, Eliot once remarked that it is the product "not of individual aberrancy but of social disintegration." The modern poet, unless he be an imposter taking advantage of chaos to dazzle and mystify, is difficult not because he wants to be, but because he must be. All the sincere writers, except those who in the end prove to be merely traditional and to lack vitality, tend to confirm Eliot's judgment. Herbert Read, for instance, means every word of his remark: "It is almost impossible to be a poet in an industrial age." Robert Graves, struggling with the problem of adequate form in both poetry and prose, points to a similar cause: " . . . the age into which I was born, in spite of its lavishness of entertainment, has been intellectually and morally in perfect confusion." William Empson, too, who has lately published a volume, as Eliot had done before him, accompanied by the author's explanatory gloss, is another poet who is not cultivating unintelligibility simply to be unique. "All that I would like to be," he explains, "is human, having a share in a civilized, articulate, and well-adjusted community." And Wystan H. Auden, also among the more difficult of the moderns, confirms the analysis: "It is impossible that a writer can do his best except in a community united in sympathy, sense of worth, and aspiration."

This whole problem of the schism between poet and public is, of course, of no moment to those who, in Wordsworth's perceptive phrasing, talk of poetry "as a matter of amusement and idle pleasure; who will converse with us as gravely about a *taste* for poetry, as they express it, as if it were a thing as indifferent as a taste for rope-dancing, or Frontiniac or Sherry." But poetry is vastly more important than that. It has its uses also in that education of man which is his end. The songs of a people have a lot to do with its laws. Shelley was quite right in calling poets the unacknowledged legislators of the world. And Arnold insisted justly enough that, what with the retirement of religion and the advance of science as a substitute for philosophy, "we shall have to look more and more to poetry to interpret life for us."

It is ironic, of course, that precisely when the people need poetry worst it is least available to them. There is no denying that the retired religion, confused reason, and demoralized ethics of the contemporary culture make for a poetry which is either unimportant or important but popularly unintelligible. Plainly, popular education must succeed where it has failed before. This breach between the poet and the people is the evidence of its failure. A democratic community must have a commonly disseminated sense of what its idea is, what its dogma, and what its tradition. When a community has such an idea and ideal, particularly when, as Yeats said, the ideal is held up by an authority, the poet and the people can meet again. The poet does not himself want to be that authority. He does not want directly to be the legislator. He does not want to be the reformer. It is, in fact, a part of the pity of the whole situation that in "unsettled ages" the poet is forced to put his poetry either to one side, or else to radical and unpoetic uses. But what the poet naturally and properly wants most to do is simply to deepen and extend the fundamental sense of life underlying a culture, and so to preserve it. Some of the poets are doing this in our time, but they are doing it with extreme difficulty, and they are not being understood. They need the support of religion, philosophy, and ethics. For, as Pound said. when something is wrong with the arts, it is not wrong with the arts only.

The Calvin Forum, December, 1949.

4

What Is Fiction For?

On a day you come upon your boy reading a novel, and you say, "What — reading stories again? You always have your head in those novels. Why don't you read something useful, something improving, something edifying?"

I understand you, I think. I understand your concern when you say that you want him to read something useful. You are yourself a working man. You have a job to do and are called to do it. You find that life is a practical affair. Subduing the earth and having dominion over it did not come easily for Adam, does not come easily for you. You honor the virtues of industry and thrift. Now you come home, tired by the labor of your calloused hand, and you find your boy sunk in an easy chair with his head in a book. It is all a little disturbing. And such a book! Fiction, of course. Another novel. Just a story. I understand you. If he must read, why can't he read something useful?

Or something improving? There too you are rightly concerned. Your interest in the boy's character is a real, almost an anxious, interest. You have been busy with the nurture and discipline of it these many years. You hoped he would be intelligent, but you could do without that. You hoped he would be efficient, able to get things done. But you could do without that also, that is, if he were not lazy. Laziness would be something else. It would be a fault in character. And for his character you have an anxious concern. For his Christian morality you have deep-seated, heartfelt concern. For this you have prayed, though you had not prayed for those other things. So I understand you when you wish that your boy would read something improving, something that will count in his character.

Again, I understand you, I think, when you use that other word — edifying. It is a good word, the word you use there:

edifying has the idea of edifice in it, and it seems to me that the
edifice behind your use of the word is a church. Good. You want
the boy to read something constructive, something uplifting, especially in a spiritual, a religious sense. The spiritual and religious come first with you. You have a concern, consequently,
for his devotional reading, for books that will assist him in worship, draw him nearer to God. You have not missed that emphasis of the Bible: "Seek ye first the Kingdom ... sell all that thou
hast ... if thine eye offend thee, pluck it out." You want him to
have a care for this above all. The spiritual, the religious, is first.
It stands higher with you than even the practical and the moral.
And it ought to.

So I understand why it is that you should be zealous for and
even jealous of the religious and spiritual development, and thence
for practical and moral concerns. What I wonder at is that this
should make for indifference to the artistic concern. Something
in your remark at least suggests that if only you could make fiction serve practical, or moral, or religious purposes you could
honor it, but that since you cannot you wish your boy would read
something useful, improving, or edifying. You suspect that
novels, when they are innocent, are trivial. At best, you feel, they
constitute mere entertainment.

I wonder at this because I know that you are not Catholic in
your insistence on the primacy of the spiritual. You do not cultivate the esoterically religious in isolation from life. The saint in
you is not developed at the expense of the man; it is indeed the
man renewed who is the saint. And it is that man, the religious
man, if you will, who finds himself called upon to be moral, social, scientific, philosophical — yes, and artistic also.

When you come to think of it, you will perhaps acknowledge
that the aesthetic, the artistic, although interdependent with them,
has a claim upon you distinct in kind from the practical, the
moral, or, in the narrower sense only now, the religious claim.
Then you will perhaps acknowledge also that the artistic need in
you can be satisfied only by art and not by some other thing. The
practical, the moral, the scientific, and those other worlds, do not
exhaust God's reality as it is revealed in himself, in life, and in
you. There is the artistic world also. You can look at a tree and
reckon how useful it would be to build a house with. You are
then being practical about the tree. You can look at a flower and

discover that it consists of stem, stamen, petals, and the rest. You are then being scientific about the flower. But you can also look at a tree or a flower without a deliberate practical or scientific thought, see it as it is, and simply enjoy it. You may call this mere entertainment if you want to. But it is not trivial. It is important.

Now, it is the artistic in him, the aesthetic, that your boy responds to when he finds that the novel which he is reading is delightful. It satisfies a need in himself, corresponds to a world and life, that is, a God's reality, outside of himself, and pleases him. Fiction makes this possible for him. In a way, the novelist is doing what Adam did in Paradise. I do not mean the pruning and the trimming. I mean the naming of created things. Words are poems really. This name-giving is artistic work. Adam was called to it. The artist in you, in all of us, is called to at least the appreciation of it. To see God's reality in the real world and beyond it, to see the ideal in and behind the actual, and so to reproduce it that all may look and enjoy, that is what happens in art. Thus to compress life till it is forced to discover its ideal, its divine reality, that is what happens in fiction. Art — the art of fiction also — is man's acknowledgement and reflection of the divine beauty revealed in and beyond nature and life. That is what fiction is for. Its function is in its own aesthetic way, not in a deliberately practical, or moral, or esoterically religious way, to disclose God's glory for God's and man's delight.

When you come to think of it, therefore, you will not so far want to deny your humanity, created and renewed in you, as not to give this world of art, of fiction, its due. It has a claim on you distinct from any other. No practical bias, or moral anxiousness, or religious exclusiveness should lead you to neglect this world, or to belittle it. That would be unbecoming to the confident Christian in you.

I see that you let the boy go on with his novel. What I hope is that you read one too. A good one, of course — there are so many bad ones. And a real novel, I mean, not just a fable, or a parable, or an allegory, indirectly again doing practical, or moral, or religious work. I hope that you get one for Christmas. I hope that you will read it, and not for mere entertainment, although a good novel is, of course, very entertaining. I hope that you will read it also to discover God and life in it. So that you may enjoy Him forever.

The Banner, December 17, 1948.

[47]

5

The Christian and His Fiction

In this matter of fiction we Protestant Christians are in something of a predicament. We do not like the fiction that is generally being written. We do not, of course, want to do without fiction. So we are trying the experiment of writing our own fiction, of writing what in the more general literary world gets to be called "religious" fiction. This designation we do not particularly like, for it seems to belittle our product and rob it of significance. Indeed, our problem comes to this: how can we create a Christian literature without so limiting it in fullness and scope, as to make it trivial and unimportant?

This problem is worth some thought. We do not like the contemporary fiction. It is usually the realism in it that we object to. We should perhaps call it naturalism, for it is naturalism of the grossest and sultriest kind that we object most to, and we object to the rest in its approach to this worst. We object, for instance, to wickedness being reproduced as something to delight in. We object to the merely filthy and unredeemed perverse being presented as though they were natural and right. We do not want to see erotic man wallowing in the slough of his self-love, or his dirty pleasures enveloped in an aura of sanctity. In our immediate reaction to such false realism, we are likely to repudiate all realism, and in our reaction to this worst of fiction, we are likely to shun all of it.

We think better of that, though, and conclude that as Christians we should yield neither the word nor the fact of realism to the enemy. We know that life is, as we say on other occasions, a pretty realistic affair. And we know, too, when we think carefully of it, that we want our fiction to be true to life. It is sin that we fear, but we do not in fiction fear life, not even life pervasively infected by sin. In our sense of life we are not sentimentalists or romanticists or tenuous idealists. We are amused, for instance, by such a superficial thinker as Shelley. He, too, wanted only the unsullied ideal. He said,

Life like a dome of many-coloured glass
Stains the white radiance of eternity.

Life does just that, of course, but such is life, and we have learned to acknowledge that this is so. And we want the real and the ideal commingled in mortal struggle. We want this in our fiction, too. It is as our parents used to say: *het mag alles niet zoo zoet-sappig mooi, het moet ook echt, het moet ook waar zijn.*

Moreover, we know what fiction is. We know that it is not abstract; it is concrete. We know that it is not a principle; it is an embodiment. It is not a theory but a manifestation. In fiction the skeleton of life takes on the body. This is a little frightening. We know that the real and the ideal in us are poles apart. We remember that except we be covered by the righteousness of Christ we shall cower, naked all, from the eyes of God. So it is a little frightening to think that in this world of fiction we leave our theoretic norms and abstract ideals and enter into the arena of experience. But we see that fiction is just this, and that we can not, may not, alter it. For, if this is the danger, this is also the worth of fiction, that it is close to life, to life concretely embodied, and to life that goes down to the root-reaches of our moral experience. We ought not, therefore, as a way out of our predicament, convert fiction into something which is not fiction by making it a disembodied ghost of life.

We shall insist on realism, then, and be as thoroughgoing about it as those others, though in a different way and towards a different end. And because it is a Christian realism that we want, our first impulse is to turn to the Christian writer and ask him to write our novels for us, to embody life for us as it really is. He, we say to ourselves, has the new heart given him of God, the eye of faith, and in some measure the mind of Christ. Let him, we say, see life for us and report it justly.

For this way out of the difficulty one can have only respect. It would seem to be a good course of action, may indeed be our best hope. But we do well to consider its limitations, too, and to ask what we mean, and what are the possibilities for success. We must ask, for instance, whom we mean by the Christian writer. For the times have so wretchedly come apart, and Protestantism has so badly gone discreet, that we hesitate to call anyone a Christian lately except we circumscribe him as a Bible-believing, evangelical, orthodox Reformed Christian. This is not being said in jest, but by way of pointing to the heart of a difficulty. We are a small Church, and we must ask whether it is likely that a person will very often appear among us who has the gift of art and the magnitude of mind required for writing fiction. That is one problem, and we have to consider it in finding ways out of our predicament. Moreover, if he were to appear, can we offer him a Christian culture, and a Christian society to feed on? Fiction does not spring richly out of the mind of man in isolation. Fiction which, as the critics say, touches on life at many points, and touches on it powerfully, must shoot its roots deeply into a tradition and a culture. If there is no Christian tradition, no Christian culture, can we from our Reformed writers get a novel which is satisfyingly Christian at the same time that it is satisfyingly full and complete? This is a prime difficulty, and it deserves to be fully considered among us, lest we expect the impossible from our "Christian writers."

A quick glance at the "religious" fiction in the Protestant world suggests that these difficulties are real. In just what does the religiousness of the religious novels usually appear? In the absence of obscenity, profanity, perversity, filth, yes; and that is substantial gain. But it is negative. On the positive side only the materials often are religious, or ecclesiastical, rather: ministers are protagonists, churches are locales, and parishioners, characters. There is also some religious sentiment woven into an otherwise characterless texture. Moreover, many of these novels are contrived and slanted to suit what the trade already calls the "religious" market. Some are, of course, worse, some better. An occasional one is good. But the case of the "religious" fiction of the Protestant world, by and large, is pathetic.

Still, our predicament is not hopeless. We do well thus to see the heart of our problem. The heart of our problem is the divorce of religion and what we call culture in the modern world. We Calvinists never intended, when we separated the Church from the State, that religion should become separated from culture. When we separated the first two, we committed ourselves also to leavening the whole society and culture with the Christian principle. We see now how indispensable carrying out that commitment is. We shall have to be very anxious about this. If the condition of a great Christian novel is both a Christian writer and a Christian culture, we see what is our duty. Except we succeed in what we sometimes call our "cultural mandate" we shall progressively be cut off from a kingdom of realization for the faith that is in us.

Meanwhile, of course, we ought not to think that the situation of fiction, of literature, in our time is any worse than the situation in business, in politics, or in social life generally, though the symptom may be more dramatic. We do not believe that the common grace of God is being so far withheld that we cannot participate in those other areas. We can participate in fiction, too. We can make use of those writers even who are not Christian but whose embodiments of life are large, just, and comprehensive. We can make use of fiction which owes much to residues of Christian life and thought in the modern culture. We can gratefully read Christian authors of persuasions other than our own, though they struggle with like difficulties. And for the rest we must get on with providing for the Christian writer a Christian culture which he can, without conflict, love and explore.

The Banner, April 22, 1949.

6

Notes on Novel Reading

Remember that a novel is a work of art, and that reading it is an aesthetic experience. Do not expect a novel, therefore, to be a scientific book, or a practical book, or a religious book. It has enough to do just being a novel, and you have enough to do just enjoying it. Naturally, once you have yielded to it, and let it have its way with you, you are likely to find that it has also contributed to your knowledge, affected your conduct, and made you more religious. But these by-products of the reading will come to you most richly if you do not try too hard to get them.

Do not look upon novels merely as an amusement for an idle hour, merely as a pastime, as something of the same sort of importance as a game of checkers. There are novels, of course, which aim at being nothing more than amusements or entertainments. These are usually innocent enough and have their little worth.

If your experience of fiction is to contribute to your education, you must make sure that the novels you read are important novels. You must make sure that they are, as we say, literature. A novel is literature if a comprehensive vision of life, sensitively perceived, is given aesthetic embodiment in it. A novel is literature if it is an appropriately embodied narrative which touches powerfully on life at many points. A novel is literature if an imaginatively gifted person of unusual magnitude of mind presents an interpretation of reality in it. Make sure that the novels you read are that kind of books.

It may be that at this point a difficulty arises for you as a Reformed Christian. The interpretation of life in some novels, you may say, and in important novels too, novels that are sensitive, thoroughgoing, and powerfully aesthetic, is an interpretation which is not or does not seem to you to be Christian. Then what are you to do? Apparently you can do four things. You can read them anyhow, if you be spiritually mature, really appropriating them. You can substitute what is called Religious Fiction for them. You can hope that Reformed novelists will soon produce an important literature out of a Reformed culture, and wait for that. Or you can withdraw from the world of fiction entirely.

Read them anyhow, if you be spiritually mature, really appropriating them. You wish, naturally, that all novelists of genius and scope who have ever written were, and in the precise Reformation evangelical sense, Christian novelists, and that all civilizations and cultures which they express in their novels were recognizably Christian. Now you find that Goethe, for instance, is mainly a humanist, Tolstoy a humanitarian, Thomas Hardy a determinist, and that although these all lived historically in the Christian era, and although their novels are visibly affected by Christian influence, these writers are not such as you would commonly think of as Christian writers. I say, read them anyhow. Appropriate them. Their novels are literature, and you need them. For there is still this important difference between them and you: they are creatively gifted, they have magnitude of mind, they have quality and range of imagination, and they are able therefore to disclose and to explore reality sensitively and profoundly. These are powers which are not conferred upon you by virtue of your faith. It is their vision of reality, consequently, that must enlarge your own, and you should lend yourself to such enlargement. It is true that in them the light falls on life from the wrong angle. You then must in the knowledge of faith make it fall from the right angle. All things are yours, you know, peculiarly yours, this literature too. Their harvesting is for your table. Their wealth is your legacy. You inherit here. Appropriate them, then, and the myriad others, ancient and modern, of whom they are illustrative.

You can read what is known in the Protestant religious world as Religious Fiction. This usually does little harm, but it rarely does much good. It comes up out of a fundamentalistic Protestantism which finds itself at bay over against modern culture. Most of this fiction is rationally confused, ethically superficial, and religiously pietistic. Much of it represents an unhappy wedding of religiousness and secularism by the bond of sentimentality. In it a merely personal evangelicism tries unsuccessfully to make up for its philosophical failure to be rational and cultural in the first place. Because it is a fiction which emerges from the outside of the total culture rather than from the inside, it has no real relations with the structure of life and reality. That, rather than incompetent technique, is what at bottom is wrong with it. Although it is read by thousands of religious people instead of literature, it is not literature. It cannot, consequently, make a substantial contribution to your aesthetic education.

Your own Protestantism, however, is neither extra-cultural nor anti-cultural; it is a cultural Protestantism. You may be hoping, therefore, that Reformed writers will emerge who will write novels that are literature and that present an interpretation of life which is Christian in the Reformed sense. Continue to look for the fulfilment of this hope. It is an ideal towards which Reformed people will all want to be constantly working. But do not be unrealistic in your expectations, and do not look for the impossible. For one thing, imaginatively gifted persons of unusual magnitude of mind are rare in general and they are correspondingly rarer in a small group. For another thing, more is required for the production of literature than an individual writer. Literature is not wholly an individual affair. It must, if it is to be important, acknowledge and maintain its relations with the total life and culture which come to expression in it. An important Reformed novel, accordingly, really requires the satisfaction of two conditions: a Reformed writer and a Reformed culture. The first is possible among us; the second must continue for a long while yet an ideal, though it desperately needs fulfilment. We have no Reformed culture now; even in our almost exclusively Reformed communities, the total cultural complex of life as it is lived there is only partially a Christian, and still less a Reformed complex. Such then are the limitations you must see in the possibilities for an important Reformed literature. Something like a Christian, a Reformed, culture is the condition of it. And it is precisely for want of a sense of this that a non-Reformed Protestant fundamentalism can make its terms with an extra-cultural Religious Fiction, and accept this fiction as an adequate art.

You can withdraw from the whole world of fiction, of course. Unless you include in this world those other books, the bad books, the perverse and ugly books, the false and dishonest books, you ought not to withdraw. You must not withdraw, unless you are prepared to withdraw from the world of business, society, and politics also. It is only when you do not acknowledge the importance of literature, when you come to regard it as an amusement or entertainment, of much less significance than those other areas of life, that you can countenance the thought of withdrawing from it at all. If the important literature of our time is bad, its badness is not owing to the peculiar perversity of novelists as a type of people, but to the condition of a total culture. Appropriate even that literature, then, and judge it, while you build for the kingdom of a Reformed complex of life.

The Banner, February 17, 1950.

7

Why Read Novels?

This is the final lecture of the 1955-1956 Alumni Lecture Series, and we may feel that, having dined on such substantial courses as theological, moral, political, and social problems, we are entitled now to a bit of dessert in the form of fine art. Certainly the friends of fiction cannot object to such a mode of speaking if the force of it is taken to be that the novel is a delightful affair. But the figure about the dessert breaks down if it is taken to mean that, although the novel may be a pleasant thing, it is not a substantial and important thing. You will see what I am getting at: I am trying to claim for fiction both the taste of the sherbet and the importance of the steak. In other words, in recommending novels to you this evening I do so on the basis of the old claim which literature has always put forward for itself: namely, that it instructs while it entertains. "With a tale, forsooth, he cometh to you," wrote Sir Philip Sidney of the story teller, "with a tale which holdeth children from play, and old men from the chimney corner." That is the charm of the novel. As for its importance, well, whom shall I call on for testimony? Jane Austen? She has some right to speak, and she was a good deal vexed by the people who were always saying that novels had their uses, presumably, as a pastime activity for idle young women, but were good for little else. She answers such people with a bit of dialogue in her *Northanger Abbey*:

> "And what are you reading, Miss Blank?"
> "Oh, it is only a novel," replies the young lady: while she lays the book down with affected indifference, or momentary shame — "It is only Cecilia or Camilla, or Belinda: or, in short only a work in which the greatest powers of the mind are displayed, the most thorough knowledge of

human nature, the happiest delineation of its varieties, and the liveliest effusion of wit and humour are conveyed to the world in the best chosen language."

That is an old complaint, of course, that one to which Miss Austen alludes, about reading fiction being a waste of time. It seems likely that, especially in America, more fiction has been read on the sneak than in the open precisely because novel readers were trying to avoid the stigma of being lazy. Especially in America, I suggest, because of the exacting practical demands made on the frontiersman, and because of the emphasis in Puritanism on diligence, thrift, and enterprise. The eighteenth century in our country, after all, was one of "useful and improving literature" as they called it, and the novel did not qualify as such. In a book by Gordon Hall Gerould entitled *How to Read Fiction* I find this interesting entry concerning his early ninteenth-century grandmother:

> According to reminiscences jotted down in her old age, one of my grandmothers made a curious and what seems to me an unfortunate vow in the year 1826 or 1827. . . . She would have been at the time 12 or 13 years old. One morning she sat down to spin in the east chamber of [her] New Hampshire farmhouse . . . but instead of keeping to her task she took up Mrs. Radcliffe's *Romance of the Forest*. She was so "enchanted" — to use her own word — that she neglected her spinning altogether and even failed to respond promptly when she was called to dinner. Presumably she finished the story. At all events, *her conscience finally awoke*. She threw the book on the bed, and resolved never again to read a novel. . . . My grandmother grew up to be an able and interesting woman, who had a wide experience of life in the course of her ninety years, but she never read another work of fiction.

This, then, is a nice instance of a thirteen-year-old Puritan conscience having done, once and for all, with the "enchantment" of fiction. One agrees with the grandson who comments, "Though my grandmother did not think so, it is good for us now and then to forget our spinning."

I was quoting Sir Philip Sidney a moment ago, and Sidney once undertook to defend poetry against charges commonly directed against it. They are charges often directed against fiction

also and I here borrow his outline for my purposes. And the first
of these charges is just this one, already in hand, namely, that fiction is a waste of time. His wording of it, though, is illuminating:
"There being many other more fruitful knowledges, a man might
better spend his time in them than in this." Well, there it is, the
implication being that although philosophy, history, and science
can give knowledge, fiction cannot. It may be able to give many
things, but knowledge it cannot give. Use all the other words you
want and nobody will quarrel with the claim: call it entertainment, amusement, diversion, play, recreation, or pastime activity.
But do not claim knowledge for it. That, so goes the argument,
is to abuse even language. *Dichtung und Wahrheit,* said Goethe,
truth and fiction, why, they are antonymns. Run up to the dictionary and look under "fiction" and what do you read? "Fiction:
a feigning or imagining." Exactly, a world of illusion is what fiction gives you, fascinating often and very diverting, and, if you
have time for such things, presumably harmless, but let us get this
clear: The world of fiction is an illusory world. For sense, the
reader of fiction is told, you go to science; it is for *non*sense that
you go to fiction. "There being more fruitful knowledges, a man
might better spend his time in them."

And now it is an interesting thing to see that Sidney's first
alleged charge against fiction — that it is a waste of time —
coalesces with the second, which is that it lies. Fiction feigns;
it lies. It misrepresents things. It falsifies. It acknowledges no
obedience to the mind in its reading of reality. Plato, they say,
was against it, because he did not trust its soaring away from the
philosopher's laws and the historian's facts. Even Shakespeare,
who put his life into the creating of fictions — or was he merely
teasing? — even Shakespeare seems sometimes to go along with
the idea that the art of poetry in the broad sense of *Dichtung* or
fiction is not to be trusted. What is poetry, asks the country
wench Audrey, in the *As You Like It*: Is it a true thing? Her
question probably gives expression to the plain man's distrust of
fiction everywhere. "Peace, peace," says Romeo to Mercutio
when Mercutio has been indulging a flight of fictive fancy,
"Peace, peace, thou talkst of nothing." And the answer comes —
but this must be irony:

> True, I talk of dreams,
> Which are the children of an idle brain,
> Begot of nothing but vain phantasy....

There you have that pair again: the indolence and the vanity. Nothing could be farther from the fact and Shakespeare knew it. He must have known, as Yeats put it, that

> to articulate sweet sounds together
> Is to work harder than all these, and yet
> Be thought an idler by the noisy set
> Of bankers, schoolmasters, and clergymen

the poets call the world. The truest fiction, Shakespeare once said in effect, is the most feigning. He must have known that so long as there were men to hear or read his dramas they would recognize in its mirror the face of reality. This is to imply also that the importance of a novelist's fiction depends in the long run upon its fidelity to the truth about life. It is because we recognize reality in the universe of fiction that we can go to it not as a way of wasting, but as a way of redeeming, time, that we can go to it also, not merely for diversion and entertainment, but also for knowledge.

This point, that fiction is a form of knowledge, seems worth making. Something has happened to the integrity of mind in our time. The time was when the analytical and speculative resources of reason, expressing themselves in science and philosophy, were allied with the intuitive and imaginative resources of reason, expressing themselves in art; all of them together were engaged in the single endeavor of mind to understand reality. Since then, as our philosophers have often and well reminded us, much of the modern mind has so defined reality that it is something which can be known only by the analytical reason of scientific method. The implication of this, too, is that the intuition and imagination are not rational at all, but extra-rational, or subrational, or irrational. It then follows very naturally that the novel is the child of an idle brain, begot of nothing but vain fantasy. Presumably you and I with our solider sense of what the nature of man is ought to be proof against this crumbling integrity of mind. If we are proof against it, we will approach a novel with the same sort of respect that we would have for a book of philosophy, of science, or of history. We will, in short, go to it for an illuminating interpretation of life as well as for diversion.

Ideally, that is. As a matter of fact, there are quantities of pieces of print which pass as novels and which it may be a waste of time to read. There are quantities of them, too, which are false products. Some are as trashy as cheap toys. Some glitter with the ungratifying glare of tinsel. Only last month a book by Quentin Reynolds came out called *The Fiction Factory*. It tells the story of the publishing house of Street and Smith, a house which fed itself fat on the "escape" market, producing synthetic romances by the ton for disillusioned people unequal to the moral struggle of life and seeking surcease from care in a pulp paper paradise. This flight from the facts of life into the glamour of romance is going on all the time. It is going on when Ma leaves the washtubs in the basement and clambers up to hear the soap opera. At its best this kind of stuff is as innocent as a game of dominoes, but the point is that it is not much more challenging either. I cannot become as angry about it as Thomas Brown in his letter to Mylady in 1697: "I have a hundred times wished," he wrote, "that these unnatural Rogues, the writers of Romances, had been hanged."

Meanwhile, though, the fiction factory keeps on grinding out the books. The *World Almanac* for 1955 reports that in the previous year approximately 1500 novels were published in this country. Most of these are what we call "mere entertainment." They are pastime books, what in The Netherlands is called *ontspanningslektuur,* innocent at best, false at worst. Among them are a considerable quantity of what is called scientifiction, books in which miracles of technological invention are the order of the day, and in which a mere natural law such as gravity is neutralized by a push-button. Among them also are the mystery thrillers, *Frankenstein, Dracula,* and all their progeny, so strident in their melodramatic passion, that I feel like writing one under the title *The Shriek of the Screaming Sheik.* Apparently the calloused contemporary sensibility requires sharp needling to respond to stimulus at all. Wordsworth once wrote that "the human mind is capable of being excited without the application of gross and violent stimulants" but he hastened to add that in his time "a multitude of causes were acting with a combined force to blunt the discriminating powers of the mind, and . . . to reduce it to a state of almost savage torpor. To this tendency of life," he said, "the literature and theatrical exhibitions of the country have conformed themselves." We can only say that they have. To these types of merely diverting or escape literature must still be added the hundreds of Westerns, successors to Zane Grey, with their Scarface Tonys, their mesas, their cacti, and their saddle leather, their hundreds of heroes unthwarted by villains and rewarded with lovely girls at lavender sunsets, whether at Sweetwater Gulch or Bullfrog Canyon. Whether written by Max Brand, or Bliss Lomax, or Philip Macdonald does not matter: their authors are not cattle men anyhow, at least not until their earnings from this market pay for their chaps and sombreros and dude ranches. Add to these the largest landholder of all in this territory of *ontspanningslektuur,* the detective novel, the whodunnit, with Erle Stanley Gardner leading the pack with his *Case of the Borrowed Brunette,* his *Case of the Drowsy Mosquito,* and his *Case of the Fan-Dancer's Horse,* and some hundred more titles in that kind. Add them and we begin to form some notion of what is meant when it is said that reading novels is a waste of time and that the novels themselves are false.

And would one be entirely out of order now if he said, speaking of this untrue, unreal, and synthetic fiction, this formula-ridden and trade-dictated stuff, this fugitive, ephemeral, and here-today-gone-tomorrow entertainment, this canned opiate or tonic for frightened or bored people, would one be entirely out of order if he said that much of so-called "religious" fiction belongs in the same general category of evasiveness? This kind has been charitably called Religious Pollyanna, the idea being that it gives expression to what people wish to think life is, not to what it is. Much, though not all of it, is produced by professional people who are slanting their product to what they call the "religious" market. Some of it is commercially produced in much the same way as the Western stories, the Screen stories, the mystery and detective stories and the like, are turned out by hacks for the pulp paper magazine market. The religious earmarks of it are mainly negative, and, as in so much of the fundamentalist cultural witness, in social, political, scientific, and other areas, this religiousness floats like a film on the surface of life. It never goes down into the root reaches of the moral experience. Accordingly, what the trade calls "religious fiction" is little more than religious gold plating laid over the rotten tooth of reality. It is the chrome facade hiding but not altering the old frame structure of the secular building behind it. It is not itself positive. A great deal of it is rationally superficial and morally evasive. It seems very likely that if ever a full-length book is written on the religious fiction of American Protestantism that book will exhibit such Protestantism in one of its weakest manifestations. Incidentally, such a book needs to be written. Perhaps it could well begin as a dissertation for a higher degree in a school of theology, say, in church history. No University Department of English would honor it, since the type of novel involved is not taken seriously as literature.

If now one leaves to one side this whole body of fugitive and commercial fiction which was just reviewed — the sentimental romances, the scientifiction, the mystery thriller, the detective whodunit, the Western, the religious pollyanna, and their related kinds — what has he left? Probably about one-fourth of the total is what he has left, and this remnant must be further subdivided into two groups. The only available label that comes to mind for the first and far and away the larger of the two kinds is the name: Popular Fiction. This name, of course, has the enormous disadvantage that it seems to carry with it the implication that the second and far and away the smaller group should be called: Unpopular Fiction. I want, however, to call it instead: Literature. I can see some of you reading a novel next week, and saying, "This must not be literature: I'm enjoying it." But the distinction between the two kinds, although it is not an easy distinction to draw, is a real one. There are borderline cases, too. Let me give you a series of names, borrowed from our American writers of day before yesterday, and ask you: Are they literature or are they popular fiction? Would you carry them into the classroom if you were a university-college teacher of literature, or leave them to one side as useful in their way and day but of no permanent significance? Day before yesterday, I suggest, and here are the names: Bret Harte, Jack London, Hamlin Garland, Owen Wister, Frank Norris, Irving Bacheller, and Booth Tarkington: these are all authors who, shall we say, are on their way out of the chapter they used to occupy in the history of American literature towards becoming a paragraph in the notes at the back. They wrote literature: *The Outcasts of Poker Flats, The Call of the Wild,* the *Main Travelled Roads,* the *Virginian, The Octopus, Eben Holden,* and *The Gentleman from Indiana* are literature, but most of the quantities of books these people wrote later were popular fiction. Something of the same kind holds true for the work of Somerset Maugham, for example, in England: he has not sustained the promise of the book *Of Human Bondage* and *Moon and Sixpence.* Such writers as Pearl Buck and J. P. Marquand are probably going the same way. Perhaps it is that the second rate as distinguished from the first rate are most liable to this deterioration from literature into popular fiction. Such writers are themselves less authentic than the first-rate writers and they can therefore sacrifice their artistic integrity more easily than those others. Ernest Hemingway says this is the reason:

> They make money. Then our writers, when they have made some money increase their standard of living and they are caught. They have to write to keep up their establishments . . . they write when there is nothing to say or no water in the well . . . Then, once they have betrayed themselves, they justify it and you get more bad writing.

If you are MacKinlay Kantor, for example, and your book of 768 pages sells 200,000 copies at five dollars a copy, in addition to being competitively bidded for by the Book Clubs, immediately scheduled for Hollywood, eagerly sought after by the reprint houses, and published at once as a *Reader's Digest* condensation . . . if you are MacKinlay Kantor in this situation it must be easy to persuade yourself that your vision of life is a little different than you first thought it was, and that although you ought to say what you see, it will not hurt any to modify it a little in the direction of what the public apparently wants. The Nobel Prize for Literature is fine for prestige, and it would be nice to be taken seriously by the English department at Yale and by the New Critics and the Little Magazines, but this Hollywood contract and Book-of-the-Month Club selection is a bird in the hand. My impression is that the luxury of integrity comes high for the American successful novelist. So much that is bad can be said about Ernest Hemingway, it seems good to report that he turned down an offer of 4,000 dollars to pose as The Man of Distinction in the whiskey advertisements and that he refused 4,500 dollars for an advisory role in Hollywood. Hemingway has on occasion unblushingly written for money, as when he contributed two pieces to *Look* Magazine about a year ago, but when he does this he practically writes on the title page: This is tripe written for money so that I can be free to write literature for fame.

There are, then, these two kinds of fiction, at some points interdependent with each other, and rather arbitrarily designated popular fiction and literature. (Since I am professionally required to deal with the second kind, I am embarrassed often by not knowing the books everybody is talking about — *The Man in the Gray Flannel Suit, The Caine Mutiny, Cash McCall, Marjorie Morningstar, The Last Hurrah,* and *Andersonville,* for instance. I read the reviews hard and have a kind of knowing look on my face when these are mentioned, but then I tell myself that I am a teacher of English and am not allowed to enjoy the books I read but have to work at them. There is the compensating factor, on the other hand, that I am not often embarrassed to find that other people have read the literature I am talking about.) The three kinds that I have been discriminating, the escape books, the popular fiction, and the literature, are roughly analogous, perhaps, to the three kinds that we distinguish in the magazine world, that is, in the same order of increasing importance, the pulps (the Westerns, that is, and the screen stories), the slicks (the Curtis Publishing Company, the *Saturday Evening Post's* stories, that is), and the qualities (the *Atlantic Monthly* and *Harper's).* I think, however, that my category of popular fiction is about halfway between the slicks and the qualities, and that the category of literature is somewhat above the qualities in worth. Can the difference between the two kinds be defined by statement? Can the difference between the novels of Sloan Wilson, MacKinlay Kantor, Taylor Caldwell, Herman Wouk, Cameron Hawley and the myriad others on that level of importance, not negligible but not great, and the novels of Francois Mauriac, Thomas Mann, William Faulkner, Ernest Hemingway, James Joyce, and their kind, can the difference be stated? One can try: the popular fiction is transient, the literature is permanent. The first usually is a book of the hour; the second often the fiction of all time. *Andersonville* and *Marjorie Morningstar* are now in the news, but the news of last year, and the year before that, and so back, is fading fast. *The Robe, The Keys of the Kingdom, The Cardinal, The Adventures of Augie March, Kitty Foyle, Magnificent Obsession,* competent books, as we said at the time, interesting, we said — and they are running on a little while in cheap reprints — but is it likely that once that momentum has stopped a later generation will ever return to them for instruction and delight? No, the popular book does not in this sense break through the limitations of the local and the temporal, the accidental and the particular, into the region of the universal and timeless and essential. Dickens and Thackeray and Hawthorne and Twain and Henry James have their permanence, but where now are Mrs. Humphrey Ward, John Galt, E. P. R. James in England, and where are Winston Churchill, James Kirk Paulding, E. P. Roe and their kind in

America? The contrast is that of transience and permanence. Yes, it is that also of the second and first rate. The style is the key to it, the distinctiveness, the earned individual accent of the style. The great book needs the new style, the style that causes imitators but no rivals. The second and the first rate: it is a question of calibre, of size, of magnitude, something including both scope and intensity. The difference is that of talent and genius. The talent of the popular fiction is often of a high order, the competence often of enviable expertness, the job is well done; there is good workmanship, discipline of a kind in it, and cleverness and wit and more. The work is obviously professional, and one can have respect for the craft of it. One can admire a good cabinet maker for the skill of his carpentry, without according him the honor of an architect who conceives a great building. The genius of literature is in this sense above the professional sway of the ordinary novelist.

And then there is another important difference between the great novel and the ordinary novel, the literature and the popular fiction. This may indeed be the biggest difference. It is this: The popular novel accepts and affirms the existing values of the people of its time, and the great literature challenges those values. The first kind is not critical, or if it is, is critical of little peripheral things; the second kind is thoroughgoing in its implied criticism of the assumptions of a period. The popular fiction follows in the wake of the dominant vogues and fashions of life and thought in a given period. That is why the popular fiction is popular: it is soothing, comforting, reassuring; the literature, on the other hand, is as often as not disturbing, unsettling, shocking even, and uncomfortably challenging sometimes. This fact precisely constitutes one of our problems as Christian readers. The first-rate literature is so deeply thorough-going and radical in its explorations that we prefer the nicer, as we say more decent, and more conventional handlings of the second-rate popular fiction. It is true that the deeper one goes in his explorations of reality, the more the difference between good and evil becomes apparent, the more the difference between the Christian and the non-Christian ways of life becomes evident. But, surely, no one would for this reason want to counsel reading only the superficial books. Just because Ibsen and O'Neill are dramatists of considerable scope, intensity, and power whose vision of life is deterministic and fatalistic, we must not substitute for them an inconsequential little comedy of manners in which the only issue is whether the girl will choose the convertible or the preacher.

Perhaps now we can sum up the principal differences between the great body of popular fiction and what is here being called literature by saying that in the literature there is a higher degree of authenticity in the exploration of the fundamental issues of life. It is a matter of genuineness, of sincerity, of honesty. There is no posturing, no manufacture, no evasion. The big ones are more than makers, that is, fabricators, of stories: they are also seers and prophets. Such are the Hugos and Balzacs and Flauberts, the Prousts and Mauriacs and Gides. Such are the Goethes and Hesses, the Kafkas and the Manns and the Werfels. Such are the Tolstoys and the Dostoevskis and the Turgenievs. Such in England are the Fieldings and Jane Austens and Scotts, the George Eliots and Thackerays, the Hardys and James Joyces. And such in America are the Melvilles and Twains, the Henry Jameses and the William Faulkners. We all recognize this, I think. To come from a novel of James M. Cain, or Thomas B. Costain, or Lloyd Douglas is one thing: Well, that was nice, we say, that was fun, and we fall asleep. But to come from those others is to have gone through something; it is, as we say, to have had an experience. We have been quite literally taken out of ourselves and it takes a while to return to them. When we do we are not quite the same. To come from the *Moby Dick* of Melville, the *Huckleberry Finn* of Mark Twain (may no one say that this novel is just a good, kind book — this Huck is we all and this river is life and this struggle of the civilized and the primitive is going on in everybody), the *War and Peace* of Tolstoy, the *Brothers Karamazov* of Dostoevski, to come from the *Amerika* of Kafka, the *Counterfeiters* of Gide, the *Portrait* of Joyce, the *Sound and Fury* of Faulkner, or *The Old Man and the Sea* of Hemingway or yet again from *The Plague* of Albert Camus or even *The Grapes of Wrath* of Steinbeck, though there is a good deal of moral sentimentality in that last one — to come from one of those is to know, as Arnold put it, that one has touched powerfully on life at many points. It is to have seen the chaos of life transmuted into the order of significant form, so that it is available for appraisal and evaluation. Life has, so to speak, been put into a forcing house in such a way that it is compelled to disclose its meaning. To read such a novel is to have entered a universe comprehensive in scope and intensive in quality. It is to have confronted the moral issues of men, not in the skeleton of theory or the bones of principle, but in the flesh and body of concrete experience. Such authentic literature is the rewarding literature. It is not fake, it is not fabricated, it is not *Ersatz*, it is not professionally made for the trade. It is a vision of life profoundly seen, greatly embodied, and valid. It is not a waste of time to read it.

This is not, of course, to say that the authentic novels are necessarily Christian. But those that are not, still require Christian reading, Christian appropriation, interpretation, and appraisal. There is such a thing as reading irresponsible books. There is also such a thing as an irresponsible reading of books. When we read the great books responsibly we can both enjoy them and learn from them. We should remember, after all, that novels are not important or great or literature unless they exhibit religious and moral assumptions at work. Oscar Wilde can say that there is no such thing as a moral or an immoral book, but if he had been serious, instead of merely clever when he said it, he would have known that that statement itself betrayed a moral attitude. What we have to do, in short, when we are reading novels is to look for the author's uncritically accepted religious dogmas. We have constantly, so to speak, to be reading between the lines to find out what the vindicating moral principle underlying his vision of life is. A significant novel is a wonderful thing in which to recognize that religious assumption is inevitable; it is, further, a wonderful thing to confirm in the Christian his conviction that his own assumptions are right. Is it not true of us Christians generally that the more of life we come to experience and know, the more we are confirmed in our Christian conviction? And where now, I should like to ask, can we turn, unless it be to poetry or the drama, for more of the concentrated essence of life than to the novel? There is a real sense in which it enables us by vicarious experience in our life to bring to bear on being Christian, myriads of lives not our own. I suppose that the way the philosophers would say it is this, that by universalizing ourselves in the significant experience of others there is more of us that is Christian, that can be Christian, than there was before. There is more of you, after reading Hardy, to be Christian with than there was before you read him, and there is also more conviction that you want to be it. In Hardy there is a comprehensive view of life, sensitively perceived, greatly embodied, by a man of considerable mind and imagination, and he can by the quality of insight illuminate whole areas of life, which, had we depended upon ourself, we would never have seen. Since Hardy's vision of life blossoms up out of the bud of fatalism instead of flowering up out of the seed of Christianity, and since the light falls on it from the wrong angle, we must in the knowledge of faith cause it to fall from the right one. But when we do this we have in his novels a legacy to inherit which it would be impoverishing to refuse.

It happens that I am a teacher of English and not a minister, theologian, or churchman, but if I were the churchman instead of the teacher, I believe I should go right on reading what my present profession happily compels me to read. I have been reading novels a good deal this year — and I now deliberately use the personal pronoun because I want what I say to carry the force of personal testimony — I have been reading novels a good deal this year, and it has been a great religious and moral experience. I do not know where the student of the varying religious and moral dogmas of men in our time could go for such swiftly rewarding insights as well as to the modern novel. It is a rich school of morality.

Here is one lesson which I learned from the contemporary fiction. I shall let the poet Eliot state it for me.

> With the disappearance of the idea of Original Sin, with the disappearance of the idea of intense moral struggle, the human beings presented for us in prose fiction today tend to become less and less real. It is in fact in moments of moral and spiritual struggle, depending upon spiritual sanctions, rather than in those bewildering minutes in which we are all very much alike, that men and women come nearest to being real. If you do away with this struggle . . . you must expect human beings to become more and more vaporous.

That is a conviction that overwhelms one after reading the modern fiction, and it is certainly a conviction worth having. It is so in the fiction of D. H. Lawrence, and of many another. Or, listen to Eliot again:

> The heroine of current fiction has no soul — she has not even a heart; she has only a nervous system. She has no spiritual crises: she has only nervous reactions. Experiences which would have made the whole of life for Jane

Eyre . . . which would have raised her to rapture or cast her into the nethermost hell . . . our modern heroine goes through these at a week-end without batting an eyelid.

Precisely, and it is so in *The Great Gatsby* of F. Scott Fitzgerald and it is so in *The Sun Also Rises* of Ernest Hemingway. And these are truths also which one knows better from having seen them in the flesh of fiction than from having seen them only in the skeleton of theory.

We no longer speak, says Howard Mumford Jones, of the moral nature of man. We talk about his reactions. We do not think of human nature as something equipped with ideals of justice, of hope, of truth, of mercy, of retribution; we equip it with social attitudes, a psychological slant, endocrine glands, and a set of conditioned reflexes.

This also is so. And that this really is so the modern fiction teaches us best. Maybe you say, but I knew that already, I knew that anyhow. But how richly, how concretely, how meaningfully did you know it? And do you not know it better after reading Dos Passos, and Farrell, and Steinbeck, and Faulkner, and Hemingway?

But enough. I wanted simply in this conclusion to testify — is that the word? — that modern fiction, if it be authentic fiction, is religiously and morally rewarding, and that everything a person encounters in it is grist for the mill of his Christian education. We have so often heard the preacher and moralist inveighing against liberalism and naturalism. But I submit that you have to go to modern fiction to learn, and to feel it on your pulses, that modern man is

merely a stupid creature whose supposed intelligence is operated in fact by forces over which his volition has no control, a mechanism motivated by primitive urges, an anatomy subject to insane moments of cruelty and fear . . . an irrational being incompetent to manage his own life.

This must suffice. You catch my drift. It is that literature can instruct while it entertains. The novel is no waste of time, unless you pick a bad one, a cheap one. It can teach you of moral evil and of good as well as all the sages can. Fiction, I submit, is a form of knowledge.

Lecture for the Calvin College Alumni
Lecture Series, April, 1956

8

A Vital Language

The plea for a more vital language in our preaching and apology arises from time to time among us. It is a plea which is ignored by some as a matter of no consequence, feared by some, too, as a threat to orthodoxy, and welcomed by others as an important and legitimate concern.

Those who ignore the call for vitality in the diction, language, or style of our spoken and written word are, it seems to me, making a mistake. What they have at the back of their minds is probably something like this: the important thing is the truth, the whole truth, and nothing but the truth. That, they feel, is the main thing, and they go on to imply that the form in which that truth is uttered is neither here nor there really. The content, the idea, the substance is what matters. To talk about the language of such content, the style of such substance, seems to them like talking about the paper on which a king's message is written.

All the same, such separation of truth from statement, of content from form, of idea from style, is a false and fatal separation. The form is essential to the meaning, to the understanding of it, and to the communication of it. The thing we have to say is inert, dead, and incommunicable until it becomes significant, gets its *sign*, assumes form. The truth, thought of as mere matter, is, if it be without form, like the chaos of Genesis. It is void.

Some have called language the dress in which thought is garbed. The figure is mechanical, and it does not go far enough. Language is not so much the dress as the incarnation of the thought. The word is truth become flesh. Language is the body of the idea, and it is only in the body that we can become aware of it. When this body of the language fits the soul of the thought, it is characteristically expressive of that soul. This is what Buffon over-stated when he said, "The style is the man."

We sometimes say that the apparel oft proclaims the man. This is so, but we should go further, still following Shakespeare. "Your face, my thane," said Lady Macbeth, "is as a book Where men may read strange matters." Or again: "False face must hide what the false heart doth know." The body, the face, tells more than the dress. Appearances are not superficial. And language, as Wordsworth hinted, is the countenance of science.

It is this integrity, this wholeness of message and medium, that puts those in the wrong who ignore the plea for vital language in our Reformed speaking and writing. In a good preacher or apologist, a person, that is, with a firm faith, with convictions really felt, with thought that is disciplined in its discriminations, the style is a telling index to the man. He must be defined man, at one with himself and in command of his thought and life, an individuality, in short, and unique, therefore. He must be a significant man. Such a man's language, such a man's style, reveals the soul of him, the spirit of him, his self.

John Milton, for example, was such a man. He had conviction. He had philosophy. He had disciplined his thinking. He was learned. After the University, he went home to his father's house to master the classics he had missed at Cambridge. He had languages: ancient and modern. He had a passion for excellence, born in part from his Puritan sense of working always under "the great task-master's eye." He had, too, a consciousness of calling, an ideal for the work he was to do, and a will for the demanding effort of preparing himself for it. Those are good qualifications for vital language. Well, someone remarked of John Milton, that almost any line of his verse would be as good an identification as his signature at a bank.

So organic is the relationship of language and thought, of language and character, even. This is what Milton had to say of it himself:

> . . . I was confirmed in this opinion, that he who would not be frustrate of his hope to write well hereafter in laudable things ought himself to be a true poem, a composition and pattern of the best and honourablest things; not presuming to sing high praises . . . unless he have in himself the experience and practise of all that which is praiseworthy.

It is the common testimony of all those who best understand the wholeness of *logos,* the integrity of thought and word. Hear

Goethe: "Altogether the style of a writer is a faithful representative of his mind; therefore if a man wish to write a clear style, let him first be clear in his thoughts; and if he would write a noble style, let him first possess a noble soul." Or hear John Newman, author of *Lead, Kindly Light,* and of moving sermons and books one after another. A man, he says

> writes passionately because he feels keenly, forcibly because he conceives vividly; he sees too clearly to be vague; . . . he can analyze his subject, and therefore he is rich; he embraces it as a whole and in its parts and therefore he is consistent; he has a firm hold of it, and therefore he is luminous. . . . He always has the right word for the right idea, and never a word too much . . . .

So it is. The moment we write a sentence or voice a statement we identify ourselves. Our speech betrays us. This is all very humbling for us men of ordinary talent, but genius must be our mentor in this. Since we are human, there is something of the artist in us all. Any sermon, speech, or piece of writing which goes to affirming the faith is in some sort a work of art. Somerset Maugham states it forcefully: "Every production of an artist should be an expression of an adventure of his soul. This is a counsel of perfection, and in an imperfect world a certain indulgence should be allowed . . . but this surely is the aim he should keep before him."

If we cannot have genius, if we do not have it, we can at least try for one of its earmarks: Genuineness. Thomas Carlyle, who was a great man for vitality, and was often preaching it, always traced the dynamism of it back to what he called the Real, the Genuine. Now it may do no good to go around telling people to be real, to be genuine, but those of us who have a Christian profession to make, in speech, sermon, article, or whatever, ought perhaps to begin there. It is as helpful a statement as any that can be made in this matter that if we are real our language will be vital, and that if we are not real our language will betray the lack.

Always this genuineness — shall I call it honesty? — lies at the basis of vital apology and witness. We all know when our language is least adequate. It is when we manufacture a sentiment instead of saying a truth. Think of the tritenesses and banalities, the threadbare phrases and stock diction, of our public courtesies. *Da spuert man die Grundzuege des Geistes nicht aus.* It is all so hollow. Language is at its worst in forced effort, in servile work, in fabricated products. The yawning editor who must get out his thousand words by noon, whether the news be susceptible to comment or not, whether he be ready for interpreting it or not — it is he who will abuse the language. His piece may be fairly convincing, and the unwary may be taken in. If they were not, none of the staff-written, formula-ridden copy, advertising and editorial both, of the big-time slick magazines would be read. But his piece is false.

There is in the jaded editorial, the puffed advertisement, the canned jacket-blurb, the mercenary ghost-writer's piece, and the cranked-out sermon of an old hand at extempore preaching — there is in all these what Carlyle would have called Sham, Puffery, Quackery, and Falsehood. The product may have a certain polish, a practised skill, a rhythmical cadence, and a reasonably good facsimile of style. But the thing remains, for want of genuineness, a No-Thing, a piece of *Ersatz*. The soul is out of it. This is what John Burroughs, the American naturalist, had in mind when he lumped the Sunday sermon with the newspaper editorial as "generally pieces of machine work, as if you turned the crank and the discourse came out."

If this be following the right line, that genuineness is the key to vitality in our Christian profession, then we shall have to take pains to be real, to achieve, so far as may be, a kind of self-integrity. We can lodge our message only if we believe. We cannot lodge it, flesh our sword in it, make it telling, if we say only what we ought to believe. This is the humbling and the denuding thing in the plea for a more vital language. This requires humble, prayerful, and determined searching. For it is a peril of orthodoxy of any kind — political, economic, D.A.R., Stalinist, Catholic, or Reformed — that the official is substituted for the real conviction, that propaganda is substituted for witness. The style of propaganda, the diction of party-manifestoes, the "line" of the dictator, however embellished and ornamented, remains lifeless and artificial. The soul of the free self is out of them. The faith believed, the conviction felt, and the truth acknowledged — these sustain orthodoxy, and from such self-integrity and honesty a vital profession is born.

Such genuineness most emphatically requires humility and requires prayer. Something akin to inspiration is needed, and inspiration, which is the breath of the Spirit, is — let us admit it — not a thing achieved, but a gift given. We Protestants do not make enough of religious exercises. We cannot come in from a week of calls, committees, affairs, and business, look at the church calendar, find the question and answer of the Catechism that is due for Sunday, proceed to the pulpit, and make something of it. We need the spiritual nurture of prayer, reading, reflection, and leisure. We teachers, speakers, and writers, too, wasting our substance in riotously confusing duty, must sit and think. "We must lie like the spider," said Sir Walter Raleigh, "until we have material to continue our web."

Being real, being genuine, with a view to being vital in our Christian profession, requires caliber, too, and it requires education. If genius has the least difficulty being dynamic in its affirmation, this is partly because genius has original force and creative reach. One cannot look for a living language from an imitative mind; such a mind tries but remains always at the mercy, in some part, of convention, custom, and habit. There is no earned awareness there to penetrate tradition and sustain it.

And education. Education, including even pedestrian learning, is indispensable to a genuineness that can last. We all know it, and we all say in one way or another that "words are grown so false, we are loathe to prove reason with them." But to learn what words once meant involves prodigious labor in many kinds, and to know what words now mean involves almost as much. We dare not blink at this fact or we shall be leaning upon words after awhile behind which there is no truth.

We have our treasure, we know, in earthen vessels. But that does not give us leave to do poor work. The plea for a more vital language in our spoken and written word is in order. We shall have to try for the genuine article. Ruskin is right: "So long as words are uttered but in faithfulness, so long the art of language goes on exalting itself; but the moment it is shaped and chiselled on external principles, it . . . perishes. . . . No noble or right style was ever yet founded but out of a sincere heart."

The Reformed Journal, March, 1952.

9

The Peril of Jargon

Jargon is a word which, unfortunately, has come to stand for almost every kind of bad diction. But when, as at this moment, I am concerned to warn against it in our Reformed preaching and apology, I am using the word *jargon* in a restricted sense. I am using it in the sense which the dictionary circumscribes very nicely as "the technical vocabulary of a science, art, trade, sect, profession, or other special group." The word nearest it in meaning, but not quite the equal of it, is *lingo,* a "foreign language or style of speech strange to people."

Such jargon is not necessarily a bad thing. It is, in fact, a necessary product of specialization. We all know how it comes into being. When specialists fence off a particular area of reality in order to study it intensively, they make fine distinctions within the limits of that area. Such distinctions require accurate delimitation, far more accurate delimitation, indeed, than the nonspecialist is used to making. They accordingly develop a terminology adequate for designating these distinctions. Such terminology, the specialized diction of scientists, is jargon.

In time this jargon becomes a thing almost secret, almost occult, to the uninitiated. Witness the language of the law, for instance. You think you have sold a piece of property, but you hardly recognize your own transaction in the way the lawyer writes it up. Witness the technical vocabulary of medicine. Look at your doctor's report, if you can get hold of it, when he transfers your case to another doctor. He may tell you that you are suffering a relapse from the flu, but see what he tells his colleague. Or look at the *Journal of the American Medical Association.* You will then see what is meant by *lingo* defined as a foreign language strange to people.

Professional philosophers, too, although they should resent my implication that they "fence off a particular area of reality" for investigation, tend to use a diction peculiar to their profession. I once spent a day at a conference of such philosophers, and I left mainly wondering whether I was still in English-speaking territory. If you want to observe what such jargon looks like, read a piece or two in *The Thomist, The Monist, The Personalist* or *Philosophia Reformata.* Here is a typical piece of specialized philosophical diction, lifted from a discussion of the English philosopher F. H. Bradley:

> This is an elliptical way of indicating something of what it means to say that, for Bradley, relations are internal to the qualities they relate. Relations contribute to constitute the qualities they differentiate, and qualities contribute to the constitution of the differentiations they terminate. Now since qualities and relations are the two inseparable aspects of incessant process, it follows that a quality transcends itself through the relations which differentiate it. . . . There is nothing exotic, occult, or academic in the fact of self-transcendence.

Now there may be nothing occult about the fact of self-transcendence, but there is something occult, and something academic, too, about the jargon in which that piece of philosophy is embodied.

Theology, too, is a specialized science, no less so because we all, as good Protestants, know a little more about it than we do about law, medicine, chemistry, or philosophy. Each of the schools of theology develops its special set of distinctions, and each of the individual exponents of a school is likely to be pinning down his discriminations by a diction partly peculiar to himself. So it comes about that there are clusters of words characteristic of Barthianism, clusters of words characteristic of Catholic existentialism, and clusters of words characteristic of Reformed orthodoxy.

Yes, there is also a Reformed jargon, as legitimate in its birth, and as indispensable for clarity of reference and precision of meaning, as any other jargon. It is scientific Reformed theological language, and these are some of the terms of it: *amillennial, covenant-consciousness, communion of saints, office of believers, special revelation, general revelation, special grace, common grace, total depravity, unconditional election, limited atonement, irre-*

sistible grace, perseverance of the saints, the sovereignty of God, the cultural mandate, and myriad others. This is specialist jargon as distinguished from the common, humanized language of men. Our children, before indoctrination has done its necessary work, come to these terms as to a foreign tongue, and they hear none of them anywhere except at church.

It would be a great gain all around if this jargon, which consists really of other men's summarized concepts of things, would call up to our minds all that the men who first shaped it intended to say. But just here lies a limitation and peril of jargon. When decades or centuries of arduous theological scholarship have finally made for the clear understanding of a matter, and have defined it with a word or phrase appropriate to that understanding, it happens as often as not that those who come after accept the word for the meaning, and the meaning for the thing.

Take such a concept and such a phrase as *common grace,* for example. The phrase is itself a piece of family language, of specialized theological science, and it is a coin so current among us that we can hardly talk of religion and life for an hour without use of it. But how many of us, if we did not have the phrase to refer to, could communicate an intelligible sense of the philosophical and theological problem to which the doctrine of common grace is a formulated solution? We bandy the phrase around so facilely, but it would be a good exercise for us all to try to communicate the idea it stands for without reference to the term.

And what I say of *common grace* is, I think, true for most of those terms listed in italics overhead. They are so often used — it is a kind of specialist's temptation so to use them — as a substitute for explanation, or as the evidence of the thing for which they are not the proof but the name. Sometimes, even, they constitute the jumping off place rather than the destination of exegesis. And it would seem to be more realistically orthodox to use them once at the end of sermon, lecture, or article rather than twenty times at the beginning. These terms come to us surrounded by the halo of classic formulation, and the aureole surrounding the classic can be a great barrier to appreciation.

Somehow we must try to come to these formulations, as for the first time, so to speak, shouting Eureka at the freshness of surprising discovery. So far, then, from beginning with someone else's finished definition, we shall have to try to recapture his sense of it. This requires something besides catechetical indoctrination. We shall have to stand by in the smithy of theological history again, watch the concept being beaten into shape, and see it plunged into the forge, whether of Council or Synod; indeed, we shall have to seize the hammer ourselves, and bend the recalcitrant stuff into this same shape, pleased that it is the same which the fathers fashioned.

And when we present our apology to the outside world, we must be doubly on guard, lest we think that our language, with which we have grown up, and which has been the medium of communication among each other for decades, means anything to others. This is, indeed, one of the educational uses of addressing ourselves to the outside world. We find that we cannot make our stock terms the basis of inference and conclusion, that we must put up an explanation instead of a word. It is a searching business, really, and is sure to show up the gaps in our self-integrity.

I venture to suggest one peril further. It is that jargon, which is the language of scientific theology, is not the appropriate medium for communication in the non-scientific contexts of sermon, lecture, and article. We must somehow get the benefit of our scientific specialization translated again into the common, humanized language of men. If we cannot do this we are partial men, and have been victimized by our specialties. I take it at least that a sermon is rather more a work of art than a body of science. And art is always and necessarily the foe of specialization.

The Reformed Journal, April, 1952.

10

Commercial Journalism

These are the days of the mass-circulation magazines. They abound in attractive display at the news-stands. Quantities of them are available at the front end of drugstores. And the carriers' bags are bulging with them.

I am thinking particularly of the smooth-paper, popular monthlies and weeklies, the so-called big-time "slicks." Among them are *The Saturday Evening Post, The American Magazine, Good Housekeeping, The Ladies' Home Journal, The Woman's Home Companion, Woman's Day, Better Homes and Gardens, McCall's, The Country Gentleman, The Farm Journal, Collier's* and, in a slightly different kind, *Life* and *Look*.

My recommendation is that if you take these magazines at all, at least do not take them seriously. It is true that they have their uses: recipes, patterns, home-making hints, suggestions for interior decorating, How-to-Do-It articles, an occasional provocative idea, and, sometimes, a rattling good yarn. It is not of course these that I object to. Nor do I object this time to particular features offensive to Christian sensibility which sometimes appear in them, liquor advertising, say, or suggestive illustrations, or the exploitation of passion, violence, and crime. Rather what is basically objectionable in these magazines is this: they represent a business usurpation of the ends of human life.

The big magazines are big business. A few of them have a circulation bordering closely on the four million. They are enterprises conducted by their editorial and managerial staffs in order to make money for their owners. Three steps are involved in this, the first two leading to the third, which is the one that matters. These are the steps: Please as many people as possible, in order to get subscribers, in order to get advertising.

This commercialism, this substitution of business ends for human ends, is the Achilles-heel of capitalist-democratic mass journalism. The result is that these magazines are at best superficial and at worst false. They operate at the rear, not at the van, of the popular culture. They follow where they should lead, and lull where they ought to challenge. They have no real independence, no objectivity, no determinate character. The editorial eye is not on reality and the truth. The eye rather is on what pleases and therefore pays. The eye is on the subscription graph. Is there a dip in the curve? Then there is a change in the popular feeling which necessitates a change in editorial position. The editor must watch the reader reaction. He must calculate the common denominator of public sentiment. He is, as he would say, in business, not in education or social uplift. The customer therefore is always right because — it pays to please him.

The customer is Everybody. The owner instructs his editor, and the editor his staff, in how best to please him. This is the burden of the instruction. Be laissez-faire individualist, especially on the editorial page, but sound quite surprisingly liberal-progressivist in the less conspicuous places. Be Republican if Dewey is sure to win, but insinuate some doubts about the platform if Truman appears to have a chance. Get religion in, for Everybody has some of it, and it seems to mean a lot to him. But avoid the controversial areas, steer clear of differences in doctrine, step on no creedal toes. Seem very definite but be loose enough to catch Catholic and Rosicrucian in the same net. The race issue is delicate: play it both ways. Exhibit a Negro serving drinks for Southern aristocrats, and feature Marian Anderson or Satchel Paige for humanitarians above the Mason and Dixon line. Despite the advertisers, go along with the liberal-equalitarian quite a way. The Have-Got momentum is in no real danger, and it even welcomes an ineffective critical brake. Only this: sound always as though you write from conviction. Everybody likes to think he is dealing with the truth. He is a born dogmatist, too. Do not bother him with complexities. He wants his truth right or wrong, white or black, is suspicious of discriminations, and blind to hues and tints. Be simple — four-letter word, short-sentence simple. Again, though, do not let him guess you are being simple. Do not say always, "Business will be good"; instead, say sometimes, "Experts are predicting an uptrend in commodity purchasing." That sounds reliable and has a ring of know-how about it which Everybody relishes. But, of course, insist that business will be good.

The editor instructs his staff. You know, he says, what Everybody likes: appeal to it. You know what he dislikes: avoid it. He dislikes ideas, especially abstract ones. If you must give him ideas, make them concrete. For the rest, give him Facts, lots of Facts. Make the Facts *scientific* — the word somehow is magic to the masses. And give him people. Everybody likes people, personalities, that is. Give him personalities he knows. He knows best the personalities of the headlines, the movies, the radio, the entertainment world generally, and sports. Give him those. It makes no difference that a man who handles a bat and ball well may not have an interesting personality. Put a ghost-writer on him and you can make him as picturesque as you please.

This, too. Remember that Everybody tends to be mainly natural, only a little human, and hardly spiritual at all. Adjust your appeal accordingly. Count on his sense more than on his mind. Feature things, surface things, things accessible to eye, ear, touch, taste, and smell. Feature the body — obtrude it. Make much of inventions, machines, gadgets, medical miracles, futuramas. By all means, stress the future. Everybody does not know the past, and he wants to think that it makes no difference. Foster the illusion of a miracle world just around the corner. Emphasize youth and hint strongly that age is only another form of it. See that the grandmothers in your stories be well below forty and capable of several careers still. The other woman, the other man, these are good story materials, but be sure to treat the husband-wife tensions in terms of incompatibility. Incompatibility implies no guilt, and guilt is always unpleasant. Finally this: cause dissatisfaction and craving. Everybody must be made to think his standard of living is absurdly behindhand. That means consumption, and consumption means production, and so comes a limitless world of wealth and plenty.

Christian, mark the evasiveness, the innocuousness of this. Mark the betrayal of reason, the collapse of ethics, the dehumanization of life of which this commercial journalism is symptom and expression. This is a thorough-going difficulty, and deserving of attentive concern. It is a difficulty which bodies forth a failure of the individual and social morale. Except that morale be fortified by a sturdier morality based on a better reason, the individual control of the mass media of communication represents no improvement upon ecclesiastical control, or state control, or the control of caste or class by way of patronage. The principle "Business is business," is a principle which, like its companion-pieces, "Science is science," and "Art is art," can safely be allowed to govern the institutions of life only in a community where the Christian idea of man prevails. Labor to define that idea, and to make it prevail. In the meantime, prefer independent to commercial journalism.

The Banner, September 9, 1949.

11

The Indefeasible Title of Conquest

Remarks made to synodical delegates and friends on the occasion of the unveiling of the corner-stone of the enlarged library of Calvin College and Seminary.

You may think from just looking at it that the new library represents an expansion, and a horizontal one at that. In a way it does, of course, represent an expansion. We need room for more books and room for more students to study them in, and this building provides it. That is expansion. But what the new library represents in another and more important way is not expansion so much as it is concentration. Let the physical line be what it will, the spiritual line is vertical. We celebrate today a growth in depth. Our motto is *Ad fontes.* We are raising a monument to scholarship. In doing it, we promise to take the higher learning more seriously than we yet have done.

I must say that the faculty is peculiarly appreciative of the resource for scholarship which this library promises to be. After all, you can hardly please a scholar better than by giving him the means and opportunity for scholarship. You are doing that in giving yourselves and us this building, and we thank you from the bottom of our hearts.

The faculty is becoming increasingly convinced that the function of the library in the total educational effort of the College is an important one. While adhering to the idea in the main that the professor and the classroom are primary in education, it is certain also that the library is an indispensable source and extension of the classroom work. In a day of small beginnings, the College did what it could with teachers who had to rely upon personal resources, and who sometimes used a merely catechetical method of drilling what they knew into their students' heads. The process of learning in that day was often little more than a matter of committing dictation exercises to what used to be called "the ventricle of the memory." Such methods still have their uses, are not wholly ridiculous, but they are inadequate, too. Then followed a heavy leaning on the textbook for the substance of learning, supported — be it meagerly or amply — by commentary or lecture. This method, too, continues operative today, and, in the right hands, with good effect. But it, also, requires the support by professor and student alike of continuous first-hand inquiry into the records of human knowledge which only a good library can supply. In fact, there is a large sense in which, on the college level, the teacher and the textbooks are but guides and interpreters for traditions of life and thought which are embodied in books.

In planning for this correspondingly greater role of the library, the faculty is not, it thinks, merely following the trend. One is a little suspicious sometimes of the dogma underlying the mushroom growth of university libraries. The expansion seems to some extent prompted by a skeptical temper and by a misapplication of "scientific method" to areas in which it is not pertinent. This misapplication has led to the proliferation of quantities of books which can be an impediment to the student who wants to get an education. The suspicion is there that the books have come to supplant the men, the hope somehow persisting that if enough facts can be accumulated, interpretation will be superfluous or at least self-evident. The suspicion, I say, is there that the men have not come clear of the books, are being victimized by accruing information, and, when asked about life's course and direction, bury themselves in the cubicles and hope an answer will emerge. You know we do not act on such dogma here. There is a world of difference between being prompted to intensive studies by faith and conviction, and being prompted to exhaustive ones by bewilderment and skepticism.

We hear a good deal lately about the increasing complexity of knowledge. The records of civilization are, of course, becoming longer, and the skills for discovering and reporting them are becoming distressingly more accurate and complete. History is all of a piece, and there are no accidents in it, and as the memory of the race becomes longer the obligation to forget nothing remains as binding as ever. It is as Christians that we are men, but it is also as men that we are Christians, and we are therefore exempt from no task that falls to scholarship anywhere. We, too, must deal with the increasing complexity of knowledge. For there is no escaping the fact that knowledge which once tended to be one has become many, much as we might wish that it had never broken up into its many-faceted modern prism. But educators presumably should remember that when knowledge becomes too complex it ceases to be knowledge. We at Calvin, at least, feel obliged to see to it that the broad outlines of knowledge, the first principles of it, the philosophy of it, remain clear, and we think that our library will reflect this conviction.

No, what we as a faculty have in mind, and what we suppose you are asking of us in giving us this fine resource, is to become scholars in our own right. We think you want our authority to be a real and not a spurious authority. You cannot be content with us merely as imitators, or merely as innovators. We cannot, catechism-wise, be parrotting other men's summarized concepts of things. Nor can we, propaganda-wise, be facilely applying biblical catchwords to textbook epitomes of knowledge. You expect us to enter upon the hard work of disciplining ourselves historically in our fields, to steep ourselves accordingly in the traditions of thought proper to them, and to emerge in command. We have no choice really in this matter. We have no university to appeal to, and must be our own university, irrespective of what degrees we may offer. Our library, therefore, precisely because it is the Calvin Library, should be larger and ampler than college libraries generally, just as our scholars should be more numerous and have more opportunity than is common at colleges generally. This is a place which must perforce be a place of universal learning. We must know all the books that matter, the makers and modifiers of the tradition in which we stand, and of the traditions over against which we stand. You want us to deal with the traditions of knowledge at first hand, and thus to make the dealing with it at first hand commendable to our students. You want us to carry our convictions to the books and through them, and so, by the exercise of responsible choice, to make our profession sure. It is this sort of scholarship that we salute as we dedicate this building.

And what a piece of Calvinistic action it is that we should be doing this, the kind, perhaps, that should precede all other. Let me tell you a story. My senior colleague, Professor Vanden Bosch, tells it of his senior colleague, Professor Schoolland. The two of them were indulging some long thoughts in off-duty hours. "You know," said Schoolland, "sometimes I think it would be better if there were no books in the world — *except the Bible*." And then, after a pause, lifting a finger to his nose in thoughtful reflection, he added, "The Bible . . . *and* Plato." That in its larger purport is, it seems to me, Calvinism speaking: the Bible, unique, its uniqueness punctuated by a pause. And also, on second thought, Plato, in whom the classic moulders of tradition are readmitted. That is a Calvinistic construction, surely: not because The Book and the books can be compared in kind, but because the two are at some points interdependent and at some points antithetical, and because, when they are antithetical, the antithesis is a real antithesis, representing a warfare, therefore, and a coming to grips with each other. Calvinism, I say. For there are Bible colleges in which The Book renders the books superfluous, as though Bible and reader existed in a vacuum devoid of historical orientation, rational context, or cultural relevancy. And there are liberal colleges enough in which the books have rendered The Book superfluous, assigning it to a place among the masterpieces of world literature or the histories of comparative religion. At Calvin we can sacrifice neither the uniqueness of the one, nor the relevancy of the others.

As a person inordinately fond of books, I cannot on this occasion leave without quoting John Milton, a man who owed to Calvinism some of his drive to learning. "A good book," he said, "is the precious life-blood of a master spirit, embalmed and treasured up on purpose to a life beyond life." That is perhaps the point. Libraries keep the dead from dying. I have some difficulty with Solomon when in that weary moment he spoke disparagingly of making many books. No matter: he had to write one to make his point, and more will have to be written, some of them by us.

This in substance is what I wanted to say: In laying this corner-stone we lay claim to the province of all knowledge, not by squatters' rights but by the indefeasible title of conquest.

The Banner, June 30, 1950.

12

Wordsworth and Hollywood

The English poet and social critic William Wordsworth, writing in the year 1800, had something important to say about Hollywood.

Not that Hollywood existed then. Wordsworth was talking about its equivalent in his own society. He was talking about the popular novels and plays which constituted the marketable entertainment of his time and country. But, in speaking of those, he put his finger exactly upon the essence of Hollywood.

This is what he said:

> ... A multitude of causes, unknown to former times, are now acting with a combined force to blunt the discriminating powers of the mind, and, unfitting it for all voluntary exertion, to reduce it to a state of almost savage torpor. ...
> To this tendency of life and manners the literature and theatrical exhibitions of the country have conformed themselves.

The emphasis is on the cause. Wordsworth is more impressed by the evil of the cause than by the evil of the effect. That is seeing the symptom of Hollywood in relation to what it is symptomatic of. Out of this social heart, says Wordsworth, comes the issue of Hollywood.

He might have said that the novelists were wicked. He might have said that the dramatists were immoral. He might have pointed out that the actors and actresses were a bad lot. He might have gone on to say that the show people were profiteering in the illegitimate commodity of harmful entertainment. He might have said these things, for the most part justly.

Presumably he did not wish to pardon those by whom the offense of Hollywood comes. But he wanted this time to stress

[87]

the other fact, counterpart to the first: namely, that it must needs be that the offense come. Hollywood is not an extravagant exception. It has a social dimension. It is a typical manifestation. Not that the environment is responsible. People are responsible. But it is the people generally who are responsible, not solely the novelists, playwrights, actors, actresses, and producers. The wages of the sin of those at Hollywood will be death; but Hollywood is itself also a spiritual death accruing to demoralized men in society.

Wordsworth speaks of a multitude of causes, an accumulation of influences. It is these, he says, which bring about a state of mind, a social morale, of which Hollywood is inevitably and characteristically expressive. These causes did not always exist, were "unknown to former times." In other words, the social trouble with which Wordsworth is dealing is a particular historical form of evil. It is a modern development.

Among those causes, those influences "now acting with a combined force," Industrialism bulks big for Wordsworth. He is thinking of Industrialism, of course, in a particular context of meaning. He is thinking of an Industrialism which has become a religion. It has become a religion in that it determines the goals of man. Those goals, he thinks, should be determined by something else, and served by business.

Wordsworth, then, sees Industrialism in the context of an atheistic Enlightenment, its dry reason now ebbing out in a normless individualism and a secularistic science. Life and manners follow in the wake of this defection. Men accumulate in cities where "the uniformity of their occupations produces a craving for extraordinary incident." The theatrical exhibitions of the time conform themselves. Hence Hollywood.

It is no wonder, therefore, that Hollywood is the kind of thing it is. Wordsworth's phrases are the right phrases for what has taken place: a blunting of the discriminating powers of the mind, unfitting it for voluntary exertion — indeed, a savage torpor. Compare the theatre advertisements of the daily paper. One exclamation point will not do. There is a screaming stridency: Terrific! Daring! Sensational! Blood-curdling! The eccentric, the extravagant, and the monstrous; the violent, and the sexually titillating — these are the regular offerings. This is a far cry from the moral freedom and creative expressiveness proper to the spirit of man. So seen, Hollywood proves to be the only potsherd left with edges sharp enough to scrape dehumanized man into some sort of response.

And Hollywood, says Wordsworth, is a social creation. In its face you see delineated the features of the society that makes it.

Irrespective now of whether Wordsworth's outline of causes is precisely such as we would ourselves draw, we cannot deny that there are these deeper reaches of implication in the phenomenon of Hollywood. Nor can we escape involvement by isolating the symptom as a pocket of wickedness in a generally decent world. Hollywood is worse than a patch of poison ivy which can be staked off, marked Danger, and so quite entirely avoided. The pagan novelists, immoral actors, profiteering vendors of illegitimate commodities, and marquee hawkers are not quite the measure of evil. There are also those "causes now acting with a combined force." We have not done with those when we see to it that the actresses "get religion" and we ourselves stay out of the theatre.

It is binding upon the Christian to live the decent personal life. But the personal is involved with the civilized. Consequently there are harder things to do than to live the decent life of what Wordsworth called a "cold abstinence from evil deeds." Civilization, especially modern civilization, entangles us in a guilt we cannot acquit ourselves of. That is the interesting thing about an acknowledgment of the social dimension of evil. It makes for a profounder sense of individual responsibility.

Who of us, for instance, though we make and promote no movies, can quite come clean from the mammonistic texture of life which, as Wordsworth saw and said, is loveless and normless in its autonomy? Who of us has so far resisted the economic momentums, business activisms, and political slogans as to keep the pristine tenderness, the wholesome sensibility, which is proper to the child of God? Presumably none. Presumably we too have not set the contemplative in judgment over the active, consulting the end to justify the process, and to harvest it. Perhaps, even while castigating Hollywood, our own reading ran to the simplistic, the digested, the pictorialized, and the striking. That too was falling short of the requirements of a Christian doctrine of man.

Thus an admission of the social implications of Hollywood leads to humility. It is just this note one misses in the attacks upon the movie industry in the popular evangelical Protestant press. The sexual immorality of the actresses, for instance, gets so much more attention than the Industry that promotes it. Presumably this is because sexual sin can be isolated as a piece of personal misconduct, whereas Business is so far woven into the social texture that it seems to lie beyond the arm of religion to touch it. As for an atheistic Enlightenment as source and springboard for a normless industry, science, and art — concerning that, in this press I speak of, Christianity is supposed to have nothing to say. Such formalism works with sin and evil on the plane of its "personal," external, individualized manifestations. The evil of Hollywood particularly is exploited, as though in search of a wicked world to be handily distinctive from.

Such a Protestantism, although it can become strident about "personal religion," and inveigh against a "social Gospel," can also end up without humility, the Catechism, and a need for the Saviour.

Social historians say that evangelical Protestantism is superficial in its social criticism. This charge does not embarrass us so long as it comes from a liberal who is looking to environmental change for his Utopia. But the charge embarrasses us when, as it sometimes does, it comes from a Christian historian. Then we allow that there is something to it. Then we admit that we have featured the isolably personalistic evils: vice, crime, gambling, drunkenness, sexual immorality, realistic fiction, and Hollywood. We isolate them, externalize them, accept the symptom for the disease. This, we say, is what evil is. This is sin. This, we say, is the world. To these mainly, to what lies behind them hardly at all, we apply our sermons, on these converge our exhortation. We can almost keep the law of decency perfectly.

The result is superficial social criticism. The result is also meager contribution to social improvement. But those are the less important results. More important is the religious loss, the loss of spiritual conviction: that our miseries are great, that we desperately need our Redeemer, and that our gratitude ought to be boundless.

The Reformed Journal, September, 1951.

13

The Metrical Versions of the Psalms

It is quite natural that in the congregational psalm singing tradition of the Reformed churches, the subject of the metrical versions of the Psalms should be a perennially fascinating one.

Those who are at all familiar with the strong feeling, animated debate, and continuous concern that went into the selection and improvement of the *berijmde Psalmen* of the Reformed churches in The Netherlands will not be surprised to learn that a similar drama lies behind the traditional evolution of the English metrical versions.

There have already been approximately four hundred English metrical translations of the whole Psalms. One might conclude that the possibilities had by this time been exhausted, and that yet another effort would be something of an impertinence. All the same, the efforts continue to be made. In 1940, for example, there came *The Lyric Psalter,* edited by Harry H. Mayer, and published by Liveright in New York. Hard upon it A. M. P. Dawson's *A New Metrical Version of the Psalter* appeared, coming from Sussex, England.

What happens is that a sort of dissatisfaction with all existing metrical translations tempts new versifiers to try their hand. The quest after improvement is perpetual. What the four hundred extant versions prove, therefore, is the difficulty of the task, and the merely proximate success of the efforts. Some very distinguished poets have responded to the challenge, among them Sir Philip Sidney, George Wither, George Sandys, John Milton, Christopher Smart, Sir John Denham, and others. And yet, after sampling the efforts of each of these, and of those many others, one feels like saying with Dr. Samuel Johnson, after he had scrutinized Denham's rendering: "In this attempt he has failed: but in sacred poetry who has succeeded?"

The difficulty for the poet-translator is formidable, perhaps insurmountable. He must satisfy two demands, one of which interferes with the other. The first is the demand for fidelity — one might say for absolute fidelity — to the inspired word of the Scripture. The other is the demand for poetic genuineness or vitality. The versifier is torn between the pull of these two forces: the necessity for being "literal" and the necessity for being vital.

It is a pleasure to see that the requirement of literalcy, of very strict fidelity to the recorded Word, has in the main been a persistent concern of the poets. Usually, when a sacrifice had to be made, the poets sacrificed the poetic quality rather than the message. The Reformed churches particularly have been anxious to preserve the faithfulness of the rendering. In their insistence on the centrality of the Word in the divine service, they authorized Psalms which so far as possible remained the Word. Such modifications as they introduced into the repertory of metrical translations were usually prompted by the felt need for greater accuracy and completeness in reproducing the basic text.

Such an insistence is sound. The Reformed churches have for the most part been proof against supplanting the Psalms by the hymns of the church, though they have not been averse to supplementing the Psalms by the hymns. Hence they objected to making the original text of the Psalms a jumping-off-place to poetic embroidery, New Testament adaptation, or sermonizing. They wanted their rhymed and metrical reading to say what the original said: if possible, no more, no less, and nothing different.

We ought to continue that careful concern for a true reading of the text. But we ought to try for the satisfaction of that second requirement also. The poetic genuineness, the poetic vitality, is indispensable too. If we cannot get it, we shall have, of course, to do without. If we can only approximate it, we must be content. If the sacrifice of the one or the other must be made, the poetry had better be made to concede to the message. But we ought not to conclude too quickly that a sacrifice is necessary.

For the poetry of the Psalms is indispensable to them as Psalms. They were originally composed as poems, and they require poetry to do them justice. Good prose is, of course, always better than bad poetry. But good poetry is better than good prose. The quality of the content and the force of the communication in these Psalms are inseparably bound up with their art. In the original they were richly charged with the moving power of poetically inspired language. And they stirred the mind, lodged their message, and fixed themselves naturally in the memory because of their poetry.

In the versified Psalms, consequently, we are looking for something more than an arrangement of words in metrical order and an outfit of rhymes. The verse must be more than a metering rod to make the statements of the original a singable affair. It should, instead, constitute the Psalm an artistic organism which, so to speak, invigorates the whole consciousness of those who hear it, speak it, or sing it. It ought by its form to recommend itself so naturally to the ear, and thence to the mind of the auditor, that it will linger on and on because of its truth and beauty.

The quality of the poetry is also, therefore, a thing of great importance. No amount of emphasis on literalcy of content ought to obscure this fact. One has only to think of the loveliness of such impressively memorable Psalms as the 2nd, the 8th, the 19th, the 23rd and 24th, the 42nd, the 90th, the 100th, and the like, to appreciate what a near crime it is to take the poetical prose of them in the King James or American Revised versions, and to torture it into bad verse. When one sees this done, he feels like looking into the possibility of chants and canticles again, and abandoning the metred versions altogether.

It is interesting to consider that if ever we should have a rhymed and metrical version of the Psalter which was convincingly vital and effective as poetry, and which was also strictly faithful to the whole and the only meaning of the original, that version would presumably become official for our authorized Bible as well as for our church song. This is, therefore, only to suggest that in the interest of singability we shall have to be content with a good deal less than gratifying adequacy in our "poetic" versions of the Psalms. The immense difficulty is, after all, one which confronts the translator of any poetry, and most particularly that of the Hebrew, whose dominant poetic principle of parallelism simply is not the dominant principle of our Western language and literature.

The whole difficulty is well illustrated in the effort of our American Puritan ancestor, the Reverend Mr. Cotton Mather. He tried so single-mindedly for literalcy that he abandoned even the formative element of rhyme to ease the burden of his conforming. In his *Psalterium Americanum,* a translation "Exactly conformed to the Original," he said: "Our poetry has attempted many versions of the Psalms, but they leave out a vast heap of those rich things which the Holy Spirit of God speaks in the original Hebrew; and ... they put in as large an heap of poor things, which are entirely their own. And this merely for preserving the Chink of the Rhyme."

The philosophy of that would seem to be right enough. But the remark about the Chink of the Rhyme is uncharitable. For, although in the worst of the metrical versions the rhyme is sometimes a mere, and sometimes a forced, embellishment, in the best of them it enters into the meaning and helps to govern it. Moreover, in his attempt not to leave out any of "the vast heap of rich things," Cotton Mather was capable of such bad blank verse as the following for Psalm 42:

> As the hart makes a panting cry
>   For cooling streams of waters;
> So my soul makes a panting cry
>   To Thee, O mighty God!

In Mather, then, as in scores of others, there is that fine concern for doing total justice to the fundamental text of Holy Writ. But there is, too, so little regard for the poetic mode of statement that the force of the original suffers after all.

The worst of the offenders on the score of content were those who deliberately read personal or official or "evangelical" points of view into the text of the Psalms. Thus, Charles Wesley practically made hymns out of them. Consider, for instance, a couple of stanzas from his 23rd:

> Jesus the good Shepherd is;
>   Jesus died His sheep to save;
> He is mine, and I am His;
>   All I want in Him I have. ...
>   Bear me to the sacred scene,
> The silent streams and pastures green!
>   Where the crystal waters shine,
>   Springing up with life divine.

But there have been worse offenders on the side of content than Charles Wesley. Here, according to H. A. Glass, *The Story*

of the Psalters (London, 1888), are some of the grosser distor-
tionists of the recorded Word:

James Maxwell, 1773, substituted "the sacrifice of Christ" for
all allusions to "brutal sacrifices."

Elhanan Winchester, 1797, adapted his Psalter to the doctrine
held by Universalists.

Joseph Irons, a Calvinist, 1847, "trusted that Socinians,
Arians, and Arminians would find no music in his version for
their falsehoods."

It must, however, be said, concerning this matter of literalcy
of content, that there is perhaps no considerable body of rhymed
and metrical versions of the Psalms which has not had to make
some concessions to the form. One way of making up for such
acknowledged defect is to compile Psalters with more than one
version of some of the Psalms, so that what is amiss in the one
may be amended in the other. Such slighter departures from "the
original" usually take the form of addition, or "padding," or
"filler" words and phrases, not present in the source, but demanded by the meter, the rhyme, the line length, or the stanzaic group-
ing. Sometimes they take the form also, if not of actual omis-
sion, then of under-development of some sentiments, and of over-
development or repetition of others. At times, too, there is a re-
shifting of emphasis, owing to the fact that the rhyme-word, although it carries the accent, is not the word which the natural
logic of the statement stresses.

On the formal side, as distinguished from that of the content,
the continuing fault of the less successful translations is artificiality. This is to say that the verse may "scan" with almost mo-
notonous regularity, and may carry its rhymes well, but in the process of remaking loses its spiritual *elan*. Very frequent, too, are
the awkward inversions or transpositions of the logically desirable word order. The natural order, for instance, at the beginning of the 23rd, is "I shall not want." In the Bay Psalm Book
versions, 1640, this becomes, "Want therefore shall not I." The
reason for this transposition — and the type persists — is, of
course, the effort to get the rhyme word for the concluding line
of the stanza, which, in this example, becomes a similarly tor-
tured "Doth cause me down to lie."

Such artificialities would seem to be too high a price to pay.
They mar what ought to be a spiritually stirring poem, in order

to make it "available" for singing to a tune. And there are numerous like infelicities. Thus the "poetic license" of the *contraction* (*o'er, 'tis, where'er, I'll*), so easily called in by the older poetasters, is greatly overdone in many Psalm readings. It gives them an archaic and artificial cast.

What is worse is that many of the versifiers have been content to do justice to the denotation of the original, that is, to its basic logical thrust, and have not explored the possibilities of connotation and suggestiveness. The play of consonance and assonance, the management of sound, generally, and all the myriad subtleties that are at work in poetry as in music — these are neglected. In fact, one is gratified when such "suggestiveness" is present at all. It is present, for example, in this nice success of the Tate and Brady (1696) 42nd:

> As pants the hart for cooling streams,
> When heated in the chase,
> So yearns my soul, O God, for Thee,
> And Thy refreshing grace.

The denotation or direct logical meaning of that is the same as in Mather's clumsy effort quoted above, but consider how richly enhanced the total impact because of the better poetry. The suggestiveness is present also in Wiliam Kethe's well established "Old Hundredth":

> All people that on earth do dwell,
> Sing to the Lord with cheerful voice;
> Him serve with mirth, His praise forth tell,
> Come ye before Him and rejoice.

It may be interesting, after all this theory, to watch the versifiers at work for a moment. We can note some of them handling the 23rd Psalm. The King James text has:

> The Lord is my shepherd; I shall not want.
> He maketh me to lie down in green pastures; he leadeth me
> beside the still waters.

Robert Crowley, in 1549, earlier than the 1611 Bible, therefore, made this of it:

> The Lord is my Shephearde, and I shall never stand in
> nede;
> For in pasture exceedinge good He leadeth me to fede,
> He causeth me to laye me downe in pasture full of grasse;
> And dryveth me to caulme waters that be so clear as glasse.

That has a pleasant rhythm, suitable to the mood of the pastoral. But its diction is now forbiddingly archaic, and the last line tapers off in a too-scientific figure.

Now follows the work of Sternhold and Hopkins, whose collection of 1564 constituted the old standby of the English Psalter until partly supplanted in 1696. This one has a commendable directness. It is, one could say, right but not rich. And it has that unconvincing fourth line:

> My shepherd is the living Lord,
>   Nothing I therefore neede;
> In pastors fair with waters calm
>   He set me for to fede.

Sir Philip Sidney's handling in 1580 is interesting, though it were hard to find the music to suit it. The last two lines, however, have the very quality of the pastoral:

> The Lord, the Lord my Shephearde is,
>   And so can never I
>   Tast missery.
> He rests me in greene pasture his;
>   By waters still and sweete
>   He guides my feete.

Next follows the Francis Rous version, 1643 and following. His work dominated the traditionally established Scottish Psalter. His product is straightforward but meager:

> My shepherd is the living Lord,
>   And He that doth me feed;
> How can I then lack anything
>   Whereof I stand in need?

Such a reading lacks the imagery of the basic text. Perhaps Rous recognized that he had stripped the tree of its foliage. He tried again, and he got the suggestiveness of the figures, but then the transpositions came in:

> The Lord to me a shepheard is,
>   Want therefore shall not I;
> He in the folds of tender grasse
>   Doth cause me down to lie.

In 1668, Miles Smyth, a type of an "elegant" age, set out to dress up his version. His ornate introduction hints at the product: "The author of this version of the Psalmes of King David, considering the Excellency, not only of the Divine matter they contain, but of the Sacred Rapture wherein they were penned, and the sublime Poetry wherewith they were set out, and adorned by the Royal and Inspired Prophet, could not but blush to think, how that Metre in which our Parochial Churches usually sing them, hath disguised so eminent a part of the Holy Writ, which bears a more than ordinary stamp of that ever-blessed Spirit by which it was dictated and given. This gave the Author occasion to make Essay, whether (without taking the advantages of an unconfined Fancy) it might not be easie enough . . . to make them speak their own genuine sense, in proper and smooth English." Well, he made his "Essay" but what it proves is that it was not "easie":

> God, by whose Providence we live,
>   Whose care secures our rest,
> My shepherd is, no ill can touch
>   Nor want my Soul infest.
> He makes luxuriant flow'ry Meads
>   Serve me for Food and Ease;
> And leads me where the cooling Streams,
>   My thirsty heat appease.

So the versions go, down the historical line. The latest which comes to hand is that of Harry H. Mayer (Copyright, Liveright), referred to above. It is forthright, true, done in modern idiom, without inversion, and simple. Its defect? Yes, it is there: that last word, *hide,* is not quite what the sense requires, and is slightly forced:

> My Shepherd is the Lord,
>   What can I want beside?
> He leads me where green pastures are
>   And where cool waters hide.

Thus the perpetual quest goes on. What one could greatly wish for is poetry so stirring, so appropriate, so redolent of its own testimony to the truth, that one could not resist memorizing it. We must work to that end. And when we are satisfied that we have the best versions available, we should publish them independently, without musical notation, and proceed to commit them to memory. We used to do it in the old Dutch catechism classes. We could do it in the English catechism classes, we could do it in the Sunday schools, and we could do it in the Bible courses of the Christian schools. There is so wide a range of the truth of Revelation in the Psalms that the minister hardly has to reach out for hymns to accompany his sermons, even those on the Heidelberg Catechism. The sung doctrine of good poems, set to good music, and thus becoming good song, would be a great force for solid good in the church.

The Reformed Journal, July, 1953.

14

Of Writing Many Books

A while back I saw a new book lying on a table. It had an attractive sort of title: *The History and Character of Calvinism.* It was a big fat book, 466 pages of it, fresh from the press, the Oxford University Press. That is the sort of book, I said to myself, that is the sort of undertaking that ought to have come from one of us. In answer to the question, Who speaks for Calvinism? I felt like saying, We do.

For a moment I hoped the thing had happened, and that one of us had come through. I looked for the author's name and found it. No, it was not a Dutch name. The author was John T. McNeill, Auburn Professor of Church History at Union Theological Seminary. I glanced at the table of contents. There was a section on the pre-Reformation church. Then followed one on Calvin's life and achievement. A third discussed the spread of Calvinism in Europe and America. A final section treated of Calvinism and modern issues. Just the sort of book, I thought again, that might have come from one of us.

Well, I reflected, if we cannot produce the author of the book, we can at least contribute the materials for it. We can supply the sources. I turned to the bibliography and index. In the bibliography of this book on Calvinism, its history and character, there was not a single contribution from a Christian Reformed source. In the index there was, indeed, a familiar name. It was Berkhof's name. I checked to make sure this was not the Barthian Berkhof of the *Hervormde*, Netherlands. No, it was our Berkhof, though his initial was given, not as L for Louis, but as D for I do not know what.

One of our men, therefore, "made" the index to this history of Calvinism, and rated one sentence in the 644-page book. I flipped the pages of the volume to make sure there was no more of us than that. Then I found a half-sentence reference to the *Calvin Forum*. Congratulations!

This was something of a shock to me, but it brought home, I suppose, a useful lesson. When a person is inside a thing or stands next to it, the Christian Reformed Church, say, or Calvin College and Seminary, it looks big to him. He lacks the perspective and misses the proportion that distance gives. Here he was thinking that Calvinism in church and religion and life meant him. And then it comes home to him from such a book as this that Calvinism, its history and its character, can be pretty adequately described without reference to him and his church at all. It is, presumably, a useful lesson to learn.

This lesson learnt, however, it remains disappointing that we have been so unproductive in the very area of our conviction and our specialty, and that we have been this just when others in late decades and late years have done much to develop precisely this area of our specialization. In fact, the author of *The History and Character of Calvinism* found it necessary to point out that it was not Christian Reformed effort which signalled the renewed interest in Calvin. He writes:

> A revival of Calvinism, modified in various ways, is also apparent in the Anglo-Saxon world. It is apparently not much affected by Christian Reformed books in English but has arisen through a discriminating reconsideration of Calvin's thought by writers such as Thomas M. Lindsay, Herbert Darling Foster, A. Mitchell Hunter, and, later, Quirinus Breen, Georgia Harkness, R. N. Carew Hunt, James Mackinnon, and Arthur Dakin. More recently the Barth and Brunner discussions have deeply affected... such Calvin scholars as Thomas F. Torrance, Edward A. Dowey, Jr., and T. H. L. Parker.

Now it may well be that not all of these books represent Calvin faithfully, and it may also be that some of our own books, such as Dr. Meeter's volume, or the *God-Centered Living* of the Calvinistic Action Committee, are as deserving as some of the books mentioned by Professor McNeill. All the same, his account is in the main fairly taken, and that statement hurts: "A revival of Calvinism . . . not much affected by Christian Reformed books . . . ." We have been spectators to all of this production.

I lingered a while longer over the book but got no consolation. What I got was further disappointment:

The harrowing experiences of World War I, and its exposure of moral bankruptcy in the West, led to a widespread new spiritual quest. There arose a craving to renew the Calvinist awareness of God and the moral tonic of the Calvinist ethic. The new interest expressed itself in an unprecedented body of historical labor on the Reformed branch of the Reformation and particularly on the thought of Calvin. Calvin's doctrines became a field of research, an arena of animated debate, but also the object of religiously motivated inquiry.

It is my impression that in the way of research and scholarly publication we have done comparatively little beyond dissertations for higher degrees. The "unprecedented body of historical labor on the Reformed branch of the Reformation and particularly on the thought of Calvin" is the work of others.

It may be useful once more to reflect on the reasons for this dearth, comparatively speaking, of general and scholarly publication in our community. The publication of books and articles is not, of course, the only evidence for measuring the vigor of a living Calvinism. Missions, education, church extension, and the personal spiritual walk are all of them evidences too. I do not care to indulge, consequently, because of a paucity of substantial writing among us, in big, broad indictments of all of our works and ways. And, as I hinted, even in this matter of scholarly and general literary activity, we have done something. There has been enough of it, and of sufficient quality, to rate even a little better than Professor McNeill rates it. But by and large he is right. We have not done much.

Nor can we say that the situation is improving as time goes on. In fact, the first and second generation of ministers and professors did rather better on this count of scholarly publication than their successors are doing. Pioneers as they were, with their frontier problems, their primitive circumstances, and their incredibly busy practical lives, they wrote books and pamphlets and articles. The reason is ready to hand. Both they and the people they served were used to European traditions in these matters. They were, both the ministers and the people, simply an extension into the new world of the continental Reformed mind. The old education carried over. It carried over for the leader who wrote and for the reader who read.

Those earlier generations had respect for learning. The preachers and the teachers had this respect and, yes, the people had it too. Since then some of the people have lost this respect. And in mistaken deference to the sense of the people, some of the leaders too have preferred ability to knowledge, and have consented to going popular. This tendency was encouraged by our total American situation. Our trouble as Americans has been that as our learning became popular it ceased to be learning. As Americans in general, and not as Christian Reformed people in particular, we proliferated schools, colleges, and universities, but we did this as often as not for something other than truth, tradition, or wisdom. It was not learning so much that we wanted as it was ability. In short, we were pragmatic. Way back in the last century Matthew Arnold, an English writer and educator, quoted the Frenchman Renan against our American education:

> The countries which, like the United States, have created a considerable popular instruction without any serious higher instruction will long have to expiate this fault by their intellectual mediocrity, their vulgarity of manners, their superficial spirit, and their lack of general intelligence.

Perhaps we can shrug off this charge of vulgarity of manners by saying that it is simply the price we are willing to pay for the democratic virtue of genuineness. But those other three defects are important: intellectual mediocrity, superficial spirit, and lack of general intelligence. And speaking now of us Christian Reformed people in particular, and not of Americans generally, it seems time to be warning ourselves about just the thing Renan mentions: *the creation of a considerable popular instruction without any serious higher instruction*. If one of us is to write sometime a big book on the history and character of Calvinism, or if such a book, by whomever it is written, is to include in its bibliography a quantity of substantial contributions stemming from Christian Reformed sources, we shall have to get on with a University.

It may be that we ought also further to rid ourselves of our provinciality if we are to make important contributions to books on the history and character of Calvinism. Provinciality is, I know, a term which can mean little more than a sort of outlandishness of manners. I am thinking of it in a different way, and I lean once more on Arnold's notion of it to clarify the term. What, he asked,

> What, now, can be the reason of this undeniable provincialism of the English Puritans and Protestant Non-conformists? Men of genius and character are born and reared in this medium as in any other. . . . Surely the reason is that the Nonconformist is not in contact with the main current of national life.

Now I know that there can hardly be Nonconformists in a country like ours since we have no Establishment to conform to. But we have this in common with the English Puritans and Nonconformists that our convictions as embodied in the creeds and standards of our church do set us off sharply from the main current of the national and international religious life.

The truth is that we have sometimes looked and acted like a sect. We have done this most when we exhibited a lack of theological poise. One thinks of this every time he hears the words of that Form: ". . . the true and complete doctrine of salvation." Presumably people in possession of such a thing should live and act as though they were in Rome and not in the provinces. We ought to have the confidence of standing in the long and solid traditions of Reformed Christianity. There is really no room for an immigrant minority, or provincial mentality in such a faith and confession.

Nevertheless our history has been marred by a good deal of polemicist pamphleteering, and we have often felt insecure and anxious lest the discussion of secondary theological considerations should jeopardize the essentials of our religion. It may be that students of theology ought to be assigned to read a half ton or so of the harsher and more opinionated *controversia* that have emanated from the "sectarian" branches of the Reformed churches. It might serve as a warning to them never, or at least hardly ever, to indulge in them. The best that can be said for such disputations and internecine contention is that some sort of price must be paid for individually, as distinguished from officially, apprehended truth. For high sensitivity to the difference between truth and falsehood, and for the individual appropriation of the truth, we are willing indeed to pay a high price, any price. Nobody, presumably, wants to leave the narrow path and crowd into the broad way. But neither do we quite want it said of us, as

Matthew Arnold said of the English Nonconformist: "He has worshipped the fetish of separatism so long that he is likely to wish to remain, like Ephraim, 'a wild ass alone by himself.'"

That other statement of Arnold haunts me, too: "Men of genius and character are born and reared in this medium as in any other." Genius may be saying too much, but men of talent and great ability there have certainly been among us, and now are. But one sometimes hears it remarked and himself also guesses that quite a few men of more than ordinary promise among us never quite fulfilled the promise. There is pathos in this, deep pathos. There has been some thwarting and frustration of the aspiring power, the original force, and the early ideal. Perhaps we can all guess at the names, and guess also at the reasons for the comparative failure. For one thing, this talent has had to live in a small community of like-mindedness. One does not expect a Dante to emerge from Mormonism, and this is not merely because Mormonism is false, but also because it is small. For another thing the demand of the horizontal has been stronger on us than that of the vertical. Our situation favored the development of practical men rather than scholarly men. We have been constantly on the frontier, expanding rather than concentrating. True, we maintained our identity by our isolation, but our isolation also impoverished us. It tended to cut us off from resources of learning and ability. Sometimes we got so used to talking to each other that we forgot how to talk to others. It was so much easier to be effective among those who agreed with us already.

And it may be that there are other reasons for the failure in fruition — if such it was — of the talent and ability and promise of some of our ablest men. Some of them felt ill-equipped to work with the primary sources because of their lack of the tongues. That is always frustrative for basic historical and theological work. Some of them were surprised by the pace of the years, and did not know until it was too late that a man must live a selective and orderly life if he is to discipline himself into solid accomplishment. Some of them — I surmise — felt intellectually compromised by the tardiness sometimes of Christian orthodoxy to confront directly all the challenges put to it by the times. Some lacked the sense of the past. Some lacked the sense of their own age. Some feared lest their inquiries disturb the theological equilibrium of their church. But be the reasons what they may, there was pathos in it. It is a pity that so much of our promise has not been fulfilled.

If men of talent and ability are born in our medium as in any other, it must be something in the situation that keeps our rightness from becoming ripeness, something that keeps us from a rich and ample productivity. I have hinted at some of the more deeply seated elements in this situation. Let me conclude this time by pointing out one more reason. It is this: our men lack the opportunity. I am thinking especially of our ministers. There is talent and enterprise among them, and also some scholarly aspiration. But we have not devised a way for them to follow up their serious studies. We make work horses out of them. We put them through a weekly round of "parish" duties, and let them come up, breathless and panting, to their sermon making during the week-end. In return we give them a stinted three weeks of vacation. This is all wrong. For the scholarly among them, this should be three months. They should go to Union, to Princeton, to the Free University, to Edinburgh, to Hartford, to Louisville or back to Calvin, or wherever, if they want to study. They require time and resources to work out their projects.

We are, as I suggested above, developing so fast horizontally that we are likely to neglect the vertical development. Presumably no one would want to impede this horizontal growth. But we must have the concentration also. Always busy taking on new territory in the open universe of the Reformed challenge we must nevertheless also consolidate the occupation of it. This whole matter of scholarly productivity is admittedly something which cannot be forced. It must come naturally or not at all. But it must come. We must begin to write books some time in which our doctrinal identity is unmistakable and of which it can nevertheless be said that they savor not at all of sectarian disease.

The Reformed Journal, January, 1955.

15

"Religious" Fiction

A review of No Trumpet Before Him
by Nelia Gardner White

Paul Phillips, a Methodist minister, is presented in this novel as a preacher hero whose personal integrity is made to win out in the end over parishioners who had supposed they would rather mould their minister than be moulded by him. Paul is no longer wanted in Aporia because the people of his little rural church suppose he is a bumbler and is lacking in social tact. The case is, however, that he thinks more highly of conscientious preaching than he does of flourishing Boy Scout organizations, and cares more for outspoken admonishment to some of the members of his church than for the Missionary Society dinners those members like to promote. So they get it communicated to Bishop Fellowes that they want the Reverend Mr. Phillips assigned elsewhere.

The Bishop acquiesces, but so far from sending Paul down to Soda Center, the one charge with fewer responsibilities than even Aporia, he promotes him to First Church, Warrenton. Warrenton is the cultural capital of the state, and First Church is rich and socially elite. Its members have dieted these many years on cultural talks mildly tinctured with religion. Moving tactfully among the people of Warrenton, consequently, while faithfully preaching the truth is a matter of some nicety for which Paul Phillips is not well suited.

At Warrenton, Paul sticks to his last, preaches what he calls "the teachings of Jesus," and for the rest sits in his usually unvisited church office trying honestly to face reality. There are points on which he will not compromise. He eliminates a professor's projected discussion of Baudelaire from the mid-week lecture series of the church. He welcomes a Negro to the congregation, and pays a social call upon the man in his ramshackle hovel across the tracks. On Christmas day, instead of pleasing the people with holiday sentiments safely remote from practical implications, he tells his audience that the disgraceful Negro slums of the town are their doing. So, and in other ways, Paul brings on the board meeting which is called to petition for his oustment.

But Paul's influence has had time to work, especially among the young who had been whetting their cynicism on the feebleness of the Christianity they had grown up in. Jeanie Fellowes, for instance, cynical, sated, and troubled by the consequences of rebel indiscretion, is attracted to the genuineness in Phillip. So is Gabriel Ficke, a smart Bohemian young blade, and so is Keziah Woodley, an idealistic young creature seeking content for her ideals. These had expected to find Mr. Phillips another stuffed shirt and are surprised to discover a man in it. They rally to him. Even Miss Pyne, who is mainly responsible for the squalor of the Negroes, gets to thinking about things. Instead of voting for Paul's release, she speaks in his defense. The petition fails, Paul is vindicated, and true religion would seem to have a future at Warrenton.

Those are the materials of the novel, and as materials they are commendable enough. This book moves in a medium of church and parsonage. It is, as we say in our demoralized times, "wholesome," and it contains no profanity, obscenity, or sex exploitation. It is the sort of book that can "safely" be put into church libraries.

Nevertheless it is a poor book. It is not authentic. It lacks, not competent craftsmanship, but artistic integrity. The ground swell of experience does not surge up in it; the right of conviction resounding from insight cannot be heard; the testament of mind and spirit are not present in it. The whole novel is contrived. It is not literature.

It is not literature: it is trade writing. It is calculated to hit as big a piece of the religious market as possible. As such, it comes off. Speaking on the level of its own importance, one can say that this "religious" novel is a slick job. The *Saturday Evening Post* spotted it right away, and serialized it: this was for the million: enough religion to appeal to everybody, not enough to embarrass anybody, a touch of Lloyd Douglas' optimism, and a reminder of Cronin's and Werfel's hero saints. Now let it be true, as Oscar Wilde said, that all art is exaggeration, and that it takes a little contrivance, something of the manipulator as well as the seer, to fit the stuff of life into the mould of fiction. But when one encounters such calculated manipulation as *No Trumpet Before Him,* he feels pretty certain that what the trade calls "slick" writing is indeed slick writing, and mostly tripe. It is the product, not of a reading of reality, but of a reading of the market. And the fact that such slanted writing is aimed at the religious market, rather than at the tired housewife, the teen-age, or the 50,000 dollar income market, makes it no better as literature.

The pity of it is that this book was awarded the 8,000 dollar Westminster Award for Christian fiction. Apparently the religious fiction awards are becoming big enough to make it worthwhile for professional writers to put out a neatly fashioned commodity according to the specifications of the prospectus. Miss Gardner at least has a practiced hand for pleasing the million, and her novel is more successful than most religious novels precisely because it is the product of an able worker. But competent or incompetent, the end is still a low one, not a high one; the result is still trade writing and not literature. In such writing the author's fidelity is a fidelity to the principle of business, and the principle of business in such matters is to touch on everything everyone wants to hear, to touch on nothing so profoundly as to cause discomfort, and yet profoundly enough to make the reader think it is literature he is reading. What the duty of the author comes to then is a duty to his employer's sense of how much reality the trade will bear.

Religious fiction awards, when they function in this way, and religious fiction, when it is conceived and written in this manner, are enough to make one wish that the adjective "religious" would never again be attached to the noun "fiction." But that is our secular-Protestant way nowadays: to sprinkle a little religious sentiment over a demoralized culture. So we get "religious" politics, "religious" journalism, "religious" education, and "religious" art. It is a question-begging performance.

The Calvin Forum, June-July, 1948.

16

A Tragedy of Pity

A review of The Heart of the Matter
by Graham Greene

General MacArthur has lately said in effect that the problem
of contemporary international politics is fundamentally theological. The same can be said of contemporary fiction. And it can
be added that such writers as Francois Mauriac, Bruce Marshall,
Evelyn Waugh, and Graham Greene recognize this. Their novels
spring from the Catholic Christian insight and commitment. Their
theologically grounded morals and morally grounded psychology
is expressing itself in a realism compared to which the realism of
the 20s, despite all of its neurological scalpel wielding and clinical
anatomizations, seems perfunctory and superficial. The Christian, apparently, is at bottom the most courageously thoroughgoing of realists, the one, after all, who dares to look the devil
full in the face, and who, having seen God and Golgotha, finds
all other glory and all other horror rather commonplace.

Green's enormously interesting new novel, *The Heart of the
Matter,* presents in very brief compass a fully orbed drama of
what Professor Parrott, speaking of *Macbeth,* called the progressive degeneration of the wilfully sinning soul. It presents Major
Scobie, a middle aged man, who has completed fifteen years as an
officer of police in the foreign service of British West Africa. His
record for careful, honest work is good, in fact, singularly unim-
peachable. Scobie is an ordinary man who describes himself as
not the kind of person who is likely to get into trouble. But in the
universe of this novel, the ordinary man, when the religious issues of life are operative in him, takes on the proportions of heroism. Scobie pities those he encounters, and feels responsible for
their happiness. His weakest point is this virtue of pity, and evil

seizes on him at precisely this point. Pity is his tragic frailty. So far from not getting into trouble, consequently, the usually considerate, cautious, and justly dealing Scobie embarks upon a program of evil comparable to Macbeth's in scope. Before the curtain goes down on the final act he has abused his office by withholding evidence from his superiors, has cooperated with a diamond-smuggling Syrian and thus aided the enemy in time of war, has committed adultery, been an accomplice in murder, used the holy Sacrament unworthily, and done the deed of spiritual despair which is suicide. Such is the enormous breach that pity has blasted through his integrity.

No doubt the interpretations of the drama in this novel, like those of good drama always, of *Hamlet,* say, or *Macbeth,* are likely to be protean. There will be readers who look upon Scobie as an unmanly man, fundamentally weak and evasive, who hasn't the character to stand up to his choices, and whose pity is sentimentally Rousseauistic. Others will say that the novel goes to show how self-conscious Catholicism is becoming, and will regard Scobie's conflicts as an expression of artificiality in the Church. Others will regard it as Greene's way of saying that the teaching of the Church on suicide in its cold rectitude and doctrinaire finality is obscurantistic, missing the implications of the religious life and doing injustice to the love of God. Some liberal Protestants may even welcome the book as a Catholic confession of humanitarianism. And others, again, will see in Scobie a kind of Catholic Puritan, who must still be saving himself by his works because he cannot rest in God and surrender his responsibilities to Him. There is some reason also to believe that Scobie's pity is a reflection of the unspeakable compassion of God and His Christ which can reach down and embrace even the pitying sinner. But the interpretations will indeed be protean. One would like to hear a few parish priests of sensitive morality and sound doctrine discuss the course of evil in Scobie's life; one would like also to see Protestant writers to whom evil is as ingenerate and puissant a force as it is in this novel, try to embody the course of its influence with as ample implication as Greene has done.

Greene's handling of this matter is absolutely dramatic. It may be that *The Heart of the Matter* is headed for the theatre. In point of structure it is perfect. The composition, what novelists nowadays call structuring, is admirable; the interdependence of the parts insures the independence of the whole. In this, Greene is Poesque according to the strictest canons of the "Philosophy of Composition." There is not a wasted line, a wasted word. His dialogue is brilliant; it is the distilled essence of dialogue, sparing and fine enough for utterance from the boards, and is dramatic in this respect also that it characterizes the characters even as it advances the action. Such writing is above experiment, is altogether expert. The action is single, the focussing sharp; all that enters into the story swiftly establishes its relevance to Scobie and his conflict. There is some setting, some atmosphere, but it is not achieved by fine writing or massed description; it is the cumulative effect of selected details, few but sharply seen, crisply reproduced, and subtly reiterated. Humid heat, malarial climate, rats scurrying out of bathtubs, a lizard idling on the wall, and vultures incessantly clanking on the roofs — these give us sense of scene enough. As for the human setting, there are the natives, the objects of Scobie's solicitude; and there is also the usual assortment of foreign service officialdom who have their stipulated duty, their waiting for leave and retirement, their boredom, and their drinks at the Club. But it is all terribly organic; the pressure is tremendous. Nothing happens in the drama that is unprepared for, and nothing in preparation betrays the end until it comes. It is important literature.

The Calvin Forum, August-September, 1948

17

The Criticism of Poetry

A review of Points of View
by T. S. Eliot

Eliot has just received the Nobel Prize for Literature. There is no new book of his to attend to on this occasion. But those who are interested in further extending his influence can do worse than present his *Points of View* for announcement. This book, which came out first in 1941 and has now reached its fourth impression, is a volume of excerpts from Eliot's previously published works of literary and general criticism. The selections were made "with the author's approval, by John Hayward." The *Points of View* is designed, apparently, to tempt the appetite. One hopes that it will lead to a consumption of the whole canon of Eliot's critical work.

Quite apart from his formidable influence on contemporary poetry, certainly the most pressing and pervasive influence in modern literature, Eliot has been enormously influential in literary criticism. In fact, most essays in the criticism of poetry of the last twenty-five years have been essays in adjustment to Eliot's theory. The influence has not always been welcome; but welcome or unwelcome it has been continuously pressing. So, for example, in Leonard Unger's *T. S. Eliot: A Selected Critique* (Rinehart), which, incidentally, is only one of five books about Eliot to be published this year, some thirty prominent men of letters can be seen hovering over his critical dicta. The spectacle resembles so many scholastics glossing the text of Aristotle.

In his estimates of others, Eliot sometimes lays bare the qualities which distinguish his own critical intelligence. He speaks of Aristotle, for instance, as one "who looked solely and steadfastly at the object," and again as one "who followed no method ex-

LITERATURE AND LIFE

cept to be very intelligent ... swiftly operating the analysis of
sensation to the point of principle and definition." And of Mach-
iavelli Eliot remarked that although he was "constructive," he
"was not a system-builder," that his thoughts "could be repeated
but not summarized," and that it was "perhaps a character of his
amazing exactness of vision and statement that he should have
no 'system'." Now those are remarks which can appropriately
be applied to Eliot's critical mind also. His is the kind of thinking which, as he said of F. H. Bradley, pursues the *via media,*
"of all ways the most difficult to follow" because it "requires discipline and self-control . . . imagination and hold on reality." He
works from common sense, but it is a common sense "not to be
got at without maturity, and study and thought."

In his literary criticism, Eliot began by regarding "poetry as
poetry, and not another thing." He held that "art may serve
ends beyond itself, but . . . is not required to be aware of these
ends . . . and indeed performs its function . . . much better by indifference to them." If that sounds like an entering wedge to a
philosophy of art for art's sake, remember that there is some truth
in that much-abused dictum. Art is sometimes given and made
to accept all kinds of work which does not belong to it. Accordingly Eliot resented the work of those critics who "busy themselves so much with the implications of a poem . . . that the poetry
becomes hardly more than a text for a discourse." We understand
him, understand him too when he cautions us to "distinguish the
appreciation of poetry from theorizing about poetry." In reaction, therefore, to the prophets, messiahs, and crusaders of literature (he sat under the catalyzing agency of Babbitt at Harvard),
Eliot felt it incumbent upon him, particularly in his early period,
to argue for the integrity of poetry as poetry and not another
thing. These are warnings and elucidations the Arnolds and Rus-
kins and Paul Elmer Mores of criticism need. It was of such as
they that Eliot was thinking when he spoke of the "temptation
of any man who is interested in ideas . . . to put literature into
the corner until he has cleaned up the whole world" as an "almost
irresistible temptation."

L'art pour l'art — surely Eliot is right in reminding us that
if this is taken to mean that the poet, like the dentist, is a man
with a definite job, it is the plain truth. Still, and this Eliot knew
and came to know better as time went on, it is a dictum which
can be acted upon only in integrated, ordered, and settled so-
cieties. Had he lived in Virgil's, or Dante's, or even Shakespeare's

age, Eliot might have remained content with regarding what he once called "the literary job" as a purely literary function. He might then, using the tools of comparison and analysis which he handled so admirably, have gone on commenting on "the felicity and blemish" of poetry "line by line," and so have maintained what is in fact an ideal "critical integrity." But in disintegrated periods such aesthetic provinciality is impossible. Eliot put his finger squarely upon this important fact in speaking of Dr. Samuel Johnson: "For Johnson poetry is still poetry, and not another thing. Had he lived a generation later, he would have been obliged to look more deeply into the foundations, and so would have been unable to leave us an example of what criticism ought to be for a civilization which, being settled, has no need, while it lasts, to enquire into the functions of its parts."

Ours is an age, of course, which was to be distinguished for achievement because we had finally got our labor divided, and so made specialization possible. What is happening, however, is that for want of a prevailing dogma and over-ruling philosophy, the functions of the parts of our society are no longer clear, and the parts are losing significance. We see the results: ministers going from the pulpit to the rostrum as social crusaders, scientists becoming philosophers without knowing the rules of the game, and poets turning into moralists and economic reformers. Everybody is leaping the pales of his enclosure and meddling in other people's affairs. This, too, is a consequence of secularity and a definition of atomism.

Eliot has therefore progressed, reluctantly because of his commendable concern for the integrity of poetry, but inevitably because of the pressures of the time, from a purely aesthetic position in literary criticism to one which "perceives the contiguity and continuity" of the several provinces of life and thought. Of F. H. Bradley, he once said: "He wished only to determine how much morality could be founded without entering into the religious question at all." It is perhaps accurate to say that in the spirit of that utterance, Eliot has for the most part been trying to found as much critical theory securely as is possible without entering the religious question. In his later period he has, however, found it increasingly necessary to enter into that question also. Thus, with a kind of flourish rare in his writings, he asked, in his Harvard lectures of 1932, "whether culture requires that we make a deliberate effort to put out of mind all our convictions and passionate beliefs about life." So his Virginia lectures, *After*

Strange Gods, were concerned with nothing less than the influence of the devil on modern literature, and in 1940 he published his *Idea of a Christian Society.* Eliot plainly does not want the needful order and integration on totalitarian or naturalistic bases. Anglo-Catholic in religion, he looks to revealed Christianity for the saving dogma, meanwhile in such books and articles as *Die Einheit der Europaischen Kultur* and "The Christian Conception of Education" reminding Western civilization, democratic or otherwise, that it had better look to the origins and bases of its tradition. A long way removed, such concerns as these, from those simply aesthetic concerns of *The Sacred Wood* published in 1920. But it would seem to be the only course which intelligence in our time can take.

Such are some of the perspectives opened up by the *Points of View.* These comments have, however, gone behind the excerpts of that volume to the sources from which they were lifted. It remains, therefore, to add that most of the Eliot rights in America are owned by Harcourt, Brace, and Co., among them those to the *Selected Essays* and the *Essays Ancient and Modern,* from which I have quoted freely.

The Calvin Forum, January, 1949.

18

The Craft of Fiction

A review of A Writer's Diary
by Virginia Woolf

For twenty-six years, that is, from 1915 up to her death in 1941, Virginia Woolf systematically kept a diary. Unlike Robert Louis Stevenson, who held that keeping a diary was a "school of posturing and melancholy self-deception," Virginia Woolf felt that it was a real benefit to a writer. She discovered that ". . . the habit of writing thus for my own eye is good practice. It loosens the ligaments." Being almost a perfectionist in her scrupulous concern for the craft of writing, she at one time forbids her future self to "let the eye of man behold" her journal confidences. Yet, at another time, she herself gives her husband, Leonard Woolf, the signal for drawing up just such a book as *A Writer's Diary* is: "If I died what would Leo make of them? . . . Well, he should make up a book. . . ."

The book Leonard Woolf made up is well named *A Writer's Diary*. His principle of selection has been to include "practically everything which referred to her own writing." The result is that this fascinating book of journal entries "throws light upon Virginia Woolf's intentions, objects and methods as a writer." And, as the Editor goes on to say in his Preface, "it gives an unusual psychological picture of artistic production from within." In kind — I do not say in quality and importance — the *Diary* belongs with Goethe's *Conversations* and Henry James' *Prefaces*. It is not often that we readers and students of fiction have a chance thus to stand by at the conception, birth, and career of a modern writer's books.

Virginia Woolf's whole life went into books. She made them also in the physical sense, at the Hogarth Press situated in her

home. She read them. Her journal shows how deliberately selective she was in her purposive reading. She criticized and reviewed them: in fact, she gave out a solid body of criticism, at
first to the periodicals, particularly to the *Times Literary Supplement,* and eventually in her first and second *Common Reader*
and in other books. And, of course, she wrote them. She did
some biography — of Elizabeth Barrett in *Flush* and of her artist friend in *Roger Fry.* She did some stories and sketches and
vignettes. But her main effort, of course, went into her novels.
They came regularly in the 20s and 30s: *Mrs. Dalloway, To the
Lighthouse, The Waves, The Years,* and the rest. This, then, is
to live the literary life. And she had the background for it.
Daughter of Leslie Stephen of the *Dictionary of National Biography* (one wonders whether he will eventually be called Virgina
Woolf's father or she Leslie Stephen's daughter), she was, as
Anne Freemantle pointed out in a recent *Commonweal,* "dandled
on every literary knee in England." She grew up to move in the
brilliant and unconventional Bloomsbury circle: Clive Bell, Leonard Woolf, Roger Fry, Saxon Sydney-Turner, Lytton Strachey,
Maynard Keynes, and their friends.

What we get in the *Diary,* naturally, is her personal shop-
talk with herself about the writing and the reception of her books.
It is valuable reading for anyone who cares about Virginia Woolf,
modern fiction, and the art of writing. The diary entries are
well written. If her random scribblings are thus shapely, one says
to himself, what must those conscientiously fashioned novels
be? Well, one has only to turn to them to find out why Virginia
Woolf is referred to as a "pure artist" so frequently. She inher-
ited the aesthetic way of life and art. The ritual that some indulge at mass, and others in the finesse of theological dialectic,
she carried out in the asceticism of a style which was agonizingly
perfected.

Her *Diary* is the best of commentaries on her work. She knows
her own weaknesses, her strengths. "But is it 'unreal'? Is it
mere accomplishment?" she asks of *Mrs. Dalloway.* It is a good
question for the heirs of Pater's aestheticism to be asking. She
delights in Fausset's comment on her in the Manchester *Guard-
ian*: "brilliance combined with integrity." In point of craft, she
had that, she certainly had it. Were her books novels? She wonders sometimes, even considers casting about for a new name, a
sort of private *genre* for the works of Virginia Woolf. She speaks
with a kind of disdain of Hardy's old-fashioned Aristotelianism in

clinging to a beginning, middle, and end in his novels. But she knows too that this is her lack: structure and architectonics. She admits it of *To the Lighthouse*.: ". . . it is hopelessly undramatic. It is all in oratio oblique." What Virginia Woolf lacked was *idea* and *purpose*. When one thinks of this, the Diary takes on tragic dimension. She is haunted by Leonard Woolf's comment on her *Jacob's Room*: "I have no philosophy of life, he says . . ." And there is pathos in her remark about Mrs. Webb's book: "But then there were causes in her life: prayer, principle." Mark Schorer once called fiction a "technique for discovery." There is a sense in which Virginia Woolf's series of novels were a technique for discovering her unbelief. Leslie Stephen, whom the *Times* calls "the parent of Bloomsbury," did not leave his daughter a good spiritual legacy. The conviction of futility seizes Virginia again and again with suicidal force as she writes herself towards progressive disillusionment.

It seems base to be quoting diary entries against a person. What would people think of any of us if all the world eavesdropped at our confessional? But it comes as a surprise to see that even a pure artist can have the feet of clay. She holds it against Joyce that he is a "self-taught workingman" but is herself about as money-conscious a writer as could be. She is terribly process-conscious, too, in her writing of books, and waits in fear and trembling for what the *Times* will say of her new book. She is a little patronizing towards the generation of novelists that preceded her — Galsworthy, Hardy, Bennett, Conrad, and the rest — and a little jealous of the praises that go to her younger contemporaries. And she easily gets off balance when the newer critics, Wyndham Lewis, Cyril Connolly, F. R. Leavis, and their kind, begin to criticize her work unfavorably in *Horizon* and in *Scrutiny*.

The importance of the *Diary* will hinge eventually on the reputation of the novels. One thing may be against that future reputation. Virginia Woolf stands at the end of the aesthetic movement. Hers was an attempt to show that you can, by artistic subtlety, make up for a lack of belief and thought and cause. It was an attempt to show that art can be a substitute for life. Two other figures of our century, both of them also heirs of aestheticism, have made the same attempt. Theirs was herculean, compared with Mrs. Woolf's. They are Joyce and Yeats. In one of her entries, Virginia writes: "I reflected how what

I'm doing is probably being better done by Mr. Joyce." This seems to me indisputable. In both, aestheticism is on trial. In both the verdict is unfavorable. But Joyce's is far the bigger demonstration of that failure.

The Calvin Forum, August-September, 1954.

19

From Atheism to Christianity

A review of Surprised by Joy
by C. S. Lewis

Ever since C. S. Lewis entertained and instructed us with his *Screwtape Letters,* we have been aware that in this gifted writer the Anglican world had the equal in Christian apology of the Roman G. K. Chesterton. In the author of *Screwtape, Mere Christianity,* and *Pilgrim's Regress* we recognized a talent for popular Christian witness comparable in our decades only to that of the author of *Orthodoxy* and *Heretics.* Both of these men, the G.K.C. of yesterday, and the C.S.L. of today, have made many a Reformed well-wisher sigh for a Reformed writer as brilliant in his mode of address to the modern mind as these two proved to be.

C. S. Lewis is a many-sided man. There are at least three of him: the professor, the novelist, and the lay theologian. As professor of poetry, first at Oxford and lately at Cambridge, he has produced two works of solid literary scholarship, *The Allegory of Love* and *The Sixteenth Century* in the Oxford History of English Literature. As novelist, he has produced such phantasy pieces full of religious implication as *Perelandra* and *That Hideous Strength* and such charming children's literature as *Prince Caspian* and *The Silver Chair.* And as lay theologian, as apologete, he has written *The Problem of Pain, Miracles, Christian Behaviour* and several other volumes of religious literature.

Surprised by Joy is spiritual autobiography. Lewis takes pains to point out that there is only so much of autobiography in it as is spiritual. Whatever in his life had no perceptible influence or bearing on his conversion is omitted. Nevertheless there is a good deal in the book which, although in the end it proves relevant to the conversion, seems at first reading to be generally autobiographical. The author feels that "the net has to be spread pretty wide" in the earlier chapters if we are to know, when the spiritual crises came, who and what the nature was that encountered the irresistible grace.

We can only be grateful for this net widely spread, for in this way we get all kinds of by-products as well as the principal commodity. We get for example, a devastating indictment of the English public schools. These schools, we must recall, are the equivalent in kind to what in our own country we call the private schools. They prepare privileged boys for the university. But first Lewis went to a boarding school which he calls Belsen and describes in a chapter called Concentration Camp. Life here was made grotesquely repulsive by the mean and wrong-headed master. The boys learned nothing but a little mathematics and lived in constant misery. Lewis concludes: "Life in a vile boarding-school is in this way a good preparation for the Christian life, that it teaches one to live by hope."

Later, Lewis went to a school he calls Wyvern, and it is in his account of this place that he mercilessly exposes the fagging system. According to this system, by no means limited to *Tom Brown's School Days* but extending right on into the twentieth century, the boys at the school below a particular level of seniority become the labor pool of the boys beyond that level. Let a fag show "cheek" or "side" or anything short of joyous acquiescence in the menialities of upperclass snobbery, and his life is made insufferably wretched for him. The system is regularly defended as excellent Preparation for Public Life, but Lewis judges otherwise:

> For the last thirty years or so England has been filled with a bitter, truculent, sceptical, debunking and cynical intelligentsia ... Those who defend the schools will, of course, say that these Prigs are the cases which the system failed to cure; they were not kicked, mocked, fagged, flogged and humiliated enough. But surely it is equally possible that they are the products of the system? that they were not Prigs at all when they came to their schools but were made Prigs by their first year, as I was? ... No one is more likely to be arrogant than a lately freed slave.

So vivid and well taken are Lewis's accounts of early twentieth-century schools that they could well be made compulsory reading for education courses. One predicts that his book will live on in the literature of education quite as immortally as in the literature of conversions. Very memorable, too, are his descriptions of two of his best teachers, Old Smewgy at Wyvern (". . . he first taught me the right sensuality of poetry, how it should be savoured and mouthed in solitude"), and "Kirk" at Bookham ("The idea that human beings should exercise their vocal organs for any purpose other than that of communicating or discovering truth was to him preposterous"). Kirkpatrick pushed Lewis directly into the body of the *Iliad,* translating a hundred lines at a time for his pupil and then telling him, be it with benefit of Crusius's *Lexicon,* to go it on his own. It worked:

> The great gain was that I very soon became able to understand a great deal without . . . translating it; I was beginning to think in Greek. That is the great Rubicon to cross in any language. Those in whom the Greek word lives only while they are hunting for it in the lexicon, and who then substitute the English word for it, are not reading the Greek at all; they are only solving a puzzle.

Such comments on education, and on many fascinating subjects besides, are, however, secondary to the main interest of the book. The primary interest is the tale, as Lewis tells it, of "how I passed from Atheism to Christianity. . . ." It may be that *Surprised by Joy* will become a classic in the conversion literature of the world. It has much of the candor and matter-of-fact objectivity of Newman's *Apologia.* It testifies of "a superabundance of mercy" as tellingly as *Grace Abounding.* It is Thompson's *Hound of Heaven* experienced in a life: his harness piece by piece was hewn from him until he waited Love's uplifted stroke. God closed in on him:

> In the Trinity Term of 1929 I gave in, and admitted that God was God, and knelt and prayed: perhaps, that night, the most dejected and reluctant convert in all England. I did not then see what is now the most shining and obvious thing; the Divine humility which will accept a convert even on such terms. The Prodigal Son at least walked home on his own feet. But who can duly adore that Love which will open the high gates to a prodigal who is brought in kicking, struggling, resentful, and darting his eyes in every direction for a chance of escape?

That was the destination. But what of the way thither? How did it all go, and what was the mode of this futile escaping from the tremendous Lover?

This retelling cannot be the original tale, nor this review the book it reviews. But here follow some of the arches of the years down which the fleeing sinner sped. To begin, he had long ago, as a child, been stabbed by the pangs of desire, been touched by the eternal, been seized upon by joy. The occasions of this visitation were slight: a brother's moss garden, Beatrix Potter's *Squirrel Nutkin,* and *Longfellow's* translated lines

> I heard a voice that cried,
> Balder the beautiful
> Is dead, is dead —

He felt the "inconsolable longing" of this joy again about the time of his going to Wyvern. The provocation this time was Arthur Rackham's illustration of the Wagnerian *Twilight of the Gods.* And to this class of his experiences, which he describes somewhere as being "of another dimension," belongs also his reading of George MacDonald's *Phantastes* ("I saw the bright shadow coming out of the book into the real world and resting there, transforming all common things and yet itself unchanged").

There is much in this concern for joy, and in this preoccupation with the hints and premonitions of glory, which reminds of Wordsworth. What is one to make of these extraordinary experiences, these flashes of mystical vision? Two things, perhaps, we can say: First that they are not quite illusory, that there is in them indeed "something very like adoration," and next, that without the fulfillment of God's self-revelation in Christ as confirmed by faith they are, as Lewis allows, "not very important." Wordsworth deplored the fleeing of the visionary gleam, complained that there had passed away a glory from the earth, and he thereupon moved closer to theistic realism. Lewis, too, takes a more tempered view of his mystical insights after his recall to God:

> I believe that the old stab . . . has come to me as often and as sharply since my conversion as at any time of my life whatever. But I now know that the experience . . . had never had the kind of importance I once gave it. It was valuable only as a pointer to something other and outer. While the other was in doubt, the pointer naturally loomed large in my thoughts.

At his home as a child in Belfast, Ireland, Lewis was taught "the usual things and made to say . . . prayers and in due time taken to church." However, it was in the misery of his life at that first boarding school that he had his first "religious" period. Prompted by fear, perhaps, as much as by anything, he took to serious Bible reading and to prayers. Because he was scrupulous to a fault about "realizing" his petitions, the prayers became a "nagging" burden, and it eased him later to have done with the whole obligation. At Wyvern the matron was a woman "floundering in the mazes" of Occultist tradition. The "vagueness" and "speculative character" of this Higher Thought seeped into the dykes of his boyhood creed. It was a delicious relief: "There was nothing to be obeyed. . . ."

The enemy had him started now. The next step is his reading of the classics. Those of us who are the friends of the classics are loathe to record the datum that these caused him doubt. Still, it was not the fact that the classics were taught that caused the trouble; it was the fact that they were taught wrong. The religion in them *was always presented as nonsense.* That *fostered* the scepticism:

> Here, especially in Virgil, one was presented with a mass of religious ideas; and all teachers and editors took it for granted . . . that these religious ideas were sheer illusion. No one ever attempted to show in what sense Christianity fulfilled Paganism or Paganism pre-figured Christianity. The accepted position seemed to be that religions were normally a mere farrago of nonsense. . . .

Moreover, Lewis had by now developed a kind of pessimism, something perhaps more psychologically than rationally rooted, a "settled expectation that everything would do what you did not want it to do."

He was confirmed in his scepticism by a number of forces. There was, for example, that teacher Kirkpatrick, a master dialectician, who, had he lived a little later, "would have been a Logical Positivist." This man provided fresh ammunition for Lewis's own Rationalism. The Materialist universe was altogether a comfortable kind of place. In it you were at worst dealing with "limited liabilities." You could at a pinch choose to step out of it with impunity. It was not so in the Christian universe: "Christianity placed at the center . . . a transcendental Interferer." And

Lewis in his "monstrous individualism" was trying to stake off a claim that would permit No Admittance.

However, the strong feet were following after, and the Divine preparation for a change of heart was beginning in the mind. There was, for instance, that vexing logical inconsistency between his Positivism and his religious Romanticism. His reading of the poet Yeats troubled him: here was a man, not a Christian, who wanted nothing to do with Rationalism and Materialism, and offered a kind of magic as alternative. Lewis was beginning to find that a "young man who wishes to remain a sound Atheist cannot be too careful of his reading." Chesterton's *Everlasting Man* put him off his poise and MacDonald's *Phantastes* restored something of that old visionary gleam. Now he consulted Idealism and the English Hegelians. He saw their Absolute but could not love it. Smaller things began mounting up.

It was so, as Lewis puts it, that "the great Angler played His fish." The labyrinthine ways were running out. The hardest boiled of atheists, he says, confirmed the historicity of the Gospels in his presence: "All that stuff of Frazer's," the man had said, "about the Dying God. Rum thing. It almost looks as if it had really happened once." From Atheism to Idealism to Theism to Christianity. Those were the steps.

> Every step I had taken, from the Absolute to "Spirit" and from "Spirit" to "God," had been a step towards the more concrete, the more imminent, the more compulsive.

Finally there was the decision, freely made, and yet made for him. "I was driven to Whipsnade one sunny morning. When we set out I did not believe that Jesus Christ is the Son of God, and when we reached the zoo I did."

Lewis is right: "The words *compelle intrare,* compel them to come in . . . they plumb the depth of the Divine mercy."

The Reformed Journal, March, 1956.

Part Two
EDUCATION

Modern Philosophy of Education

If an ardent progressivist, or experimentalist, or functionalist, were to describe a traditionalist, he would, particularly if he
had just been nettled by another book, say, from Mortimer Adler,
probably come through with a picture something like this. He is a
medievalist. He arrogates authority to himself because of something he calls reason. But you must know that this reason of his
is anything but the scientific verification of evidence. It is a sort
of hypostatization of his own *a priori* and factually unsupported
personal opinion. He is also a blind conservative whose attitude
towards all proposals for social change is *caution*. He talks such
jargon as mental discipline, formal discipline, memory, faculty
psychology, transfer of training, ancient languages, and good
grammar. He talks also about the training of the mind, as though
the mind were an isolable entity which, like the blade of a knife,
can be sharpened by repeating the paradigms of Greek verbs. He
thinks of that mind, not as an active principle of dynamic energy, but as a warehouse that must be stuffed full of data. He
holds that it makes sense to teach a boy Latin, though the language is dead. Apparently, therefore, he wants to teach it on
the ground that the boy hates it, and that it so constitutes excellent frictional material for generating what he calls discipline.
He is an intellectualist. In blunt imperviousness to modern psychological inquiry, he seems never to have discovered along with
the late Professor Dewey that "mind is primarily a verb" if, indeed, it be distinguishable at all from experience itself. He makes
much of individualism, having apparently never heard that man
is a gregarious animal whose natural habitat for growth is society. He holds to a sort of archetypal model of ideal education
which he considers just as suitable for a kid in Chicago in 1953
as it was for an uppercrust Greek in Plato's Athens or an Eng-

lish gentleman in the reign of Elizabeth. He is always talking books, great books, classics — paragons of excellence, apparently — most of them ancient, and recommends these as the best medium for education. So he ignores the environment, the situation, and our actual needs for life-adjustment, and for swift adaptation to the changing needs of a changing society. He likes to quote the oldtimers: Pope, for instance: "The proper study of mankind is man," or Roger Ascham: "Learning teacheth more in one year than experience in twenty." He is the sort of fellow who might have had a place in the closed universe, the closed society, and the closed mind of Medieval Europe. But since modernity has opened these up, we shall have to abandon Ascham in favor of Pater who said, "Not the fruit of experience but experience itself is the end."

Such the *cartoon* that a nettled progressivist might draw of traditionalism in education. What is the *portrait* like, what is such traditionalism really like?

Its main feature, I think, its leading idea, is its idea of man. That idea is, frankly, a religious and philosophical idea. It assumes man's relationship with an eternal, and it is not entirely verifiable in sense experience. It represents more than a linking together of observable and measurable data, and presents man, consequently, as more than an assembly of physical, biological, psychological and other phenomena. Traditionalism knows, of course, that man is natural, and that in this nature he is a creature subject to the laws and circumstances of the natural order. It knows, too, that in this nature, man is as suitable and rewarding an object for study by an empirical scientific method as any.

But traditional education is insistent that man is an horizon in which two worlds meet, the natural and the spiritual. And it holds that it is in his spiritual character that man's characteristically human nature consists. This is his uniqueness. It gives him his independence and his wholeness. It constitutes him a self. He is not, therefore, accounted for as a piece of the continuum of nature. He is a whole, a little universe, a microcosm. He has consciousness, rationality. He lives in two orders; he can penetrate phenomenal reality, sense experience, get behind them to universals, laws, principles, causes, and ends. This it is that makes knowledge, science, philosophy proper, satisfying, exuberating, and possible to him. In fact, he seeks his freedom, his fulfillment as a human being, precisely in such progressively realized knowledge of reality. It is this uniqueness of the human being in the created order that we Christians know as man's lordship, or sovereignty, owing to the endowment, at creation, of the image of God. Such human freedom is the thing that gives culture its large importance, it being only mind that can make culture.

Something like that, presumably, is the idea of man which governed his education in its essential structure, from Plato and Aristotle, on through Augustine, and Calvin, into the Renaissance of Bacon and Milton, and beyond that to Matthew Arnold and his kind in the last century, and to Sir Richard Livingstone, Jacques Maritain, and, yes, Mortimer Adler in ours. Maritain, at least, thinks that he can give out a definition of man which could serve as a basis for the civilization of our Western World, and be accepted by Greek, Jew, Protestant, and Catholic Christian. This is his definition: "Man is animal endowed with reason, whose supreme dignity is in the intellect; he is a free individual in personal relation with God whose supreme righteousness consists in voluntarily obeying the law of God; and man is a sinful and wounded creature called to the freedom of grace, whose supreme perfection consists of love."

If this idea, an idea which, in short, I shall call the idea of the freedom of the mind of man, is the leading idea of traditional education, be it as assumption or as articulated philosophy, then traditional education will object to experimentalist, progressivist, functionalist, or the New Education, only in proportion to the extent that it no longer makes that assumption about the nature of man. That at bottom is the only question I am asking about the New Education: does it do justice to the freedom of mind, to the fulfillment of man's characteristically human destiny to know? Some of us think that it does not. It is the sort of thought one of my colleagues at the College had when he said, in reference to the title of Mr. Randall's book, *The Making of the Modern Mind,* that he would like to write a book with the title *The Modern Unmaking of Mind.* What he was thinking of also was the threat, as he supposed, in modern educational thought, to the specifically spiritual character of that mind, to its naturally human aspirations to freedom, and to its progressive fulfillment in the knowledge of reality.

I for one, together with many observers, see something of such a threat to man's humanity in the educational philosophy of the late Professor Dewey. This thinker, following in the wake mainly of William James, is of course regarded as the key figure in the New Education. What goes on for a human being when a person learns is something like this for Mr. Dewey. As an experiencing creature a man runs into a difficulty. This disturbs his equilibrium, his poise, his sense of well-being. He then makes use of something he has in his organism, which is called his intelligence, to take the measure of the obstacle and find resources for removing it. He emerges from the problem thus solved, ready for another embarrassment, another difficulty of the situation, another rub in the environment, and another solution. Now this sort of use of the intelligence can hardly be called, as Maritain puts it, a "progressive grasping of the object of knowledge," or as Plato puts it, "an inner beholding of the truth." This testing of validity by consequence, by the degree of success attained in adjustment to environment (and such is the notion lying behind the phrase, "education for life adjustment") is to make of the mind a means, a technique, and a tool. There is no freedom here, no rationality, no possibility for recognizing, determining, and judging ends. It assumes that experience is self-vindicating, and that education can only assist the human organism to grow, as Brubacher puts it, "in whatever direction a novelly emerging future renders most feasible." The second term of that phrase, "the human animal," seems appropriate now, for animal growth is nothing more than morphological development along fixed lines, and animal growth is assisted also by resources native to the organism for coping with obstacles and taking advantage of opportunity, whether by sharp quills as in the porcupine, or swift feet as in the rabbit. This notion of cleverness owing to intelligence in the struggle with nature for life is therefore exactly described as evolutionary, in that there is no fulfillment in ends, as pragmatic in that the test of intelligence is consequence, as skeptical in that there is in it no such thing as philosophical proving, and as deterministic in that the situation, the environment, whether natural or social, is the real governor of life.

To revert now to the idea of traditional education — the idea of the free human mind by education progressively realizing the truth of reality, I call attention to some of the major traditionalist emphases, some of those, namely, in which there is often a clash with the emphases of the New Education. Let me put the first one this way: *Knowledge is more important than ability.* Because it is by truth, by reality, by revelation, that man's mind is formed, is patterned, is fulfilled, traditional education holds that content is important, that subject matter matters. Now this idea that an organized program of studies, representative of reality, representative, too of a hierarchy of importances, should be followed out in schools and colleges, is an idea which is under very formidable threat in American education. We in Michigan have in recent years got a phenomenon, known as a college agreement plan, by which the colleges of the state are asked to agree that they will admit students from high schools irrespective of the content and organization of courses pursued. The idea is: not what a student has had, nor in connection with what he has had it, but what ability he generated in handling it. That's animal training — you can do it with a horse. History? No, couldn't see any use in it. Foreign languages? Look, I'm going to be a business executive. I can hire a Mexican if I have to know Spanish. Science? A little physiology. English? Yeah, I had some of that. But the grade is good. The boy must have handled his social attitudes skillfully. What can you do with him in college? Why, whet some more ability, of course.

Traditional education never operated that way. "The crucial error," says Mr. Hutchins, "is that of holding that nothing is more important than anything else, that there can be no order of intellectual goods . . . nothing central, nothing peripheral, nothing basic, and nothing superficial." Nothing but method, technique, ability, and training, without any mastery of basic instrument-knowledges, without any discipline in either scientific or philosophical-theoretical thinking, and without any confrontation of the student by that world of history and culture in which the mind can realize and universalize itself and fulfill its humanness. "In such conditions," says Hutchins, "the course of study goes to pieces, because there is nothing to hold it together." It does. Lacking the principle of the underlying unity of all knowedge, the curriculum breaks the bounds of rational system and spreads out over phenomena. Scales, hierarchies of importance go by the board. Mr. Tenenbaum, biographer of Kilpatrick, exponent in turn of Mr. Dewey, records this experience: ["I have] seen a class of 600 and more graduate students in education, comprising teachers, principals, superintendents, vote their opinion in overwhelming numbers, that Greek, Latin, and Mathematics offered the least likely possibilities for educational growth; and with almost the same unanimity they placed dancing, dramatics, and doll dressing high on this list in this regard." The curriculum goes to pieces. I suggest that traditional education with its imitation of nature, its intrinsic respect for reality, rightly insisted on a rationally determined content and organization of courses. It was right in preferring natural philosophy, moral philosophy, and divinity to courses in practical skills, in social attitudes, in community values, and in "character education." It is reality that patterns the mind; it is truth that forms and fulfills.

That takes us to a second emphasis, a corollary of the traditionalist insistence that content matters. It is this, also greatly threatened by the contemporary educational theory and practice: namely, that *the object of education is more important than the subject in the. training of the teacher.* I mean that in the training of the teacher, history is more important than Johnny. Modern education owes a great deal to the psychological study of the pupil and the correspondingly required methods most effective in teaching him. I, too, blush for some of the crimes committed by stupid traditionalists on the dawning intellect, and the spiritual intuition, and the creative reach, and the aspirations to the freedom of understanding, of the young schoolboy. Shakespeare suffered it out, and spoke afterwards of "the whining schoolboy with his satchel and shining morning face creeping like a snail unwillingly to school." We have learned from some of the moderns that interest is indispensable to learning, though many an ancient, Socrates, for example, including that old Roger Ascham, had guessed as much. But the source of the interest is not the pupil, nor the teacher, but the truth. A man has an affinity for the truth. The teacher must stand before the pupil in the authority of the truth. He begins with insights, not merely with difficulties. He must be educated in truth before he is trained in teaching. Johnny, as an object of known man, is not as important a subject as Homer, and the teacher should know Homer before he knows Johnny, and indeed, in order to know Johnny. The tendency and the fact in our time of some teacher training schools to segregate people who plan to teach from other people, to give them psychology limited to empirically observable data about pupils, and to support this by as many methods courses as there are subjects in the modern curriculum, is well calculated to produce teachers who do not have the authority of mind. For it is the object of knowledge, rather than the pupil, the teacher, or the method, that must do the education.

A third traditionalist emphasis is its predilection for what are called the humanities. As I see it, traditional education considers culture a more important medium for education than nature. It also fosters natural science, of course, for natural science richly rewards the student with a human knowledge of phenomena and of the principles which explain them. But nature as an object of knowledge can be regarded as standing lower in the order of reality than culture as an object of knowledge, for the reason that in this subject the human, the moral, the free, the rational element is itself present. The substitution, therefore, of an exclusively scientific education for a humanistic education, or the subordination of the humanities to the sciences, or the teaching of the humanities as natural sciences — and one or another of these possibilities obtains in many schools — can represent an abandonment of the traditionalist idea of man. The last is perhaps the greatest threat, namely, the naturalization of history, society, politics, law, literature, and the like, by transforming them into studies of natural, cultural, or social circumstance.

That point, too, as a fourth consideration, has a corollary, perhaps, in the traditional insistence on the educational value of books, letters, humane letters, great books, classics. These seem to traditionalists to have authority, to be their own embodiments of what a colleague calls the "funded wisdom" of the ages, vital, quickening, redolent of truth, the sort of thing to which mind leaps up in recognition of mind, in which mind enlarges and deepens itself, realizes itself. Of course you can ask on whose authority they are so great. Arnold called them the best that has been said and thought. Huxley in philosophical skepticism turned away from them as being matters of opinion. Huxley said, "Science appeals not to authority," as humane letters do, "but to nature." He identified nature with phenomenal, empirically observable reality. He was wrong. First, because nature is not science until mind has intervened. Next, because good mind is a good authority to appeal to. Now the classics are precisely large and comprehensive human readings of life. They chart the course of the human spirit, and exhibit alternative answers to man's religious and philosophical quest. In them, as Wordsworth said, there is the breath and finer spirit of knowledge, the soul of science, the steady and whole view, the harvesting of history in its concrete actuality. It is just the thing to quicken the mind's yearnings for fulfillment, to satisfy the inner beholding of truth. To supplant them by experience, life, laboratories, or textbooks, though they may well be supplemented by these, is to denominate something other than knowledge the end of education.

One is not, naturally, going to have access to such funded wisdom in the classics unless one can read. I make it a fifth point. The traditionalist holds that the three R's make sense. Consider then whether there be not some departure from an idea of the uniqueness of human nature in such an utterance as this, which was addressed by a principal to the National Association of Secondary School Principals. He was being progressive with a vengeance: "When we come," he said, "to the realization that not every child has to read, figure, write, and spell ... we shall be on the way to improving the Junior High School curriculum. We shall some day accept the fact that it is just as illogical to assume that every boy must be able to read as that each one must be able to perform on the violin, that it is no more reasonable to require that each girl shall learn to spell than it is that each one shall learn to bake a cherry pie." Certainly it would seem that when the doctrine of individual difference, of unique aptitude and interest reaches such a point, it cuts itself off from that common core of studies so long held to be the *sine qua non* of the education of democratic people.

The traditionalist, to make another point now, wants foreign languages in education as part of his learning the first R, that is reading. He wants them not for reasons of trade and holiday. He wants them not solely for their utility in research. He wants them mainly because he thinks that an adequately philosophical mind is not possible unless it is disciplined by the rationality or logic of the literature of our civilized West. It wants foreign languages, and particular foreign languages, for Arnold's reason when he said: "The civilized world (the only kind in which mind can be educated and community is possible) is to be regarded as now being, for intellectual purposes, one great confederation, whose members have for their proper outfit a knowledge of Greek, Roman, and Eastern antiquity, and of one another." Presumably this knowledge is not just a knowledge about, but a knowledge of. It is not just information. It is a sharing of mind unified by something like a common idea. This idea forms us. We need it for our self-fulfillment. The best cultures represent that idea best. They would seem to be the Greek, the Roman, the German, and the French. And this too. Language, unless one abstracts it from reality to the point at which it becomes a mechanical signal system, is one of the spiritual arts. It reveals reality, truth: it speaks to mind, mind responds to it. But then there must be no divorce between the sign and the thought signified. Traditional education thought of the two as a unit, so that as Shakespeare said, language can be called the discourse of reason. "I endowed thy purposes with words that made them known," said Shakespeare. There is rationality in language.

A final emphasis. The new education makes so much of the social situation. That is good. The older education made much of the social in man also. But at this point we must be careful lest the social become again nothing more than a conditioning environment, such as the soil is to a plant. One does not get humanity, in the sense of the freedom of the human spirit, back into education by simply assuring himself that the environment is not natural but social. For the social is hardly distinguishable from the natural if one does not acknowledge that society, human society, as distinguished from instinctively gregarious animal groups, is achieved by free consent. There must be interiority of the personal self, personal conscience, deep-seated independence if there is to be society. Hence, as Maritain puts it, the essence of education does not lie in adapting a potential citizen to the conditions and interactions of social life, but in *first making man,* and by this very fact in preparing a citizen. Otherwise society is a force, and man is its victim.

But I must be breaking off this talk, till you probe me for explanation. My drift is that an idea of man is at stake in the difference between the older and the new education.

Address, Principals Convention, September, 1950.

2

Christian Education

My subject tonight is *Christian Education*. Perhaps I ought first of all to give you in a single sentence what it is I mean to say. It is this: Christian education must be both education and Christian if it is to justify itself and successfully meet the secular challenge. That is the thrust of what I have to say. Our schools must be schools — that for one thing. And then they must be Christian — that for another thing. And in making these two points I shall want to insist, of course, that they must be both at once.

I speak of these obvious considerations again, because it is easy to have the school without the Christian. All we should have to do then is a fairly competent job of handling the curriculum as it is done in any good school, and do it in what we might call a Christian atmosphere, and so justify ourselves. That would be easy. It would be easy, further, to have the Christian without the school, that is, to make what we call the "devotional" element the principal thing, and to pay little more than lip service to the subjects of the curriculum. Either of these would be easy. What is hard is to have the Christian and the school in vital and vigorous interdependence with each other all the while. But that is precisely what we are trying for, and what we must have, if our schools are to solve the problem which secular, neutral, or public education cannot solve.

Our schools must be schools. Let us look at that first. It is worth a good deal of attention. I hope, in fact, that you will think it hardly less important than the other point, namely, that they must be Christian. It is well, I think, to be reminding ourselves constantly that ours is an educational enterprise. It is not, at least not primarily, an evangelical enterprise. We call this work of our schools kingdom work, and rightly so, and the kingdom of

Christ is, of course, a spiritual kingdom, and it is most certainly the business of our schools to train our boys and girls, our young men and women, for responsible citizenship in it. But to say that it is the function of our schools to train for citizenship in a spiritual kingdom is not to say that the schools ought so much as possible to be churches. They are not churches. They have their own function, and it is a different function from that of the church, although, happily, not unrelated to it. It is at church and not at school that our children are by the grace of God made members of the covenant in baptism. It is at church and not at school that the offer of salvation is presented, the word of truth is preached, the communion of the saints is exercised in the sacrament. These things, and more, are proper to the church as church. They stand high in our hearts, higher than anything else. We think them the most important things. In this we are right. However, it is by no means an implication of this that we can think of the schools as Christian and important only insofar as they extend into the week-days the offices of the church.

There are Christians, though usually not Reformed Christians, or at least not mature Reformed Christians, who cannot get very excited about Christian schools as schools. They are so eager for the honor of what they call the religious and the spiritual in life, that they hesitate to think anything else of much importance. Such Christians are as likely as not to be comparatively indifferent to the curriculum, to the cultural subject matters. We understand such Christians, feel something of the attraction of the same idea, perhaps, in ourselves. The Christian, after all, finds himself called to the Christian life in the midst of the world. When regeneration, conversion, sanctification begin to operate in him, he finds himself, particularly in some times and places, estranged, opposed to, the culture, the whole complex of life, that presses in upon him from all sides. It bears down upon him mercilessly from every quarter, from the business, the social, the political, the military, the scientific, and aesthetic worlds. We therefore understand the Christian who is inclined, especially at first, to apply his faith in negative ways, and to look upon science, and culture, and history, and the rest as things alien to his religion. There is, I say, something appealing about it that those who seem sometimes to be the most saintly among us, who prize a close walk with God in mystical communion with Christ, should not only by-pass culture, but even attack it as a worldly idol. Then texts begin coming to mind, and beckoning for distortion, like that one "but not many mighty and not many noble," and "If thy right eye offend thee, pluck it out," and "Seek ye first the kingdom and its righteousness," and "Sell all that thou hast," and many besides.

Such Christians are rightly aware of an antithesis between Christian and world. They see the line of it running between Cain and Abel, between Noah and those drowned in the flood, between Abraham and Lot, Jacob and Esau, Israel and the peoples around her, between Christ and her persecutors, and they hear their Master saying, "My kingdom is not of this world. Not as the world giveth, give I unto thee." And this antithesis such Christians are as likely as not to interpret as an antithesis of Christian versus culture, Christian versus learning, Christian versus science, Christian versus reason, Christian versus literature and art, and so, wittingly or unwittingly, Christian versus school. In the end religion becomes something isolated from life, and in the name of religion the school as school is sacrificed to something not a school: be it a Biblical institute, an evangelical agency, a center for religious instruction, a place of worship, or a missionary enterprise.

We understand, I say, and are sympathetic. All the same, it is not our view of either Christianity or education. We, too, insist on the primacy of the religious, the spiritual, in life. Ours is also the conviction that regeneration, that the choice for Christ, that the turning from sin and self to God and his kingdom, that this is the primary thing, without which indeed nothing else matters, from which everything else issues. We, too, have our special revelation: Christ, and Bible, and church, and sacrament, and worship, and soul, and we refuse resolutely, of course, to identify these with any natural or mundane thing. They are spiritual, they are the one thing needful, the pearl without price.

But we are Calvinists. Our Christian conviction is a Reformed conviction. And it is part of that conviction that the religious and spiritual cannot exist in a void, in isolation from life. It is part of the Reformed conviction that the spiritual in us requires human fulfillment, human embodiment. It is part of the Reformed conviction that the religious in us is part and parcel of the rest of us. We maintain that, so far from identifying science, and nature, and culture, and literature, and history with the world, and so expressing the antithesis of Christian and world in ignoring them, we must know, judge and appropriate these all, and express the antithesis of Christian and world through them. We are not Barthians in this sense that we think God's will is unknowable to man, "wholly other," as the phrase is, and virtually irrelevant to history. We are not Manicheans: the world is not the Devil's; the earth is the Lord's and the fullness thereof, the world and they that dwell therein. True, we know the kingdom is spiritual, and not to be identified with any historical cultural product; but we know that we have no means of building for the spiritual kingdom except by cultural means as human beings living on this earth at this point in history. Hence we are not anxious about civilization, as though in this life only we had hope. We are not liberals, identifying the task of the church with, and losing the Gospel message in a preoccupation with cultural concerns. We are not monastic. We neither retire into monasteries, nor into small scale social orders of our own. As a matter of fact, ours is not the facile dualism between church on the one hand, and practical life on the other, the practical life construed then as a way of making some money to continue the work of the church. For us something stands between the church and practical life, and this something is the school. Motivated by Christian conviction, it can, if it is a school, keep religion from becoming a disembodied ghost, and can keep practical life from becoming an irreligious, secularized, and commercialized thing. We take the Calvinist challenge seriously, namely, that the Christian must bring the whole range of life — science and art and society and government — under the sway of Christian principle and purpose as an expression of the kingly rule of Christ.

I repeat: the schools must be schools. It is the very strength of the Reformed profession of Christianity not solely in the isolatedly religious but in the religious commanding the naturally and culturally human. It is as human beings that we are Christians, in our human nature expressing itself in a natural environment, expressing itself also in cultural activity of all kinds, and, further, in a particular historical situation here on earth. Our being called to be saints does not exempt us from being human, nor exempt us from cultural activity, nor exempt us from social and political obligation, nor render reason superfluous, nor permit an indifference to art and literature, nor lift us out of history. On the contrary, it is in and through these things that our moral and religious choice for the spiritual kingdom of Christ becomes concrete, real, and meaningful. And that is why our schools must be schools, our education education.

Or put it this way — a kind of figure of speech. Quite apart from the religious question now, we could all manage to become some sort of men and women presumably without ever going to school. It is by virtue of our birth that we become human beings. What the school does, then, is that it takes this humanity, this humanness of ours, and makes it more intelligent, more aware of itself and its environment, makes it, so to speak, more effectively and more consciously human. It does not, in short, give us our humanity, but it develops, disciplines, and matures it, makes our choices and actions more significant, and equips for ampler and better oriented cultural activity. Just so the Christian in his Christian education. The education does not in the first instance make us Christians. It assumes, as it may assume in what are Covenant schools, that the Christianity is ours by virtue of the grace of God in regeneration. And the education now, the school as school, addresses itself to the task of making this Christian humanly significant. I say humanly significant. I have no objection to saying spiritually significant, if it be understood that it is through all of reality — natural, cultural, historical, and supernatural — that this must happen. The school addresses itself to the task of taking the Christian pupil and making his profession of Christianity a significant profession. The school, in short, teaches the pupil how he can express and gives him the means to express a responsible human citizenship in the kingdom of Christ.

You know that the public schools often designate this as the function of their education: to train for responsible citizenship. They mean, in our democracy. We have that same duty, of course, but we think it is best performed when we denominate the purpose of education, as, yes, responsible citizenship, indeed, but in the spiritual kingdom of Christ. Our responsibility in society inevitably issues from that.

But then our schools must be schools. If it is at church that we make our choice for Christ, it is at school that we keep making that choice always more humanly and culturally and practically significant. Citizenship in the kingdom requires this kind of education. Else we should be dwarfed, stunted, meager, and only partially-conscious Christians. The question after all is not one of how little we can get by with and still be essentially Christians. The question in education is one of how strong, how aware, how full, how rich we make this profession. And, as I say, we have no choice, since we are the kind of creatures that we are, but to do this in our human nature, in our natural environment, by means of cultural activity, in a particular moment of history, and always in reference to a spiritual kingdom. The materials our schools as schools must use, therefore, are not ecclesiastical, or devotional, or always primarily Biblical materials. Our schools are not in this sense Bible schools. We ought not to regret this or proceed unconfidently, as though the cultural curricula of our schools are regrettably necessary for practical reasons, but a kind of interference really or at best addenda to the religious work. Nor ought we even so one-sidedly to prize, shall I say the *devotional* element at school, the religious atmosphere, as we say, the chapel exercises and such, that we suppose the distinctive part of the school inhered in these, and the rest were neutral or religiously indifferent.

You will understand me at this point, I take it. I think that devotional exercises, Bible reading, prayer, meditation, the service of song, and Biblical study seriously pursued, pursued also with evangelical emphasis, and not merely as so much scientific data — I think that these are very precious. Without them a school could hardly be designated Christian. But my point now is that they do not constitute the school a school: for this precious devotional element is just as proper to the home, to Christian industry, Christian recreation, places of Christian mercy, and the like. Understand me further in this insistence of mine that the schools must be schools. I honor the teacher who, when she has reason to suppose that a pupil or student is not a Christian, drops whatever she is doing, her arithmetic, or geography, or history lesson, to press the Gospel message upon him. That teacher has her values in the right order. She puts first things first. So much is absolutely true. But we ought not to go on to infer from this that a Christian school is a Christian school because it offers such wonderful opportunities for church or missionary work. It is a precious by-product. It is a true description of our schools to say of them that they come up out of the church, are supported by Christian parents, conducted under Christian auspices, taught by Christian men and women, include in their curriculum more than the public schools by virtue of Bible study, church history, and doctrine, and are carried on in an atmosphere of worship guaranteed by devotional exercises. Every one of these things is important. No school could be effectively Christian without them. And yet the essence of the distinctive in our schools lies not in these important circumstances but in the character of the education itself.

Our schools must be schools. They must subject the Christian student to as thorough a discipline as he is capable of in the natural, cultural, historical, and spiritual life of man. It is as human beings that we are Christians. All that is human concerns us. That gets us into all the subjects of the curriculum. It involves us in the whole of reality. Unawareness of any part of it, the failure to appropriate any part of it, to know it, and to judge it, and to refer it to a spiritual kingdom for justification, this by so much impoverishes our human expression of our Christian choice.

Now this humanness of ours in which we must be educated, through which we must express both our opposition to the spirit of the world and our choice for the kingdom of Christ, includes a lot. It includes, for instance, that part of us which we share with inorganic and organic nature. We are chemical and physical and biological in part, and so is our environment. Thence the natural sciences in our curriculum. We have, further, a nervous organization, akin to that of an animal, and yet differing from it, and so we learn psychology. And at that point the uniqueness of the human creature among created beings asserts itself rapidly. We are conscious. We have mind. We can think. We are moral. We can make choices. We have creative freedom. We can make things out of things, expressive of higher things. You will remember that second chapter of Genesis: "And God formed every beast of the field, and every fowl of the air, and brought them unto Adam, to see what he would call them." There lies the human uniqueness, the gift of reason, the expressiveness of language. And it is in this area of our humanity that most of the subjects lie: science, government, history, mathematics, literature, social studies, and the rest. There are the materials proper of school education. By means of these, religious man enters into scientific man, aesthetic man, social man, practical man, and the rest. All of these are involved in the shaping and maturing of the Christian choice for God. These are the main business of the school as school.

And it is the teaching and learning of these that must be Christian. That is my other point. For insisting that the schools must be schools I do not mean to imply that ordinary academic competence is all that is required. No, no, the education as education must be Christian. The quality of it, the character of it, the soul of it — that must be Christian. In this lies the distinctiveness of our schools.

The fact is that education is a human affair. It represents a human awareness of reality and a human appropriation of it. And this is a further fact: whatever is human is religious. The religious in us is as natural and as real to us as the moral, or the rational, as the scientific and aesthetic, as the biological and psychological, as the social and historical. This religious in us, I say, is a part of our being a creature; it is, I say, natural to us. And this continues so in spite of the pervasive presence of sin. Just as we continue to be human beings now that sin has invaded us, so we continue to be religious beings. We say sometimes that man has become a beast because of the presence of sin, but that is only a way of speaking. Man cannot escape being human; if he could, his approaching the bestial would not be a gross disgrace to him. And so he continues to be religious, though to be sure, except for the intervening grace of God, the religion will be false. We sometimes say of people also that they are irreligious. We understand each other when we say that: we probably mean that they are profane, or pay no attention to the things of the church. But there are no irreligious people. The question is one only of a false or of the true religion. And, again, we sometimes say of a book that it is a godless book, or of a nation that it is a godless nation. There, too, we understand what is meant, and there can be no particular objection to such a way of speaking: we mean of course that the god who is served in the book or the nation is not the one true God. But that is the limit of the figure of speech. The fact is that wherever there is a man, there a God is worshipped. All men require a God for the vindication of themselves, the justification of their thoughts and actions, the justification, too, of their cultural activity.

To be human is to be scientfic, yes, and practical, and rational, and moral, and social, and artistic, but to be human further is to be religious also. And this religious in man is not just another facet of himself, just another side to his nature, just another part of the whole. It is the condition of all the rest and the justification of all the rest. This is inevitably and inescapably so for all men. No man is religiously neutral in his knowledge of and his appropriation of reality. The preamble to the Decalogue does not read, "Thou shalt serve a God," as though there were any choice about that. It is a natural reality, even now, that we shall serve a God. No, the preamble to the Decalogue and the foundation stone of our Christian schools is this: "I am the Lord Thy God . . . Thou shalt have no other Gods before me." Belief is a basis of all learning, faith is inevitable in man, men are fundamentally dogmatic. All this I know is rank heresy to the secular mind, but it is the secular challenge I am trying to answer. And the answer I think very satisfactory is this answer: Christian schools in which the God behind the reality there explored is the one true God.

You see, though, that this makes of Christian education a much harder thing than that other method of conducting curricular affairs secularly and neutrally and then bringing in the distinctively religious by way of chapel exercises and the devotional element. It is hard work to prove the spirits whether they be of God. It is hard work to be in the world, really in it, I mean, fully aware, that is, of the religious and prophetic tensions and pressures of it, the ultimate loyalties and allegiances of the various cultures in it, the religio-moral choices of men in the past that make the cultural challenge of the present what it is; I say, it is hard work to be in the world that way, and then not to be of it. And yet this proving or testing or trying of the spirits whether they be of God, this being in the world and yet not of it, this, precisely this, is almost the whole business of liberal education in our schools. That is really what we are always busy with in the classroom. That makes our schools distinctive.

One hears such strange stories sometimes of how far afield an occasional teacher will go in his eagerness to establish the distinctiveness of the Christian school. Understand, I honor and reverence them all for wanting to be distinctive. The whole burden of what I say here is to establish the need of it. I hear of teachers who suppose they are making arithmetic Christian by having the pupils take dimensions of the local church instead of a farmer's corncrib. There are others who refuse to give a pupil an *A* for excellent work on the ground that according to the Christian view man is imperfect, and cannot therefore be excellent. It is reported of a teacher of geography that he spends more time on the geography of Palestine than of any other country including our own, and of a teacher of drawing who will have the pupils draw nothing but the animals in the ark. There are teachers of literature who choose only novels which treat of ecclesiastical subject matters, and have nothing to do with poetry unless it be a rimed version of the judges of Israel or the names of the apostles. You will have heard your own stories: I report these, salute these teachers for their manifest eagerness to be distinctive, and yet say unreservedly that this is not getting at the essence of the Christian in education at all.

Christian teachers, Christian friends: it is so easy in the name of Christianity to turn one's back to art, to science, to politics, to social problems, to historical tensions and pressures, in one word, to culture, if you will. But once the conviction seizes on you that these all, precisely because they are cultural realities, exhibit a religious allegiance and an ultimate loyalty, that none of them is neutral but rather that all of them are faith-founded, all laid on an altar, all dedicated to a god, then you realize that they are at the very least important. Then you realize, too, that the true discernment of the God behind the culture, the assumption underlying the thought, the dogma beneath the action, the soul in the body of the thing, are precisely what it is the business of our schools as schools to disclose and to judge. In that lies the strengthening of the moral sinews of our young Christians. It is so that their choice for Christ and God can become a meaningful human choice. Christianity versus culture: no, it is the fundamentalist heresy. Culture alone: indeed not; it is the liberal heresy. Christianity through culture: the religious in man governing, shaping, determining the scientific, artistic, social in him, precisely; it is the Reformed truth.

But if this kind of education is to be accomplished in our schools, then it is an implication of Christian education that it be not merely general education but also liberal. By this I mean that our passion should be not so much to try to get everything in that has cropped up on the face of the earth, as to get everything in which exhibits alternative gods, alternative moral choices, alternative beings and principles of cultural vindication. Our education, in other words, must be liberal in that it ministers to the freedom of moral choice. For us that means that it ministers to the choice for Christ already made before we come to school, reinforcing it all the while and making it always anew and always more consciously and more maturely. <u>Devotional exercise plus vocational training is not Christian education</u>! I do not think this is possible if the sum total of our education consists of shop, home economics, typing, stenography, hair-dressing, pile-driving, bookkeeping, accounting, mechanical drawing, and similar vocational skills. I have no objection to the inclusion of these in the schools, provided they are not regarded as adequate substitutes for what are called the humanities, sciences, and social studies. For if this sense that I speak of, the sense of the religious in man, and the religious in every cultural product, and the religious in the various cultures and epochs of history is to be borne in upon us, we shall have to be shaped and disciplined in the spiritual history of man, that inheritance in which and over against which we choose for Christ and against the world. An educated person will then know, for instance, how a Greek looked at reality and to what God he appealed for its vindication, and how a medieval Catholic looked at it, and how a renaissance humanist looked at it, and how an eighteenth-century deist, and a romantic pantheist, and a modern naturalist. It is only so that the student will learn that all things human are religious, that human culture, while inevitable, is not in itself enough in that it requires religious justification. And it is so that the Christian student will be taught and confirmed in his conviction that the religion of Christianity is the only adequate religion. Some equipment, some skills, some tools for the better making of a livelihood, my dear Christian friends, that has a little, but only a very little to do with the Christian in education, and it has very little to do with education. And it is justified in our schools at all only if it is a subsidiary part of a major program of studies in what we call the cultural subjects.

Reverse of current trend in public education

As to that secular challenge, I can, happily, be very brief about that now. Very brief, for it issues from what I have said already. You know that it is the going theory of secular education in public schools that education must be neutral. I do not say that the advocates of secular education, of public education, deny that man is fundamentally religious. They probably acknowledge that he is, some of them at least. But they are forced from their position to take the stand that this religious claim cannot be allowed in public schools. They must leave it, therefore, to private, and personal, and individual choice of the student, and deal with the curriculum, as they say, neutrally, that is, without exhibiting a religious allegiance or loyalty. This is the Achilles' heel, the vulnerable spot, of public education. I do not gloat over their predicament; far be it from me. These schools are necessary in such a society as ours, and we require a society to live in also, and so we are too involved in their predicament not to share even a sort of responsibility for it. Predicament it is, though. Professor Trueblood said of it: "In our democracy we proceed on the assumption that it is illegal to teach the faith on which it rests." That, in a word, is the predicament our idea of Christian schools avoids. We hold that the education being a human enterprise is inevitably religious, that except it be religious it is not education, at least not moral education, and that the alleged neutrality of the public schools must — if their education is to be real education — turn out to be a mere allegation. Our answer to the secular challenge is this answer: Being neutral is impossible for man as man, certainly impossible in so fundamentally human a thing as education. It is this answer: We believe in order that we may know, for belief is the condition of knowledge. As for those secularists who maintain that the thing to do in education is to adopt scientific method, to adopt an hypothesis and then refuse to adhere to it until the facts make it impossible to disbelieve it, we say that this is making doubt and skepticism the basis of knowledge. And it is not to be so objective and neutral as it sounds. It is a protestation made in the name of a god, the god of scientific method. That, too, when you come to examine it closely, is a profession of faith. The god is false. We know whom we have believed, and in His name we appropriate the whole of His reality in our schools.

Address, Teachers Convention, September, 1951.

3

What Kind of Education?

An Open Letter to Veterans

This is written on the assumption that you have decided to take advantage of the educational benefits of the GI Bill of Rights, but that you have not yet determined what kind of schooling to get. You know that several kinds are available to you. Thus you have heard of general education, of vocational, professional, and pre-professional training, of commercial and business courses, of trade schools, and the like. And you understand that, irrespective of what level of training you had reached when you entered the service, you will have to select one or some combination of these, now that you mean to continue at school.

You may care, consequently, to take a full look at each of these kinds of training. It will simplify matters a little and do no important injury to the truth to say that three kinds of schooling are available to you: vocational training, a general education, and professional training. Unless you have already completed college, the alternatives for you will be to pursue vocational training or a general education. Inasmuch, however, as your choice of one of these affects the possibility of your entering a profession later, it will be well to consider the implications of professional training also

Vocational training is job training. It aims to help make you a skilled worker. It teaches you a trade. Obviously, training for skill, for competence, at a job is desirable. Much of what used to be "common labor" has in the world of your time become skilled labor. The intense development of the natural sciences, particularly as applied to invention, and the highly departmentalized division of the world's work which has resulted, have created thousands of jobs for which a degree of specialized skill is necessary. Lathe-operating, tool-making, book-binding, copy-editing, electric welding, pipe-fitting, and piston-drilling are a few of these "jobs" for which some technical skill is required and for which courses are offered in schools. You have only to look at the curriculum announced in the catalogue of any large school of applied science to be impressed and perhaps a little appalled by the number and variety of job skills which have developed in our highly industrialized society. And it is technical competence in one of these skills that vocational training can give you.

You may want to acquire one of these skills. You may feel that you have been set back by the war years, that the time you might otherwise have had for a general education has been sacrificed to the service, and that you now have no choice but to hurry up and make some money. For it is true that vocational training bears more directly upon making a living than any other kind. Before you settle upon this, however, consider the alternatives, and remember that vocational training is only job training. All kinds of influences are at work trying to convince you that it is something more than that. A business establishment which teaches sign painting will call itself a University or perhaps an Institute of Arts and Crafts. A school whose speciality is electric welding will recommend itself to you in its catalogue as a College of Applied Science. Besides, many educational institutions, eager to please, will offer courses as directly limited by considerations of vocational utility as those given in trade schools, and yet describe and reward them as parts of a liberal arts and sciences program. Such confusion of means and ends is likely to give you the impression that acquiring a job skill is tantamount to becoming educated. It is not.

Now professional training has this in common with vocational training that it also aims at competence in the performance of work. The differences are, however, more important. The training differs because the work differs, and a profession differs from a job in that it requires a greater calibre of ability, a different kind of preparation, and a nobler motivation.

Surely it is simply being clear-headed, and not undemocratic or snobbish, to say that the work of doctors, lawyers, teachers, ministers, nurses, engineers, architects, scientists, and business administrators on the higher levels of policy presupposes a caliber of ability greater than is needed by barbers, bank tellers, or stenographers. Removing brain tumors, determining the constitutionality of laws, planning the Stilwell road, or projecting the national census requires gifts of mind and imagination which are not essential to cutting hair, making change, or taking 130 words flawlessly a minute. This is a qualitative distinction between the profession and the job, and you will do best to acknowledge it.

As for the second difference, it is clear that professional training differs in kind from the vocational. The competence aimed at is more difficult to achieve. Accordingly, professional schools, schools of medicine, law, engineering, and the like, usually do not give degrees short of the completion of at least three or four years of work. Consider the doctor of medicine, for instance: he goes through high school, through college, through three or four years of medical school, follows that by a year of internship, and that very often by two years of residency in a hospital. So, he finally dares to begin his practice. Most teachers, the best taught lawyers, architects and engineers, and the learned clergy graduate from similar programs of sustained study. Moreover, this study is not merely "vocational," not wholly limited by the considerations of the use to which it will be specifically applied. It is disinterestedly broad, scientific, objective. Because professional training is thus exhaustive, it is usually preceded, not by pre-professional training, but by a general education. In this sense, it is the absence of the preceding general education in the training of the West Point cadet which keeps him from quite making good his claim to being a "professional" soldier. His work has all the earmarks of a profession except this, that his professional specialization is not preceded by a disinterestedly broad and objective course of study. And it is this broadness of background and exhaustiveness of preparation which causes the work of a doctor, lawyer, or teacher to differ in quality of competence from that of a plumber, shipfitter, or linotype operator. In fact, in this sense, it is possible to say that a profession is the "job" which an educated person does.

That leaves the third difference — nobler motivation. *Nobler* sounds out of key in this matter of fact context and in a world which has come to prefer competence to motive as the hope of peace and progress. But *nobler* is the word. A man is not a professional man unless he is motivated by something besides the need for making a living and the love of making money. He must be motivated by the love of the truth, the love of the work, and the love of the service. Read the oath of Hippocrates to which doctors subscribe, and you will catch this note at once. Consider that as a professional man, Einstein earns less than a draftsman in an aircraft plant. The professional man is not in business. He does not get wages: he gets a salary, a fee, or an honorarium. Although he sometimes publishes a professional card because he has services to offer, he does not advertise, he does not hawk his wares. But for the usual exceptions, he does not go on strike. And although some may advise you to take up law or medicine or preaching because "there is more money in it" than there is in a job, do not, if that is what motivates you, plan to enter upon professional training. For without this element of noble motivation, the job, unfortunately, may still be a job (something to get away from after thirty-two hours a week, according to the latest ideal of organized labor), but the profession is not a profession.

Such distinctions between the profession and the job are not the less real because they are often confused. We are all democratic and properly hesitant to point out difference in kind among us. So we tell each other that it is all a matter of skill, aptitude, or interest, and if your aptitude is for brain surgery and mine is for well-drilling, who has the right to be haughty? This commendable eagerness to be democratic explains some of the confusions in education among us, but it does not excuse them. We cannot ignore the differences between the profession and the job unless we are willing to pay the scientist who achieved the atomic bomb the billions in war costs which the early capitulation of Japan saved the country. We cannot ignore them unless we want doctors to look into our bill-folds before they look into our throats, and unless we want nurses to be as gentle as their fees are high. We cannot ignore those differences unless we want scholars to withhold their monographs until arrangements with the manufacturers for royalties have been completed. The fact is, you see, that the world cannot wag without the professions as professions; and until we are ready to welcome the sight of teachers conducting picket lines in front of the schools, and biochemists hoarding their vaccines against a price, we shall have to acknowledge the qualitative differences both in the practice of and the training for the professions as distinguished from jobs.

Most janitors, then, are not plant superintendents, garage mechanics are not engineers, and certified public accountants are not business consultants, though it usually does no harm to think of them that way. Pharmacists who after a six-weeks' course in filling prescriptions proceed to sell hot water bottles and ice-cream are not professional men, any more than those who can whirl the acids and test cream in the country towns after a week-end at school. Nor, for the matter of that, are the lawyers who dash through a year or two of law after high school, "cram" for conventionalized bar examinations, and hang out a shingle. But worse, much worse, in promoting the confusion of the profession with the job is the attitude often of those who practise the professions. There are doctors, lawyers, engineers, and others who suppose that competence in one art or craft confers upon them wisdom in all matters, but who at their conventions talk politics in the same kind of lobbyist fashion as Legionnaires in the last hours of a smoker. Thus these all encourage the muddle-headed notion that education might as well be vocational training and nothing else.

You may care next to consider the meaning of a general education, for it is between that and vocational training that you will be concerned to choose immediately. The phrase "general education" is not altogether satisfactory, but it is perhaps better than any other. It is general not as opposed to intensive, for an education must be intensive if it is to be an education: it is general as opposed to vocational. And it is general in that it comprehends everything that concerns everyone most. Accordingly, the content of a general education comprises studies in the liberal arts and sciences, commonly but not necessarily divided into three groups: the humanities, the social sciences, and the natural sciences. To say that these are the subjects which concern everyone most is simply to say that they comprehend one's relations to God, to one's self, to others, and to nature.

It is an earmark of such a general education that it is vocationally disinterested, that it is ideal, that it is normative. A general education does not aim at competence. Competence is not now the word. It aims at developing your capability for responsible living. The responsibility it helps to develop is not the responsibility for doing a job well, for that is competence, but responsibility for human living under God in a human society and a natural environment. Plainly such an education addresses itself to you as something more than bread-winner, wage-earner, worker, or professional man.

It is precisely over against this that the whole matter of whether or not you feel skeptical about the value of an education comes in. You may even agree that the whole of your spiritual, intellectual, moral, emotional, and physical life is very important, and yet not choose to get a general education. Convinced as you may be of the worth of vocational, applied scientific, or professional training, you then feel that in what you probably call your "personal" life you can rely on your self, shaped as it has been by instincts and habits, by home and church, by natural sagacity and "experience," and by reading the news magazines and hearing the commentators.

However, if you rely on such resources for the values and virtues, the judgments and decisions, and the thought and action of your life, wishing school only to help you make a living, you miss, without even touching on it, what is at bottom the main purpose of a universal education in a democracy. A democratic society is not something you can be thus skeptical or cynical about, for it is not something that goes on in spite of you. You have not the detachment to be cynical; you are too involved to be skeptical. You cannot say that what is wrong is the Communists, or the Jews, or the Catholics, or the Negroes, or the Administration, or the labor unions, or They, or Them, or It. You are not looking on at an experiment. You are in control, and your thinking, choosing, and acting make democratic society what it is.

In the Army and the Navy, the word *responsibility* was also used. But military responsibility is of another kind than this at which a general education aims. It is so different in character that it can almost be called a formal, conventional, or artificial responsibility. In the military you were irresponsible in every creative sense, even though you had to be prompt and punctual and competent in the performance of stipulated duty. You worked on order, did what you were told to do, and did it in the prescribed way. Such responsibility was comfortable. The military world was a world in which competence was enough. You did your job and were through.

It might be pleasant to think that democratic society is the same kind of world the military was — that it is simply the sum of thousands and thousands of workers, each competent in his work, of millions of experts, each doing his job expertly, of a fool-proof organization made flawless by volumes of regulations, and the whole held together by a General. In the fascistic world which you have just pulverized there were such workers, so organized, under such totalitarian control. That is why you destroyed it. But democratic society is not so. There are no expert thinkers to do the thinking, expert voters to do the voting, expert governors to do the governing. Public life is not a matter of prescription, civil service, and police. And you are the General. You must do more than your job. You must determine policy.

You know how it is said that the tendency of the returning veteran, what with his long independence from civil obligations, is to be skeptical about the reality of human purposes and the progress of human society. You may share this skepticism to some extent, even though it is not more perceptible than the absence of this sense of the worth of a general education. This skepticism may be no more evident than the longing to "get into business for yourself," or to build a home and let the rest of the world go by. You may feel as though the world and its perennial problems are past finding out, that you want to plunge into some job, any job that pays and offers some security and a little time for a hobby. You may, speaking figuratively, want to give your wife the pay-check on Saturday evenings, and then, your whole duty done, hide your head behind the comics and not be bothered with family affairs. You will remember, however, that such skepticism is fundamentally irresponsible.

For responsibility in this larger sense, vocational and even professional training have only a little to offer, but a general education has much. A general education can not give you good will, for that is the gift of God. But it can cultivate the feelings, enlarge and exercise the imagination, discipline the mind, train the judgment, provide historical perspectives, and shed light on the nature of every reality. Such an education is an invaluable aid and corrective to the instincts and habits and the natural sagacity which experience without school can give you. You ought not to forego it, for freedom depends upon it, and freedom is more than security.

The Calvin Forum, February, 1947.

4

"Interests" and Education

A number of ill-considered ideas about education threaten sometimes to filter into our Reformed community. One such idea that we should take pains to counteract is the idea that school is a place to coddle people's interests.

Interest is most certainly a condition of learning. Interesting subject matter, the interesting presentation of it, and an interested student — these are the very culture, perhaps the only culture, in which education can thrive. Even so, however, in speaking of interesting subject matter, we should distinguish between a natural and a disciplined interest. We like the colored comics until we discover the *Reader's Digest,* and the *Reader's Digest* until we earn our way into *Harper's.* This represents a kind of progression from a natural to a disciplined interest, and "interesting subject matter" is therefore not entirely an instinctive affair. All the same, interest is a condition of learning, love a condition of insight. It makes sense, therefore, to take some account in our schools of the individually differing interests of students.

But there is a point at which this idea of "interests" invites anarchy. It is getting so now, for instance, that some high schools and colleges advocate paying no mind at all to what a student takes, and in combination with what else he takes it, provided only that he takes something, and does well in it. This, in educators' phrase, is called "ignoring content and pattern" of courses, and "stressing achievement." Just what alien principle this notion is an expression of, I cannot say, though it seems to blend well with that other modern excrescence, the doctrine of "pupil-centered education," and with its corollary, "the elective system." All three of these ideas seem to me the last infirmity of naturalism. Reality being so very bewildering — such the underlying dogma — maybe we can get somewhere by identifying it with its victims, and studying them. I say again that this extravagant preoccupation with interests should not occur where the Christian idea of man and his education is operative.

I feel keenly about this again just now, fresh as I am from a tour of professional duty at assisting students in their registering at college. We have a green book there, called College Catalogue, in which there is a tabular listing of the courses offered. In the front end of this book there is also some advice about what the students ought to study, and in what order, and in what combination with other subjects. This advice is a distillation of traditional sense, and has been mediated through a good many educators' minds. It outlines a considerable range of possibilities, makes allowance for individual differences, is flexible, and undergoes revision when new occasions teach new duties. All the same, there is insistence in it on "content and pattern" of courses. So far, indeed, from being mere advice, it lays down the conditions for graduation.

Many a student, when he comes to register, chafes under the restrictions of a prescribed course of that kind. He has his eye on the second half of the Catalogue, that is, on the offerings. He pores over it like a kid at the confectioner's with a nickel to spend, pointing to the delicacies he's been pining for. He wants some of this, a little of that, and, look, could he have a couple of those? When he encounters resistance (because I am sitting there) he looks at me as if to ask whether this is not a free country. This, then, is an instance of someone who looks upon school as a place to have his "interests" tickled.

Many a student, too, be it said, comes well-girded, and seems of his own volition, and not perforce, to select a content and order of courses such as the most veteran counsellor would recommend. There is also the occasional one who makes out a program of studies that is surprising in its quality. I recall one such a year ago. It was a model performance, heartening to any teacher with some Reformed sense in his system. I looked at the name — it was not Dutch. The man had "fundamentalist" antecedents.

There are, however, those too many others. Fresh from high school, hardly emerging from a semester at college, the "natural science" and "foreign language" limping in on a "D" or an "E," they are eager, now that they have "worked off some requirements," to get at their "interests." "I made a little schedule," says the girl, and there it is crumpled in the purse:

> Music Appreciation
> Story Telling
> Interpretative Reading
> Art
> Contemporary Poetry

Clearly that will not do. There is of course no objection to any one subject as such. There is nothing wrong with Music Appreciation. Music has always been expressive of spiritual man, and the appreciation, form, and history of it are as good a way as any to reach through to that moral education which turns out in the end to be the purpose of life. Story Telling, too, the art of story, was fundamentally significant well before Moses could say of life that we spend it as a tale that is told. Interpretative Reading, the art of expression, is that discourse which, in well-regulated schools and lives, goes inseparably paired with the spiritual reason. So Shakespeare:

> Sure, He that made us with such large discourse,
> Looking before and after, gave us not
> That capability and god-like reason
> To fust in us unus'd.

Music, story, speech, and those others, laid in God's reality for discovery, use, and praise, belong in the curriculum. But what bothers me in my student is that her "little schedule" is top-heavy on the aesthetic side, and that it provides little opportunity for historical discipline. I fear, too, that she looks upon herself as a creature mainly organic, and full of sensibilities which she now wants coddled, entertained, and at best "refined." This is nice, but is it moral education?

The student is not so much, not solely, to be blamed for a still disordered and immature sense of what man is, what life is, and what education is. What I wish for on such occasions is a more generally active idea of Christian education in the community as a whole, an idea going out from the center to the periphery, from the periphery to the center, and involving everybody — teacher, minister, board member, pupil, and people. We have such a fine chance for maintaining the spiritual dignity of man and his education by way of nature, culture, and history. There is the first question and the first answer of John Calvin's *Genevan*

Catechism to challenge us: What is the chief end of man? To know God and enjoy him forever. The thrust of that, when we come to reflect upon it, is that man is spiritual and moral, not merely natural and organic. There is also the counsel of the Ecclesiast: The fear of the Lord is the beginning of wisdom. That makes education dogmatic; it does not make education unnecessary.

We shall insist then on "content and pattern." Our object is morality, not efficiency. We want character more than calibre. We have no objection to the term "development" as an aim in education, provided it means moral development, and not merely a refinement of crude sensibility, or a better organization of impulses and instincts. We are not so bewildered by reality as to find ourselves adrift on the stream of nature. We cherish "personality" because of its "interests," yes, but even more because these lead us to the moral decision of spiritual freedom. Hence we shall want content, want to be disciplined by reality as it is. That reality must be representative reality. The curriculum will therefore include nature, culture, and history. And it will provide historical discipline. Else there will be no opportunity of showing that man in his life chooses for God or against him, and that this choice is the significance of life.

That takes me back to the solid advice at the front end of the Catalogue. I explain to the girl, and give her the usual:

> Bible
> Biology
> Latin
> Grammar, Rhetoric, Composition
> History.

"Okay?" I ask.
"Okay!" she says. These students are susceptible to ideas.

The Reformed Journal, March, 1951.

5

Formal Discipline in Our Schools

It is commonly observed, and with a good deal of justice, that contemporary students, by and large, exhibit a lack of formal discipline in their oral and written expression. This absence of "good form" comes out in such ways as these: faulty grammar, poor spelling, unconfident punctuation, illegible penmanship, shaky logic, fragmentary utterance, incoherent composition, slovenly pronunciation, colloquial and slangy diction, and the like. Such "bad form" is bad enough in itself. What makes it worse is that it is symptomatic of something. It is symptomatic of disintegrated morale in our educational idea and practice.

THE CAUSES

Presumably the causes for this lack of formal discipline in the contemporary student are as complex as the causes of other inadequacies in modern education. Some of these can be named here, not all of them mutually exclusive:

1. The absence of any really operative, over-ruling idea, defined objective, or undergirding philosophy in education generally. The result is bewilderment, confusion, experimentalism, and subjectivity in the schools.

2. Democratically conceived "universal" education which seems to imply "passing" pupils at all levels, irrespective of calibre or evidence of achievement. The result is a levelling of standards of excellence in accommodation to the many.

3. The "elective" system in schools at all levels with its implied pick-and-choose attitude towards educational wares, and its repudiation of prescribed content and pattern in study programs.

4. The abandonment, presumably on "pragmatic" grounds, of sustained work in foreign languages, or, at best, the teaching of these as utilities rather than disciplines.

5. The newer psychologies, expressive of religio-moral and rational decadence, with their exaggeration of *pupil-centered* education, their emphasis on self-expression at the cost of self-discipline, and their substitution of a personal world of self for an objective world of reality.

6. The encroachment upon educational methods in all fields of the dogma of "scientific method."

7. The fetish of "enriched curricula," that is, empirical expansion at the expense of concentration on essentials.

8. The thinning out of properly educational effort by reason of the so-called "broadened responsibility" of the schools.

9. Premature "specialization" for which in teacher and pupil we have had to pay the price of "a full and harmonious development of all sides of our nature."

10. A false division between content and form, thought and expression, "fact" and statement. Such a dualism leads, on the one hand, to an *Information, please* approach to knowledge, and, on the other, to feverish busyness with what are then called "communications skills and techniques" as panaceas for the general disintegration.

11. Under-staffed schools, over-crowded classes; mass methods of teaching and testing; emergency, practicality, and hurry as opposed to leisure in education.

12. Hastily trained and ill-qualified teachers.

13. Home backgrounds characterized by under-developed lives, "peasant" practicality, suspicion of culture, meager thought and reading resources, and a brash "What's it for?" and "Does it pay?" attitude.

THE SOLUTION: IN GENERAL

Such causes, it is true, might be expected to operate more effectively in the schools generally than in our Christian schools. But more than one of these causes are undermining the formal discipline of the pupils and students in our schools also. By our schools I mean all of them, from kindergarten through seminary. By and large our graduates, too, lack that formal discipline which is the natural accompaniment of successful education.

We have, therefore, a job to do. The following are, I think, some of the steps that can be taken towards solution of this symptomatically serious problem. I list them again in outline fashion, though each bone of the skeleton could, I think, be fleshed in a full-bodied article. My concern at the moment is for a bird's-eye survey.

These, then, are the remedies that suggest themselves:

1. Further development, but more particularly, further appropriation, of a sound and operative Reformed or Christian idea of education:

a. To provide the basis in conviction for thorough mastery of the essential subject disciplines of the school.

b. To counteract the tempting subjectivity, self-expression, and pupil-centered drift of the contemporary schools; and to counteract also, therefore, the substitution of habits for understanding, techniques for knowledge, skills for disciplines, and the like.

c. To substitute for a superficial "culture" spread thinly over a "practical" or "vocational" course a rationally defensible discipline of the pupil by means of a science of reality.

2. Reduction of the teacher's pupil load and course load so that mass methods of teaching and testing can be supplanted by satisfying methods.

3. Liberation of the teacher from financial care so that he can address his life professionally to plain, ordinary competence in his important work.

4. The development and selection of teachers for appointment who have themselves been solidly taught — teachers, therefore, who in their own speech and writing exhibit a unified, as distinguished from a fragmentized, education.

5. A general, and a practically implemented, acknowledgment that the "formal" work of students is the corporate responsibility of all teachers at all levels and in all subject matters, and not that of "English" teachers alone.

6. Resolute opposition, by all hands, and in every way, to the reigning dualism between fact and form, science and art, knowledge and statement, lest the "sciences" go one way, the "arts" another, and the pupil remain a barbarian.

7. Concentration of effort upon reading, thinking, and writing, instead of the dispersion of attention over "broadened responsibility" areas (personal conduct, character building, social etiquette, Indian pottery, municipal administration, catechism, and interior decorating).

8. Fostering general school pride in excellent formal accomplishment (spelling bees, speech and essay competitions, honor-student awards).

9. The re-introduction into examinations of the old-fashioned, essay-type question, emphasis on well-organized class reports and papers, and the evaluation of student work on the basis of form as well as content.

10. Confident, practical reassertion of the value of foreign language study as a scientific discipline (that is, for its grammar, rhetoric, logic, and literary significance, not simply as a useful tool for tourists, salesmen in Latin America, or employees of the State Department).

11. Some attention again to individual "recitation," the student standing, if need be, and committed to full-predication replies.

Towards Solution: In "English"

1. Thorough execution of systematic work in grammar:

a. The repudiation of "functional" and "experimental" approaches in favor of a legitimately scientific approach.

b. Reference continually to the relationship of logic and right thinking to grammar and right statement.

c. Repudiation of the notion that anything in grammar is a matter of "mechanics"; grammar is integral with meaningful form.

d. Accent on right and real understanding quite as much as on drills, workbooks, habits.

e. Re-appropriation of such tried avenues to right understanding as diagramming and parsing.

f. Clear presentation of minimum essentials, and frequent repetition of these at various stages of the educational program.

g. Satisfaction with nothing less than the nomenclature, recognition, and application of the science of grammar.

h. Recognition that punctuation, and even style, depend upon a mastery of grammatical principles.

2. Thorough execution of systematic work in composition:

a. An emphasis on "imitation" quite as much as on "expression."

b. A use of all three ways to teach composition: theory (principles of rhetoric), example (literature), and practice (student composition).

c. Continuous work in logic and outline, in abstract and condensation, in precis and summarization, that is, in the objective forms of composition.

d. Acknowledgment of the individual student's "uniqueness," but insistence also that he continually mould and remould his thought until it conforms to reason.

e. Subjection of the student again and again, as his spiritual horizons widen, to the purging discipline of giving shape and form to his elusive thought.

f. Confidence in the fact that it is inescapably human to make things, to mould things, to create.

Summary

In summary, let me report an incident by way of exhortation. I lately encountered a college student, one therefore who had achieved twelve years of "English." I asked him to write on a piece of paper what a substantive was. He told me what a *subintive* was. I asked him for three kinds of nouns when classified according to form, and he wrote (my transcription is literal): *Three kinds of noun as to form comon, sinple, phraal.* I then called for the four genders and got this: *mascilein, feniante, neutur.* My next question: Which are the three cases in English? And the answer: *There are there. cases in English: Comon, proper, abstract.* One question remained, a call for four uses of the nominative case. Came the response: *Four uses of the. nonative case: He went to town-objectiv.*

Must I append a peroration?

Presumably there is no such thing as a Christian semicolon, or a Calvinistic participle. But there is such a thing as a Christian view of life. According to this view, God is rational, His world is a *universe,* and the mind of man is capable of order. It may be that a Deist could say as much. We should say no less. We have therefore a job to do.

The. Reformed Journal, November, 1951.

* * *

The above. article, "Formal Discipline in our Schools," elicited a reply from Dr. John J. DeBoer, College of Education, University of Illinois. In this reply Dr. DeBoer presents the case for descriptive as opposed to normative grammar. He calls into question the implication he sees in Dr. Zylstra's article that there is a set of a priori grammatical principles, transcendental grammatical archetypes which are everywhere and always the same. He contends, further, that Dr. Zylstra, in his opinion, pays too much deference to the theory of formal discipline, a theory which, he says, has been largely discredited by modern experimentation. He insists, too, that the study of language can and should be studied as a body of knowledge which partakes of nature as well as of grace; that the scientific method has validity in the study of language; and that only by resorting to the highly dubious method of appealing to "revealed principles which supersede the facts of observation by finite creatures" can such findings be ignored. Dr. Zylstra replied to Dr. DeBoer in the article which follows, "Formal Discipline Reaffirmed." [Editors]

6

Formal Discipline Reaffirmed

That was a spirited letter which Professor John DeBoer of the University of Illinois wrote (the *Journal*, December, '51) in comment on my "Formal Discipline in Our Schools" (the *Journal*, November, '51).

There seems to be a difference between us, and as I see it the point at issue is this: What in language teaching constitutes the norm or standard of expression? I proposed *reason* or *logic* as this norm, and Professor DeBoer proposes *usage*.

Journal readers may care to know that the tussle Professor DeBoer and I have got going here is only a faint reflection of a long debate among the professionals. It can perhaps be called a debate between the formalists (the *logic* men) and the functionalists (the *usage* men). These terms are flattering to neither party. Perhaps it would be kinder to call them the philosophers and the scientists, respectively: or yet again, those who talk principles, and those who talk practice. The formalists, further, tend to lean to the old, and the functionalists to the new. The formalists speak of *normative* grammar. The functionalists call it *descriptive*. There is more than a little of the classical in the formalist, and, as this formalist sees it, there is a good deal of the romantic in the functionalist.

Anyhow, quantities of writing have gone into the discussion during the last half century. Most of this came from the functionalists, who, making use of the rising sciences of psychology and sociology, assumed the role of challengers over against the entrenched formalists. Their challenge was successful. Functionalism is now the prevailing attitude in language teaching. The formalist is at bay.

As I hinted in my first piece, my objection to functionalism comes down to this: It defines language as a natural activity of man. Or, if you prefer, it defines language as an activity of natural man. I, to the contrary, hold to the view that language is a rational expression, an expression of spiritual man. From this, it seems to me, emerges the difference between proposing *logic* as the norm of expression, and proposing *usage* as that norm. From this emerges also the tendency of the functionalist to use "scientific method" for getting at the nature of language, and the tendency of the formalist to use science or philosophy for getting at it. For the first, grammar becomes a form of applied psychology and sociology; for the second, it becomes a form of applied logic.

I think a good deal hangs by this difference. Language is, of course, also a natural activity; that is, it has a natural dimension. The ear and the eye, the lip, the larynx, and the tongue enter into it. In this sense language is biological. It is natural, further, in that the psychological — nerve and synapse, motive and feeling, disposition and temperament — enters into it, even when the psychological is equated entirely with the natural in man. Again, language is natural in that the "speech environment" or the "sociological situation" conditions it. And to the extent that language is thus an activity of the natural man, "scientific method" is valid and useful for getting at its nature. But these natural dimensions of language do not exhaust it. There is that about it which reaches beyond the natural into the rational or spiritual, and it is precisely this aspect of it which is normative, definitive, and ideal. What I object to in functionalism is that it ignores this spiritual reach of language.

Let me say that I am quite willing to undergo what Professor De Boer calls "the kind of 'intellectual discipline' which insists upon the validity of the observed facts of language." I am willing to do this, that is, if the force of the "observed" is not limited to what "the scientific attitude" and "scientific method" have it within their power to disclose. For it is certainly a "fact of language" that *besides* being natural, and *in* being natural, language is free, rational, spiritual. This, its rational being, is its essential part. In studying language, consequently, one is studying something more permanent and universal than popular speech practice. One is studying the truth of that reality which reason apprehends. Only — and this may be the nub of the matter — the reason which thus apprehends the *principles* of language is as different from the reason which observes and reports popular usage as the reason of Aristotle is from that of John Dewey.

That is my whole case: that reason informs language. Language has therefore a contact with the realm of law, and is expressive of principle. In this, its rational freedom, it escapes from the bondage of circumstance, transcends climate, geography, race, milieu, environment, and participates, as the older philosophers said, in the universal. In this sense, psychology and sociology, most particularly when these are regarded as empirical sciences, naturalistically defined, cannot disclose its nature. The law to which the uses of language are obedient is ultimately the law of reason, and not the law of nature. And hence it is that the principles, or essentials, or science of grammar can provide a structure and an architectonics (something different, now, from a "language situation" or a "speech environment") which *disciplines* the pupil by reality.

This point of view, out of favor as I know it to be in contemporary education, has nevertheless the bulk of traditional sense behind it. It is a view, simply, which insists on the integrity of *Logos*. *Logos* is only half translated *word* (language), the other half being *reason* (thought). It is the keyword to the rational nature. It is the keyword also to the human being. This is to be human, to be spirit speaking, to be expressive mind. Language therefore distinguishes man: it proves him rational, free. Compare man as a speaking creature with Carlyle's definition of man as "a tool-using animal." Note the collapse of dignity. It does not define a man that he can manipulate techniques. What defines him is that he can express thought. *Ratio* and *oratio,* the Romans said, following in the wake of Aristotle, reason and speech, these complement each other, and are consonant with each other. Hence, in the older education, grammar had its place next to *logic* and alongside of rhetoric in the *trivium* or basically disciplinary core curriculum of the pupil. It is there, next to logic, that I wish to keep it. I think it represents a derationalization of man to transfer it to psychology and sociology. "Sure He that made us" says Shakespeare, "with such large *discourse/ Gave* us not that capability and god-like *reason/* To fust in us unus'd."

Functionalism, on the other hand, unless I entirely misread its origins and career, is preoccupied with the accidental rather than the essential in language. Those terms, I admit, are Aristotelian. Functionalism is preoccupied with the element of change, not that of permanence. Professor Charles C. Fries' *American English Grammar* (Appleton, 1940), a book produced partly with the assistance of the National Council of Teachers of English, is an instance of it. A right or wrong, a correct or incorrect in grammar? There is no such thing. Such a way of talking is a vestige of the eighteenth century when people preferred mental constructs to realities, and formal stereotypes to actual practice. Right or wrong? No. The best one can aim at is "language nicely adapted ... to the circumstances of the occasion." The thing to teach, consequently, is not principles; the thing to do is to describe trends of practice. The thing to develop is the sharp eye: "the actual observation of usage." Given free rein, such an emphasis makes of the traditional class in grammar a research seminar in public utterance, and sends out field workers to record and report what particular people under particular circumstances say. The report thereupon is normative for usage. "We cannot hope," says Professor Fries, "to change the practices of a language; we can only help students to learn what those practices are." On such a basis yes, "scientific method" is perfect and adequate for language study, and grammar cannot be a science. It is not the rational in language that impresses Fries; it is the natural: "the most important facts of language are the circumstances under which it is usually used."

What the English class in such a context of meaning ought to be doing is something quite different from studying the principles of grammar. It should instead be cultivating "the scientific attitude," alerting itself to change, that is, to sociological change. This is the most precious lesson "grammar" has to teach. It must "cultivate sensitiveness to speech environment." What is this but the collapse of reason and the attempt, as Walter Pater undertook it, to live always at that point of a moment at which it ceases to be itself?

The customs change, of course. The differences between the English of *Beowulf* and the English of our time are legion, and they affect every phase of language: diction, spelling, inflection, syntax, accidence, construction, punctuation, and the rest. But what of the principles? Do they change, or are they only newly illuminated by varying custom? Since it is knowledge, science, that we should aim at in school, knowledge rather than skill, science rather than habits, ought we not, in grammar also, to teach principles? I for one would be content if the contemporary pupil were to learn the principles of language construction which operate in and are illustrated by the *Beowulf*. In that poem, as well as in the latest speech of Drew Pearson, the pupil can come to grips with the essentials of grammar. There, for instance, he can learn what the sentence is, magnificent embodiment as it is of mind speaking, seen as a whole and in its parts: substantive, predicate, complement, and modifiers. These would, I think, be an adequate discipline in this phase of rational reality. The pupil could then pick up people's habits after school, and adjust himself accordingly.

It was in reaction to functionalism, that I drew up that skeletal piece on "Formal Discipline." I was concerned then to warn against "disintegrating educational morale" owing to the absence of an undergirding philosophy other than "the scientific attitude." I felt that something like a proper respect for language, a proper respect for also that phase of it which is grammar, is part and parcel of the Christian sense of man. And so I was concerned to advocate that we do not reduce it to the level of a tool, a technique, to the level, that is, of nature. If we do that we shall end up without any possibility of making our teaching Christian.

If this be mere "vigorous assertion" accept it as that. It is "undocumented" I know. I cannot be expected to use the method to which the term "documentation" belongs when I think this method cannot get at the essence of language. Anyhow, these ideas are frankly something of a testament of faith.

The Reformed Journal, January, 1952.

7

Thoughts for Teachers

In these days registration is due again. We shall have to be concerned once more, both on the school and college levels, to see that our students get a solid core of liberal studies. There will be that tremendous pull towards the practical. The Commercial Course will seem to make so much more sense than the Classical Course. Somehow, in practice, Carlyle's old definition of man as a tool-using animal appeals to us just as much as Calvin's idea of a God-knowing creature. It is an old tension, this one between the practical and the liberal arts. I quote from the younger Seneca as Macaulay quoted him in his essay on Bacon:

> In my time there have been inventions of this sort, transparent windows, tubes for diffusing warmth equally through all parts of a building, shorthand, which has been carried to such a perfection that a writer can keep pace with the most rapid speaker. But the invention of such things is drudgery for the lowest slaves; philosophy lies deeper. It is not her office to teach men how to use their hands. The object of her lessons is to form the soul.

The object is to form the soul. That will be a good phrase to have in mind as we sit at the registration tables arranging the schedules of our pupils. Which shall it be now, Latin or Gregg? The object is to form the soul.

Two hundred years after Seneca old Plotinus gave out his idea of the relative value of liberal and vocational training:

> For who that is strong enough to meditate upon the original turns by choice to its phantasm? Witness the circumstances that among children it is the dunces who betake

themselves to the crafts and manual employments, because they are not competent to learning and meditation.

That is by now a quaint way to put it: "who that is strong enough to meditate upon the original turns . . . to its phantasm?" But this is to say that the thing is no substitute for the idea, and that there is a difference between the servile and the liberal arts.

We have been using the word *integration* a lot in our discussions of education. It is a great word and no doubt we shall have to use it some more. Personally, I like the word *orientation.* It may be that we have spoiled it a little with our university Orientation Week and the like. Such a week is devoted primarily to helping the student find himself on the campus. But even the meaning of that is not bad for getting at what education is. For once I shall quote the dictionary to help establish a point. To orient, says Webster, means *to cause to face toward the east.* It means *to ascertain the bearings of a thing.* How much more important those bearings are for us teachers than the thing itself. We have to get squared around towards God if the universe is to make sense. Life is bewildering and meaningless without the fixed reference point. And how were one to find his way in a life of eternity with a map of time except he have a polar point, a Bethlehem, an Incarnation? Orientation: that is our work as teachers. We must give our pupils their bearings in life by causing them to face towards the east.

Arthur Koestler, in his novel *Arrival and Departure* (Macmillan, 1943), powerfully illustrates how a differing assumption or dogma changes the picture of reality. The facts we look at in our schools are very much the same as those that are studied in other schools. But the patterns we see — and life, like a painting, is a muddle until we discern the pattern — are different. Koestler says:

> As children we used to be given a curious kind of puzzle to play with. It was a paper with a tangle of very thin blue and red lines. If you just looked at it you couldn't make out anything. But if you covered it with a piece of transparent red tissue-paper, the red lines of the drawing disappeared and the blue lines formed a picture — it was a clown in a circus holding a hoop and a little dog jumping through it. And if you covered the same drawing with

blue tissue-paper, a roaring lion appeared, chasing the clown across the ring. You can do the same thing with every mortal, living or dead. You can look at him through tissue-paper and write a biography of Napoleon in terms of his pituitary gland, as has been done; the fact that he incidentally conquered Europe will appear as a mere symptom of the activities of those two tiny lobes, the size of a pea. You can explain the message of the Prophets as epileptical foam and the Sistine Madonna as the projection of an incestuous dream.... The clown and the lion are both there, interwoven in the same pattern.... Since the Renaissance the red tissue-paper of our scientific reasoning has obtained greater perfection than the blue of our intuition and ethical beliefs.... But prior to that, in the Gothic age, the scales moved the opposite way; and I believe that this process will soon be reversed again.

"If you just looked at it you couldn't make out anything." This, then, is the necessity of dogma in education, grounded in the religious nature of man. There is no possibility of finding oneself in the universe, of getting one's bearings, of being oriented, in neutral education. After that the question becomes, Through the tissue paper of *which* dogma is one reading reality?

The point of departure for several of these ideas is my reading of Professor Frederick A. Pottle's book, *The Idiom of Poetry* (Cornell University Press, 1946). He has some good things to say also about a problem which is recurrent among us in our schools: namely, What may our students, our pupils, read? On this point of Christian liberty in the reading of books, Professor Pottle takes a strong stand. It might well serve, it seems to me, as a statement of our own ideal in this matter. He says:

> We protect children from books that might cause trouble, as we keep certain kinds of food from them, but when they grow up they must decide by the testimony of their own lives and their own consciences. It was profoundly said by St. Augustine that all morality can be summed up in the injunction, "Love God and do what you will." The saying could as well take the form, "Love God and read what you will."

Dr. Pottle understands the considerable threat to the morality of the young in some contemporary literature, but he thinks that the best way to deal with it is to build up positive resources of strength:

> The church would do well to worry less about the demoralizing effect of contemporary literature and more about the sincerity, persistence, and competence of its training of the young.

Dr. Pottle is one of those modern minds who have the honesty to admit that "Every man, without exception, has his orthodoxies...." There is always an area of dogma, an area of things which we take for granted. For most people of our time this uncritically accepted area is the scientific one. "Without being taught to do so," he says, "we assign all 'truth' to the province of science. Whatever science cannot manipulate we feel to be unreal or untrue." But other basic assumptions lead to a different kind of quest from the modern, and to the acknowledgment of a different kind of evidence. "How could men," asks Professor Pottle, thinking of the Middle Ages, "be content to remain so ignorant of ascertainable facts?" The answer is clear:

> Because they were "making sense" of nature in a framework [the theological] which interested them more than the scientific....

The same was true of the Greeks, though their dogma differed from that of the Middle Ages as well as from that of the Modern Age:

> Is it not clear that the ancient Greeks could have made every discovery in science on which we pride ourselves, if they had thought it worthwhile?

This is perhaps our hardest work as Christian teachers and the most inescapably obligatory: namely, to discriminate dogma, to discern within which framework a particular book, or period, or author is "making sense" of reality.

It may be that this use which I am making of the word *dogma* in these notes is a little singular. It is not synonymous with doctrine. It leads to doctrine when it is articulated but it is not itself the doctrine. It is the faith behind the creed but it is not itself the statement of the creed. V. A. Demant used the term a good deal in his *Religious Prospect,* and my impression is that men of letters are using the term to designate a category of assumptions or "framework within which to make sense of reality" rather more than theologians are. Anyhow, the idea is more important than the term, and the reality than the idea. I borrow some further account, therefore, of this whole matter from T. E. Hulme. Hulme explained in his *Speculations* (Harcourt, Brace, 1936) that in order to get at a period or an age one must get at its dogma:

> In order to understand a period it is necessary not so much to be acquainted with its more defined opinions as with the doctrines which are thought of not as doctrines, but as FACTS. There are certain doctrines which for a particular period· seem not doctrines, but inevitable categories of the human mind. Men do not look to them merely as correct opinion, for they have become so much a part of the mind, and lie so far back, that they are never really conscious of them at all. They do not see them, but see other things through them. . . . It is these *doctrines* felt as *facts,* which are the source of all the other more material characteristics of a period.

Once more now, I suggest that dogma in this sense, though you may call it what you will, is the thing that we must be always getting at in the classroom. People who feel that Christian school teachers do not need a thoroughgoing education do not understand this.

Another example of how differing assumptions about life make for a different reading of reality is the nice contrast between Thomas Henry Huxley's and Herman Bavinck's accounts of the physical earth and its importance. Huxley followed in Darwin's wake and argued that "general conceptions of the universe . . . have been forced upon us by physical science." Among these general conceptions which Huxley felt "forced" to adopt because of his scientific framework of making sense out of reality was the following:

> It is very certain that the earth is not the chief body in the material universe, and that the world is not subordinated to man's use.

And here is Herman Bavinck, for whom the "theological dicta" that Huxley scorned entered into making sense of nature. Here is Bavinck, looking at the same data through the other tissue paper, as Koestler would say, of revelation *(Magnalia Dei)*:

> And man is and remains the crown of creation; the dressing and cultivation of the earth ministers to man's benefit. That is why Scripture says so little about the creation of the heavens and of the angels, and limits itself mainly to the earth. In an astronomical sense the earth may be small and insignificant; in mass and weight it may be surpassed by thousands of planets and suns and stars: but in a religious and moral sense the earth remains the center of the universe. It and it alone has been chosen as a dwelling place for man. It is the arena in which the great struggle against every evil power is conducted. It is the place for the establishment of the kingdom of heaven.

Except in the sense of the 8th Psalm, there apparently is no reason why, for a person governed by religious dogma, the immensities of the physical universe as demonstrated by science should diminish the significance of man. It is a kind of false modesty to think less of ourselves because the physical world is so big.

Koestler thought that the scientific framework by which in the modern time men have chosen to make sense of life and reality would give way again to one of "intuition and ethical belief." We teachers should be alert, I think, to this change which has been heralded by many prophets of our time, particularly by men of letters, and which does indeed seem to be already well under way. A new and different dogma, in the sense of these notes, is shaping up in the middle decades of this century. The change seems to be a change from Liberal Man and Natural Man to Religious Man. Some think of it as likely to be a bigger change than that which happened at the French Revolution, and as big a change as that which took place at the Renaissance. We seem to be moving from an age of science into an age of faith.

Perhaps, though, I should not call it an age of faith that we are entering upon. I remember being admonished against it by Wystan H. Auden, a writer who has been especially sensitive to just this shift of dogmatic climate here under discussion. He once called such a designation a misnomer. He said it in a statement which pretty well characterizes the scientific assumptions within which the modern world has heretofore elected to confine its truth. He said it in his Foreword to Emile Cammaerts' *The Flower of Grass* (Harper, 1945);

> It is wrong to speak of ages of faith and ages of doubt, as if a man could ever be without either, but each has its favorite idol, and of the late age it may be said that it had a belief, approaching superstition, in the presentational immediacy, the being-thereness of a fact, and a doubt, approaching denial, of its having any further meaning or value.

But this mentality which Auden here speaks of he assigns to "the late age." The implication is that this age is no longer here. He characterizes its successor, too, in an off-hand clause which seems to be happily struck off, and one of the most important sentences recorded in our decade. It comes at the end of his book, *The Enchafed Flood* (Faber and Faber, 1951):

> We live in a new age in which . . . the necessity of dogma is once more recognized, not as the contradiction of reason and feeling, but as their ground and foundation.

It may be that before century's end — and, after all, dates do not govern spiritual epochs — this of Auden, and its equivalent in, as I say, many other writers, will be the text to exegete in characterization of our time. Those of us, if any, who have practically as well as theoretically escaped the liberal and positivist dogma of a scientific framework of interpretation, will presumably welcome the return of an acknowledged religious dimension. For it is dogma that determines what we mean to recognize as evidence.

The return to the religious way of making sense of reality will not, of course, solve all of our problems. Being religious is not synonymous with being Christian. A whole new set of advantages and disadvantages may be ahead of us. There will be disadvantages, too: irrationalism and resurgent naturalism can come back in the guise of religious affirmation. But when the issue no longer is whether or not there is to be a faith, but rather one of which faith it is to be, we shall be more honest and direct with each other all around.

Meanwhile we teachers must be alert to the changing soul of the times.
                    The Reformed Journal, September, 1954.

Part Three

RELIGION

1

Eccentric Religion

By and large, the trouble with religion in our age and country is that it is eccentric. It operates from the periphery rather than from the middle of our national life. It is there all right, but it does not affect much of anything one way or the other. And just as religion is eccentric in our society, it is eccentric in ourselves. It operates from the periphery rather than from the center of the individual. In society our religion is a kind of "pocket" Christianity; in ourselves it is a kind of "faculty" religion.

Look at the religious situation generally in our country. Look at it objectively as the visitor from Mars would look at it. If he were asked to report back to his planet, he could do worse than take a copy of *Time* magazine with him, point to its table of contents, and say that what he had seen down here was a lot of people interested in: Art, Books, Business, Cinema, Education, Medicine, Music, People, Personality, Press, Radio, Religion, Sports, Theatre... and the rest. If he were then asked whether the item called Religion, tucked in there between Radio and Sport, were the governing thing here as it is in Mohammedan Asia, Confucian China, or Shintoistic Japan, he would have to say that he thought it was not. He would have to say that Religion was operating alongside of those other things rather than in them and through them.

Presumably the man from Mars would have to report that religion, so far from serving as the leaven which keeps the body of the national life from crumbling, is itself one of the fragments. If he were observant, he might discover that it had once been an important organ in civilization, but that it had since atrophied, its functions having been taken over by other organs. Religion, he might say, seemed to him like nothing so much as a vestigial appendix or supernumerary wisdom tooth, still present, but unsure of its job, and more of a nuisance than a help.

Pressed to say which organs had taken over the position of centrality in the government of things, the Martian might be puzzled to reply. He could say that something called Art had sometimes put out its claims to be the redeemer and restorer of Life, but that these claims had never received much popular support. And he might add that Science and Business, doing their work without much reference to the religiously defined purposes of man, were now pretty largely putting their stamp upon the national culture, and were making almost everything else follow in their wake.

Something like that would be the Martian report. For the fact is that religion in our age and country is insular. It is very largely disengaged from life. It seems to acknowledge no essential involvement with what we call civilization. It floats as a detached cell in the bloodstream of practical affairs. It is a department among departments, a specialty among specialties. Instead of counteracting disintegration, it has itself disintegrated. It stalks like a disembodied ghost among the secular shadows.

In the individual life, in the life of the self also, religion has unwarrantedly isolated itself. Even Christians in our time have begun to feature Christianity as "personal religion." There was good reason for so denominating it, and that reason continues. For one thing, it was the truth. It is the person of the individual believer who by faith, through grace, makes the commitment to his Saviour and Lord, and so is reconciled with God. For another thing, it was a necessary protest against the opponents. Over against the hollowness of official religion, it became necessary to stress the genuineness of personal religion. And over against the falseness of a Liberal social religion, it became necessary to emphasize the truth and purity of personal religion.

The isolation of religion from life, therefore, does not spring from the fact that religion is personal. It springs, rather, from the fact that the person is no longer whole, is no longer a single state of man. It is so that the personal has come to be identified with what is left of the self after its practical, social, and cultural relationships have been cut away. This is a meager person, a fragmentary self, and in it the Gospel of the true religion, be it pure and undefiled, has no field of operation. There too religion is eccentric religion.

The problem, plainly, is the problem of secularism, for this is secularism defined: the separation of religion from life, that is, from all phases of life except the isolably personal phases. The problem of secularism is peculiarly a problem for Christians: those who have no *sacred* have no need for distinguishing a *secular*. And the problem is most particularly a problem for the orthodox, because these, in their necessary concern for the purity of religion, are tempted to isolate it and to deny it practical, cultural, and social relevancy.

Our best resource for counteracting the eccentricity of religion, for staying the subtle encroachment of secularity, is, of course, the Gospel truth. It is our Reformation legacy of a pure and undefiled religion ... *and* ... that religion operative in the life. We are forced by our time to attach the word "evangelical" to the word Christianity, but in doing this we do it to delimit its meaning, not to limit its scope. There is no limit to the Gospel. Think again of that one word among the twenty in *Time's* index, think of Religion finding a crevice between Radio and Sport, as an area all its own. Then think of the astonishing magnitude of religion as seen from the vantage point of the Prologue to the Gospel according to St. John: "In the beginning was the Word, and the Word was with God, and the Word was God. The same was in the beginning with God. By Him were all things made that were made . . . In Him was Life and his Life was the light of men . . . ."

Our religion is by the grace of God planted and seated in our humanity, and must be central in it. And our humanity is involved up to the hilt in life. We cannot then accommodate this religion to a crumbled society. We cannot accommodate it to a disintegrated self. We cannot regard practical life, in its historical involvement and in its cultural and social extension, as something independent from our personal religious life.

Ours we say, and we believe, is the whole Gospel for the whole man, and through him, for the whole society. We must let it possess us at the center of our self, and then we must bear it in upon our time: its feeling, its motive, and its idea. For the time, as the poet Yeats said, is out of joint:

> Things fall apart; the centre cannot hold;
> Mere anarchy is loosed upon the world,

The blood-rimmed tide is loosed, and everywhere
The ceremony of innocence is drowned;
The best lack all conviction, while the worst
Are full of passionate intensity.

The Reformed Journal, February, 1952.

2

The Contemplative Life

Contemplation is a word which sounds badly out of key with the noises of our time. It savors, even to us religious folk, of hymn-book archaism. It suggests old Plato, the Pagan Orient, and the Catholic Middle Ages. A good many of us, it may be, are content to leave it to Athens, Buddah, and the monks.

We have no right to do this. The contemplative life is the God-conscious life. It is the life that knows its end and can rest in that knowledge. The Psalmist spoke of it: Be *still,* and *know* that I am God. We read of it in Hebrews: There remaineth a *rest* for the people of God.

John Calvin put it into the first question and answer of his *Genevan Catechism.* His question was fundamental: What is the chief end of man? And his answer was crystal-clear: To *know* God and *enjoy* Him forever. That is the eternal Sabbath which begins here: *Delight* in the *knowledge* of God.

Modernity, by its neglect of God, has idolized the active life. John Dewey, lately deceased, was typical of this idolatry. He glorified process. He deified experiment. He championed evolution. His action lacked its reason. His reason lacked its worship. His worship lacked its object. Such action is not contemplative. It is blind. It is activism. The punsters teased him with their "learn to do by Deweying," and the jest fitted him.

Well before Dewey, the German Goethe had set the pace for the modern activism. He put his Faust to work translating the prologue to the Gospel of St. John. That meant finding an equivalent for the Greek word *Logos.* Faust experimented with several possibilities. He tried *Thought,* and concluded it would not do. He tried *Word,* and rejected it as inadequate. He tried *Energy,* felt he was getting closer, but remained unsatisfied. Then he hit on it, and ushered in modernity: *In the beginning,* he wrote, *in the beginning was the Act*. The creature had taken over, and God was an exile from His world.

Such has been the modern temper. Service, humanitarianism, the second table of the law divorced from the first, evolution, process, change, experiment, motion — those are the keywords to the age. Carlyle, a disciple of Goethe and a rebel to Calvinist doctrine, applied it all to religion: "Whatsoever religion," he said, "is not work, may go and dwell among the Brahmins ... or where it will; with me it shall have no harbour."

The result of this neglect of the contemplative life has not been satisfying, even for moderns. There has been no *rest* and there has been no *enjoyment*. Ernest Dowson spoke of its endless activity:

> I cried for madder music and for stronger wine,
> But when the feast is finished and the lamps expire....
> I am desolate and sick of an old passion,
> Yea, hungry for the lips of my desire.

That old passion, were Dowson and others honest in analyzing it, is the human passion for the knowledge of God. It is the longing of the creature for communion with his Creator.

The whole story of the sinner's pitiful flight from the grace of a satisfying communion with God is told in Francis Thompson's poem *The Hound of Heaven*. There is no poise in such flight, no shelter, no harborage, no contentment. There is only the blind activism of the panic-stricken outlaw from God. You remember the lines:

> I fled Him, down the nights and down the days;
> I fled Him, down the arches of the years;
> I fled Him, down the labyrinthine ways
> Of my own mind; and in the mist of tears
> I hid from Him, and under running laughter....

And as his panic increases, the fleeing sinner hears his Lord:

> Lo! naught contents thee, who content'st not Me.

Mr. Eliot, the contemporary English poet with the Catholic temper, summarizes the modern predicament:

> Endless invention, endless experiment,
> Brings knowledge of motion, but not of stillness;
> Knowledge of speech, but not of silence;
> Knowledge of words, and ignorance of the Word....

> Where is the Life we have lost in living?
> Where is the wisdom we have lost in knowledge?
> Where is the knowledge we have lost in information?

Action must spring from thought, from thought that is seated in worship, in worship that is worship of God.

The knowledge of God is proper to us as creatures, and it satisfies. That is the finest fruit of the contemplative life: to know and enjoy God. No one will care to ask what such enjoyment is for. It is enough for us. So far from being caught in the web of natural process, snared in the fatality of endless busyness, we can rest in that knowledge.

For man is a creature who can know. Animals cannot, though animals can be magnificently efficient. We people cannot for all our years fall as gracefully as a kitten at two weeks, or fly as well as a bird at its first attempt, or build a house in the ground as competently as an ant. True, the ingenuity and skill with which men in our time have learned to do things is amazing. But such efficiency, skill, or power does not make a man a man.

We see that at once back there in Paradise. When God had done making the animals, we read this: "And the Lord God formed every beast of the field and every fowl of the air, and brought them unto Adam to see what he would name them." There we have it: a mind to know and to name. The capacity for conscious appreciation. The leisure, the spiritual freedom, to enjoy. Man, conscious reflector of the glory. *Homo sapiens,* man knowing, not quite submerged in *homo faber,* man doing. *Homo ludens,* even, man as artist, man playing. The knowledge of God, which begins in the saving knowledge of Grace through faith, makes for rest and enjoyment. That is the finest fruit of the contemplative life.

Contemplation itself, of course, is not indolence; it is not idle. The saints work hard. Mary's effort at the feet was no easier than Martha's in the kitchen. Gethsemane is unique for its ardor. Jacob wrestled in prayer. Contemplation represents not an escape from drudgery into entertainment, but the positive education of leisure. Some people are too lazy to engage in it, too bored to be still. It embarrasses them, the confrontation in solitude of self, and God, and destiny. Robert Louis Stevenson, perhaps with tongue in cheek, once wrote this of such persons: "There is a sort of dead-alive ... people about, who are scarcely conscious of living except in the exercise of some conventional occupation. . . . They have dwarfed and narrowed their soul by a life of all work, until here they are at forty, with a listless attention, a mind vacant of all material for amusement, and not one thought to rub against another while waiting for the train."

In its deeper levels this of Stevenson is a kind of boredom too, a boredom springing from neglect of the contemplative life. For boredom also is an earmark of life in our day. The poets have seen it and are good reporters. "Ennui, ennui, ennui," says Christopher Fry, in a recent drama, and he toasts the vanity of a purposeless life with a yawn. It had been Oscar Wilde's final dread. "The only horrible thing," he had said, "the only horrible thing in the world is ennui." It is horrible, of course. When we cannot find God, we cannot find his world and his wonders. Or finding these, we can only use and exploit them; we cannot appreciate and enjoy them.

I thought of that when we crossed the Pacific, some of us, on military duty during World War II. There were five hundred of us crowded into the bowels of a hold in the ship. It was hot there. We travelled on or near the equator the better part of a month. Some of the men played cards all day every day. Finally we caught the first glimpse of our tropical island. It lay there sublime in its splendid beauty. Those men landed . . . and began playing cards. I remembered some lines I had once read. This was one of them: "He is an uneducated man who is fettered to a process." This was another, Thompson's again: "'Tis ye, 'tis your estranged faces, That miss the many-splendour'd thing." And these from Wordsworth also came to mind:

> The world is too much with us; late and soon,
> Getting and spending, we lay waste our powers.
> Little we see in nature that is ours;
> We have given our hearts away, a sordid boon!

If the neglect of the contemplative life can lead to such an abuse of nature, it can lead also to an abuse of work. Few will deny that work in our age needs the sanctifying influence of contemplation. The harshness of secular exploitation must be taken out of it, the tenderness of religious purpose restored to it. Men have made their work their end. Their work is therefore their fate, and they are victimized by it. No wonder: work that is not free, that is not oriented to final purpose, that provides no knowledge of God — such work violates the spiritual nature of man who was born for this end that he should know and enjoy Him.

Ruskin in romantic longing for the old religious poise said as much in the last century. We take a lovely landscape, he said in effect, breath-taking in its beauty, and exploit it. We put the belching chimneys and ugly factories with their accompanying slums and smoke into it. Then, when we see what we have done, we clear an acre or two, and decorate it as a public park. We take the freedom of individual expression out of the work on the conveyor belt and at the buffer wheel, and then, when we see what we have done to the artist in us, we hire a group of people to make art for us, and pile it up in museums. We take the positive leisure, the contemplative quality, the education out of our work, and then we tire ourselves on holidays and holydays laboring hard at our recreation. We try for a civilized house, with all the trimmings of a machine civilization — the garage, or garages, have of course supplanted the library — and then, when we have the house, radiant heat and all, we plan for a summer cottage where we can rough it for a while. There is some divorce of work and worship in all this too, and not enough consideration, not enough purpose.

Contemplation can sanctify work, provide its reason, give it purpose, harvest its fruits. I have seen it in a farmer. He was a good farmer, he enjoyed farming, but he was not a soil-grubbing, money-mongering farmer. For him the purpose of work was not to make money. It was not even to provide food, shelter, and clothing. Those were but the means. What he got from his work was the knowledge of God. After supper, evenings, he liked to saunter around his fields (that word *saunter*, incidentally, once meant going on a religious pilgrimage to St. Terre). He did this not to satisfy his "acquisitive instinct," as if to say, "This is mine; I own this." Those evening jaunts of his were a kind of Sabbath journey in which he placed his effort on the altar, and gleaned its spiritual benefit. How different, such leisure, from the entertainment we moderns have provided as an escape from the drudgery of work.

The neglect of contemplation results also in the long run in an abuse of art. On this count, as I see it from my present vantage point, Puritanism has a burden on its conscience. It has sometimes ignored art, sometimes opposed it, and sometimes bent it to practical uses. Art is in this respect like religion: it does not want to be vindicated by its usefulness. It wants to be itself. The songs, the psalms of David, are fruit of the contemplative life. They express the enjoyment of the knowledge of God as He is revealed in the Word and the world. Such indispensable leisure is the condition always for the production and the enjoyment of art.

If we have not yet a literature, and an audience for the enjoyment of literature, comparable to that of the Catholics, or comparable to that of our kind in The Netherlands, this is to be ascribed in large part, perhaps, to the comparatively greater neglect of contemplation among us. We do not *enjoy* knowledge so much, and we *use* it more. And thought — in so far Carlyle was right — thought without Reverence is barren.

The point in this connection is not, of course, that we should engage in the contemplative life for the sake of the arts. The point is rather that the presence or absence of the production and appreciation of them is an index to the quality of our enjoyment of God. For art is precisely the kind of thing which, disengaged from the processes of work, stands by disinterestedly harvesting its spiritual fruit. And the enjoyment of art, like the enjoyment of other kinds of knowledge, is at bottom not a practical but a contemplative affair. We shall sometime have to become concerned, as they in The Netherlands are already concerned, about what is there called the *manco* (it has almost become a technical term in Reformed circles there) or *lack* of a convincing Protestant-Christian literature.

We shall have to cultivate the contemplative in life, finally, if we are to maintain our respect for education. We have sometimes dealt too cavalierly with knowledge. We have talked too much about knowledge *for,* and too little about knowledge *of.* If we see to it that our knowledge be knowledge of God, we need not be so greatly concerned about what it is for. Knowledge for effective citizenship, knowledge for power, knowledge for efficiency, knowledge for social usefulness, knowledge for economic competency, knowledge, even, for service — these have crept into our defenses of education also, and they are not warranted.

Sometimes at college we get students who are always chafing at their seats because they cannot see what all the Bible, philosophy, history, literature, language, and science are for. They want — sometimes, one guesses, by parental prompting — a fast course in business correspondence, double-entry ledger keeping, shop techniques, secretarial etiquette, and the like. Such an attitude, it should suffice to say now, is hard to relate to the first question and answer of John Calvin's Catechism. They have not fathomed the question, What is the end of man?, nor its answer, To know and enjoy.... They do not understand the Psalmist's injunction: Be still, and know....

Our life is not a treadmill, but a journey, and we should be sometimes arriving. Essence of the contemplative life is delight in the knowledge of God. Because it begins, as I said, in the saving knowledge of faith, I am minded to reproduce here a poem which comes up out of a contemplative age, the eleventh century. It is the 410th number of the *Psalter Hymnal:*

O Jesus, joy of loving hearts,
Thou fount of life, Thou light of men,
From fullest bliss that earth imparts,
We turn unfilled to Thee again.

Thy truth unchanged has ever stood;
Thou savest those that on Thee call;
To them that seek Thee Thou art good,
To them that find Thee, all in all.

We taste Thee, O Thou living bread,
And long to feast upon Thee still;
We drink of Thee, the fountainhead,
And thirst our souls from Thee to fill.

Our restless spirits yearn for Thee,
Where'er our changeful lot is cast,
Glad that Thy gracious smile we see,
Blest, that our faith can hold Thee fast.

The Reformed Journal, August, 1952.

3

Liberalism and Dogma

Dogma is a word that is falling into disuse among us. It is kept alive in our language mainly by the liberals. To them it stands for the worst of bad things. Liberalism thrives on its opposition to dogma. Take dogma out of the world and the liberal collapses for want of anything to be or to do. His whole case is the case against dogma. Hence he sees to it that we hear a lot about the Nazi dogma, the Communist dogma, the Catholic dogma, and the fundamental Christian dogma. He sees to it also that we hear little about the liberal dogma for that, he maintains, is a contradiction in terms. So he keeps using the word, loading it with bad meaning.

I have an instance of it before me as I write, and it nettles me into reaction. It comes from the inside flap of a book-jacket:

> In an age of dogma, controversy, and persecution, Browne had voiced one of the first pleas for religious tolerance.

That is a typical piece of liberal *dogma.* Consider it. "In an age": that age is the past, of course, an age now well behind us, thanks to liberalism and Browne's share in it. "An age of dogma, controversy, and persecution": where you have the one, you have the others — if dogma, then persecution, and then also a passionate bickering about things that cannot be proved. "Browne . . . voiced one of the first great pleas for religious tolerance": as always, so here, religious tolerance is assumed to be a liberal accomplishment. As a matter of fact, religious tolerance comes precisely from dogma, conviction, and principle. Its basis is the conviction that religious allegiance is the most precious of man's properly spiritual freedoms. Behind the tolerance lies a faith and a principle, not a critical temper or a skeptical philosophy.

Christians, no doubt, nominal and real, have contributed their unfortunate part to the disrepute of dogma. Because religion is radical, conviction is liable to danger. When it is wedded to bigotry, it gives ground to the liberal protest. Even so, the bigotry is not to be identified with dogma. There have indeed been historical periods of inquisition, persecution, and intimidation, all three conducted sometimes in the name of dogma. But the solution cannot be reactionary liberalism. The solution cannot be: no dogma. The issue is not dogma or no dogma. The issue is: What dogma? Being human, we cannot abandon principle, live without it. We must choose for God and the governing principle, the determinative dogma. That is the way to religious tolerance. That is the way to religious freedom, and every freedom properly moral.

The noun *dogma,* then, owing mainly to the liberal protest, is in disrepute. So is the adjective *dogmatic.* We have yielded it to the enemy, have followed in the wake of the popular usage. The word is now a term of opprobrium. It stands for a mentality that is as blind as a mole in its wrong-headed bias. We bring it out, steeped in vitriol, when we tire of arguing. We say, "He is dogmatic," and so condemn without trial. We fetch the word down from the liberal's line, where it stands alongside of those others: communist, fascist, authoritarian, dogmatic. This is a regrettable decay of meaning, and something like a fall from grace.

The point is that dogma is inevitable. It is belief, religion, dogma, principle that is the fundamental thing in human life. And this thing is spiritual; it is not organic, not natural. The biologist cannot say, Out of this tissue it grew. The neurologist cannot lay it bare. It is altogether spiritual, and is common to everyone. It is a meaning of that line in Genesis: *And God made man. . . .* Dogma is basic to both the human dignity, and the human heroism. It makes man moral. In the Christian, by the grace of God in Christ, it becomes the Christian dogma, the precious *Beginsel* of our elders.

Does it solve all the difficulties thus to affirm the dogmatic basis of life? No, it does not. The theologians, the philosophers, have wrestled long, will wrestle longer with the problems such an affirmation raises. And they will work fruitfully, if they proceed from principle, and acknowledge that they do. To reaffirm the dogmatic basis of life is not to solve all the difficulties of faith and life. It is, however, to confront the right ones.

"Dogma" and "dogmatic" in disrepute, *dogmatics* threatens to follow. For some of us, even, it stands for little more than a big book full of catalogued doctrines. Well, the life of dogmatics is dogma, and the life of principles is principle. Cut off from its root in dogma, dogmatics can become as unprophetic, unheroic as the liberal's "ideologies." Against that word too we should be on guard. It tends to take the faith out of philosophy; there is something wrong with the dogma underlying its rise to currency. When a man's dogma becomes ideology, his religion becomes something he can stand outside of, and be spectator to. In the end he finds himself judging it by something he calls "free scientific enquiry." We do better to acknowledge the moral rooting, the foundation in belief, the dogma. It is the religion in the thought behind the action. Our lives issue, as our elders said, *uit beginsel*, out of dogma.

Now take another look at liberalism. It filters in subtly, and when it comes, it wastes the Christian heroism. Dogma is to the liberal what is wrong with people, what is wrong with the world. His quarrel is not with a particular kind of dogma; his quarrel is with any kind of it. The fear of it is for him the beginning of wisdom. Belief, if it is to have place at all, is to come only after the inquiry, not before. He maintains that his thought is not religiously founded, faith informed, moral. By the "free" of his free scientific inquiry he means unenslaved by dogma. So he substitutes a technique for a faith and a philosophy. This is a far cry from the evidence of things not seen. It is the plain acceptance of experiments proved.

In the long run, however, the liberal's effort at evading dogma is as futile as it is ill-disguised. He too is a man committed to religious decision, and he makes this decision. A dogma underneath the reason, a faith that informs it, is active in Pagan, liberal, Catholic, and fundamental Protestant alike. There is no such thing as irreligion. There is false religion, and retired religion. But irreligion? No! The liberal has his basic allegiance. It is as absolute as the Communist's, as active as the Catholic's. His refusal to say by what dogma he professes what he professes is a ruse. His crusade against dogma emerges from dogma. His neutrality is a pose. Watch him in crisis. He bristles like other authoritarians at what is opposed to his vindicating creed. In the end he will name his god, and but for the restraining grace — quite different from the liberal tolerance — oppose heroism to heroism.

The liberal gives out his manifestoes, voices his witness, and so do we. In a time when some of the principles for which we stand appear to be the same as those for which the liberal stands, we shall have to inquire into the underlying dogma. It is only in that area that we can determine of what principle the principles are expressive. This is the hard work of trying the spirits to see whether they be of God. This is the hard dogmatic work of living out of principle, *uit beginsel leven.*

The Reformed Journal, March, 1951.

4

Hospitality

...There was no room...in the inn.
—St. Luke.

> Come, Thou long expected Jesus,
>   Born to set Thy people free;
> From our fears and sins release us;
>   Let us find our rest in Thee.
> Israel's strength and consolation,
>   Hope of all the earth Thou art;
> Dear desire of every nation,
>   Joy of every longing heart.

—Charles Wesley.

Among the older American Christmas classics, none is more charming than Irving's *Sketch Book*. I was reading those five Christmas chapters in that book again a while ago, and I found myself longing for the ingratiating warmth and liberality in the manor houses of yesteryear. The thing that comes to grand expression in Irving's sketches is the old time Christmas virtue of *hospitality*. Said the old Squire of Bracebridge Hall: "I love to see this day well kept by rich and poor; it is a great thing to have one day in the year, at least, when you are sure of being welcome wherever you go, and of having, as it were, the world all thrown open to you."

It is quite right that this virtue or grace of hospitality should be so firmly associated for us with Christmas. The association is a natural one. Two of the things, certainly, that make for hospitality are the *guest* and the *gift*. Both of these were uniquely present at Christmas. St. Benedict set it down as a rule of his order: "Every guest who comes to the monastery shall be received as if he were Christ Himself." Such, surely, is the basis of the generosity and love we show *our* guests at Christmas, and such, rightly taken, is the foundation of all Christmas hospitality whatever.

Time was when the very word *guest* quickened the pulses and set up a high expectancy. One sees eager children, wistful at the window pane, awaiting the cutter's arrival. It may be that we have lost something of the keen edge of this expectation in the humdrum of our secularized lives. But time was when distances were long, travel was hard, and visits were a privilege. It was then that the host appreciated the guest, and the guest the host. And if we have lost the fine edge of expectation in our regimented holiday procedures, this may also be because not everything is in order with our charity. One of our American poets, Mr. Auden, at least, writes of clearing up the debris after a trying holiday:

> ... Now we must dismantle the tree
> Putting the decorations back into their cardboard boxes —
> Some have got broken — and carrying them back to the attic.
> ... There are enough
> Left-overs to do, warmed-up, for the rest of the week —
> Not that we have much appetite, having drunk such a lot,
> Stayed up so late, attempted — quite unsuccessfully —
> To love all our relatives, and in general
> Grossly overestimated our powers.

We ought all, of course, in this Christmas season to be those children at the window impatiently asking again and again, "Is He coming?" And if ever there ought to have been an excitement of expectation it was when, in the fulness of time, prophecy yearned for fulfillment in the coming of the Divine guest. This was He who was announced in Eden as the One that should bruise the serpent's head. The procession of the prophets marched towards Bethelem from Balaam to Malachi with a mounting crescendo of urgency. The whole past was converging upon this present. This was the Branch, the Root, the Stem. Micah had been very specific: "Thou Bethlehem Ephrata, though thou be little among the thousands of Judah, yet out of thee shall he come forth that is to be ruler of Israel." But there is no need here for calling upon the prophets for further witness: the words of Handel's *Messiah* are ringing in our ears. The point is clear: Our Lord ought to have been an *expected* guest.

But what now of the hospitality, the welcome, the entertainment He received? Think again of Washington Irving's words: Christmas the one day on which we can be sure of being welcome anywhere, and of having, as it were, the world all thrown open to us. The world, all the world, was most certainly our Lord's due. "All things are delivered to me," He said. "God," wrote the author of the Book of Hebrews, "hath in these last days spoken unto us by his Son whom he hath appointed heir of all things." Long ago, in the Book of Genesis, the father Jacob had sent his son Joseph to his own, and they had said, "This is the heir: Let us kill him." Our Lord explained it in a parable: "Surely they will reverence the Son." But they did not accord Him this welcome. They put Him to death.

Joseph and Mary came to the inn, and they were waved away. Such was the Christmas Eve hospitality accorded the Heir of all things, Him to whom the world should have been all thrown open. Later He would give some hint of His natural right to the things that were refused Him, as when He sent His disciples for the colt on which to ride triumphantly into Jerusalem. If they were prevented from loosing the animal, those disciples were simply to say: "The Lord hath need of him." But this hour was not now come. There was no room at the inn.

We need not, at this late date, be berating the desk clerk in that old Palestinian hotel for his lack of respect. The natural man, of whom there is much in us all, does not easily recognize spiritual things. The poor man did not guess that eternity might have impinged upon time in the guestbook of his establishment. He did not know, as a poet would put it later, that twenty centuries of stony sleep were about to be vexed to nightmare by a rocking cradle. He may have come with our best world's wisdom, and mumbled something about first come, first served.

First come, first served indeed. This was the Alpha, and He should have been served first. But there was no room. So it was that our earth received its honored guest. Afterwards, on occasion, it is true, He found hospitality in that friendly cottage in Bethany. But that was an oasis in the desert of general neglect. "Foxes," He said, "have holes, and the birds of the air have nests, but the Son of man hath not where to lay his head." The expected guest was a *rejected* guest. He came to His own and His own received Him not.

Obviously, our own Christmas hospitality will be merely sentimental unless we begin by opening the homes of our hearts to this royal guest ourselves. Someone wrote a verse about that:

> They said the Master is coming
> To honor the town today;
> And none can tell at whose house or home
> The master will choose to stay.
> And I thought while my heart beat wildly,
> What if he should come to mine,
> How would I strive to entertain,
> And honour the guest Divine?

Joyce Kilmer put it this way:

> Unlock your door this evening,
> And let your gate swing wide;
> Let him who asks for shelter,
> Come speedily inside.
> What if your yard be narrow,
> What if your house be small:
> There is a guest is coming
> Will glorify it all.

Consider, finally, the words of our Lord: "Behold, I stand at the door and knock. If any man hear my voice, and open the door, I will come in with him and sup with him, and he with me." That is the penultimate word on hospitality. May we pray for the grace to receive Him into the homes of our hearts. May we praise Him for the great grace of condescending to us, entering into us, and lodging with us. May we unbar the gates of our pride, and kindle within the hearths of our souls a love that can respond to His own. May He himself prepare within us a table of offerings acceptable to Him. And may He dine with us now and evermore.

The Reformed Journal, December, 1955.

5

No Concern of Ours

The situation being what it is, I was feeling worried lately, really down in the mouth. I wanted some advice. So I looked up a scientist, because I have heard that scientists know the answers. "The situation," I said to him, "is bad and what's more I believe it is getting worse. What do you mean to do about it?"

"I just work here," he said. "Ask him."

He took his hand off the test tube he was holding and pointed at his employer, a business man. "Things are bad lately," I said to him, "and I was wondering what you were thinking . . ."

"I simply tend to my business," he interrupted. "But for something like that now you ought to go over to the University. They get paid there for thinking about things."

The first man I found at the University was a professor of history. I figured he ought to know, and I said to him, "I don't like the trend lately, and I want you to tell me what ought to be done about . . ."

"About Russia," he said. "I know, everybody's wondering. Ask me next year, second semester; just now I'm doing the Graeco-Roman period."

Then I met that writer whose picture I had seen in the paper. I went up to him and said. "You're an artist, I hear. What are the artists saying about the state of the world lately?"

"Artists," he growled, "have nothing to do with the state of the world. Their responsibility is to their art." And as I left he barked after me, "Why don't you ask a preacher?"

That was an idea. They used to send us to the Chaplain in the Army too. I looked for a preacher and found one. He had his arm full of hymn books. "The world," I began, "is cracking at the seams, the bottom is dropping out, the . . ."

"I know it," he said, "but speak to me about it later. We're having a rally at the park tonight, and I haven't arranged for the song service yet."

It was plain I wasn't getting anywhere. I went back to the scientist in a huff, and came upon him talking to the business man, very friendly. "Who is responsible for things anyhow?" I demanded.

"I told you," he said, "that I just work here. The government maybe."

"But that's commu-fascism, isn't it?" I was shouting now.

"Could be," said the business man, "but it's no concern of ours. We just tend to our business."

The Calvin Forum, October, 1948.

Part Four
LETTERS

1

Letters from New Guinea

How vividly and intensely you are present to my mind during these days at sea . . . I have a kind of heightened sensation, a ferment of thought and feeling. Two things bring it on: the magnitude of this big affair, and the vagueness and indefiniteness of it. I want to be spared for time and opportunity to make it all articulate. This is not the time or place to write well of it. The days are long. I wish some old friend were with me. It would ease the weight of the significance. Your realistic imagination can guess what this life is. Like we anticipated. But living it is nevertheless a crisis. It brings me face to face with the elemental realities. I am confident in my spirit of God's leading, that He has command of me. I would like to know the purpose clearly (not that I doubt) but because the vagueness hurts my poise. They are His appointed trials, though, and I will take them on His own terms . . .

May 9

I do not have that sense of a scattered personality usual to travel. The old steady interests and values continue. The bigness impresses me. The bigness of the physical and moral worlds. That and the puerility of the Army, the pettiness of the average man. "He that sitteth in the heavens shall laugh." The important things about this trip are satisfactory. There is great discomfort. God bless you.

May 22

I am in New Guinea. There has been no opportunity to write before this. We have had a long hard time and will have more.

By the grace of God our ship came safely to port, and by His grace I still have plenty of heart for the job. This is no place for a frail body or a dainty stomach. Nor for the soft-hearted. Our circumstances are at the moment elementally makeshift. Living is very uncomfortable; quite possible, though. Nothing is clear in the confusion of these first days. I shall fight for health and life all day, almost full time work. I was going to write frankly. This is certainly the hour of sacrifice. Tell my colleagues, living in comfort, and my weak contemporaries that this is so. That they can never pay for it. Good will be born from this, if I am individually spared . . .

May 23

I am sorry that I could not write daily on the vessel, for my life then stimulated an excitement of mind which made me want to write. However, writing even for myself was physically awkward. Excitement of mind I have had — enough to leave me almost tired . . . The days have been significant, full of fecundating stimuli, pleasant and often unpleasant. O for a desk and privacy rather than my knee by candlelight! I could make some speaking thing out of this new matter. I am glad my mind has been active. It is because of mental inactivity, the deliberately cultivated emptiness of mind which the army breeds, that military men fall on cards and dice and use the language of affected Dead End kids . . . I am gradually making myself more comfortable and look for substantial improvement. My natural milieu is not unlike *Green Mansions,* but there is a realistic as well as a romantic side to tropical life and jungle areas. The coconut tree is picturesque, the cassowary has a crude call, the lizard is a slithery thing . . .

May 24

I have finally found a place where I can write you a longer letter . . . This day, that is, the weather, was uncommonly pleasant compared with all previous ones. There was sunshine instead of rain. A man next to me is reading to-day's Detroit *Times* avidly. It is dated March 17. It got here quick at that, he says . . . It is pleasant to see that a group of men can be admirably resourceful in making a spot livable against bad odds. The more clever and industrious soon appear. My own tent-mates are of the middle kind. I wish they were eight go-getters. Living at such close intimacy is a delicate matter and needs tact . . . The common man thinks he is realistic and he is always skirting around the truth of his extremely evasive moral self. How kiddish many of these men are, even the older ones. With tattooed chests, their manliness is skin deep. They punctuate their silly childish outbursts, their raw elemental expressiveness with a "hell of a this" and a "damn that" to show that they are "he-men." Most of them have an ethical religion, with a very broad notion of ethics. There is no grace in it, no notion of ingenerate quiet, no sense of a right or wrong juridical relationship with God, no need for worship: hence all very sentimental . . .

May 25

Except for setting and a general primitiveness my life these days is not unlike that at my last two stations. It is as I had anticipated and is only a prelude to the real purpose which is I know not how far in the offing . . . I shall have to educate you and Tukie to a life in the rough, to wood and water and makeshift comforts. Burroughs and Grayson and Thoreau will have nothing on me. I really weather these slings and arrows of an outrageous nature unusually well. For this I am grateful to rugged origins. Existence is almost full time work here. I want most now slightly better conditions. Keep for me a clean towel, sheet, shorts, and socks, a clean basin, and I will love you hard and deep forever. Do not be anxious . . .

May 26

. . . Do not jeopardize my life with fears, anxieties, and bootless cries, desiring this man's scope and that man's place. Character only dignifies us, and the rest is only instrumental to it. Failure in ourselves commits us to another war, as past failure commits us to this. Wars are chastisements and must beget remorse and amendment. That is the good they can do. Let's not lose that good . . .

May 27

I have rigged up a kind of table here in my tent and it makes writing easier. I begin this before supper, having just completed a disagreeable fatigue detail. I have shaved and washed. We are having white grapes tonight. I nibble at coconut during the day. I had a chance to dry some things this afternoon . . . I long to graduate from the vagueness of the replacement status. I want to do a job. I cannot at my age and with my equipment merely exist. I will feel demoralization setting in if this goes on . . .

May 28

By some ironic contrast, I was thinking just now after supper, of our Harvard experience . . . This writing by candlelight at an improvised desk near my own cot is pleasant. The group has gone to see a picture: I appreciate this solitude. I continue to wish that I could be alone more. I do not believe that under these circumstances introspection, and even introversion, is unwholesome . . . Sometime I shall explore: for coral figures, the chambered nautilus and other shells. And I mean to see what we foreigners call natives. There too the squalor and privation will probably outweigh the tourist-folder charm. But they probably will be more fully human than the soldiers. Have I ever told you how a routine job is done in the Army? Something needs doing: an area cleaned of rubbish, a latrine dug, a supply tent put up. Such work is called a "fatigue detail." Some twenty men are haphazardly designated at this detail, put "in charge" of a non-com. You take off for the job. By the time you get there, four or five of them have "goofed off." Others glide away in process. A few are urbanites, used to pavements and ledgers. They try, complain about the tools, the place, the weather, and move no dirt. Two or three, rough bred, unobtrusive, have the steady swing, the long stroke. They do the work. These three might better have been selected in the first place. The other seventeen might better have been left at home. An old Army man is useless. The oldest I know — he knows all the modes of evasion — arrived late today. Tugged a moment at a rope. Goofed off. Came back, and grabbed a tarpaulin. The rotten thing tore. He got disgusted and left in a huff. I hear his dice now striking a crap board. He is the typical Army product. Only those men are any good in the military who were lately civilians, and they are good only in so far as they have resisted the military way — if something of the old go-getter is still there, the old love of thorough work, the old enthusiasm and resourcefulness. They do the work. I know now that I shall, if I can, oppose all propaganda for a large standing Army. A good Army is a citizen Army; a bad one is a military one. But there will, of course, be much maneuvering after the war, for there are a lot of merely physical bodies, dull heads, who want the front, the dress uniform, the balls, and the power of force which peace time army men have. Such boys must all be taken care of, and will be. And all their puppets, the G.I. Joes, who "bitch" now, will then "gold brick" in their factories, argue wages and hours, figure everybody owes them a living because of what they "went through," live mechanically as they were taught in the Army, and play at cards and dice. How puerile, how downright childish men are. Always at cross purposes with their loose and meaningless selves, they still flare up when at some unguessable sensitive point, they decide to be tough. They are very naive, very amusing, and very petty. There must be exceptions, but they are not the evident ones, they are not typical . . .

May 29

It may be that I shall learn to go to bed earlier from my Army life. Our candles are limited, there are mosquitoes, and under cover on my cot is a good place to be after dark. I'm so used to leggings that I shall want them to trudge to school with after the war. They are an excellent all around protection against rain, mud, and creeping things with legs . . . I was to have done some postal work today but it seems to have fallen through. Well, I can always boil fatigues by the stream's edge . . .

May 30

There has been some routine work around here lately. Evenings have been mine, but I have not yet been able to get to books or magazines, and candle rationing has set in. I save the wax, melt it with a piece of rope in a peanut can and use it again. The bags of mail reported waiting have not yet reached us. It is well over a month now that I have heard from you. I get no war news, have heard nothing of actions since I reached this place . . . My shipboard tan is giving way to the ugly atabrine yellow. The men know the new currency values now and play dice without hesitancy again . . .

June 1

If my handwriting is a bit irregular this morning it is because I am back to my knee again. I changed location slightly, having just made the last one habitable. Here, though, I have a better floor, better lavatory, and expect today to get it into line with the last . . . My main peeve here is the mud, the rain, the mud, and the incessant need for washing clothes. It's always bricks without straw. One must find the nails and knock them in with a stone . . . I see enough for volumes of gall, but have the lucky detachment called humor. This means there is still pride in me. There should be. I'm very probably the most highly educated man in New Guinea.

June 2

June 1 was for me a vexatious day because of a local tussle with an authority: he had the Nazi mind that loves "duty by directive" and regimentation, and I thought what hope against such typical obtuseness. Then at 6 p.m. it became a gala day: your many dear letters from 26 April through 16 May, sent to the old address, came. This note is simply an acknowledgement; I shall read and re-read, try soon to give you a long one in return . . . Your letters are all I have, for the old stupidity goes on.

June 3

I am at a Red Cross institution, rough-hewn but comfortable. Your many fine letters inspired me to make a writing desk, my second — the other stayed behind. But I wanted even better than that tonight, and here I have chair, table, and light. You wrote of a change in me, of experiences you are not sharing and are never to fathom. Yes, there will be disturbing changes. But love is not love which alters when it alteration finds . . . At bottom I am not different here. A bay is a bay anywhere, and trees are trees, and roughing it is something I can endure. I am educated, you know, and although I am often wrought up, and anxious, and much shaken, I retain the poise. Yes, in this there is a religious element. Especially on shipboard you know full well that precaution, and many men are not enough, and I was able sometimes then simply to relax in a kind of surrender to God's leading. Providence is not a fiction. Here I want to be careful not to boast of an unreal serenity. I have hard times. And certainly His people must acknowledge Him and give Him way or there is no praise, no worship, no glorification . . . Milton's sonnet on his blindness struck me with force on the sea and since. So passionate and self-denying in his endeavor to have God's will done "on earth" as well as in heaven, he is so sure in that sonnet that over against the grandeur of the Divine sovereign his own rule should be one of relaxation. His understandable arrogance here wholly gives way to the Christian humility. It is a beautiful thing. I sometimes have an overweening, illegitimate anxiety to be greatly useful. Now that I simply cannot in these days, weeks, months perhaps, I should not fret too much. For this uselessness in view of the sacrifice of the situation chafes me most and wears me down at times. My attempts to escape it are almost pathetic. I must wait with calm and indifference, with something of the fat apathy of the typical soldier . . .

June 4

There has been some activity about my function; it is favorable, definitely, and appropriate. Its importance I do not yet know and its nature I cannot state . . . Among the officers I have met there are some gentlemen who know the inequality of sacrifice among the military men, and are not so bar-conscious or directive-ridden as to ignore the qualifications of the enlisted man. There are some who go the extra mile, trudge about in the rain with you, because they are interested. And there are others who already have the regimentation, the artificiality of a tradition-laden military convention in their marrow . . .

June 6

Sunday evening, at the Red Cross retreat, I began a letter to you and then became interested in negro spirituals. These colored men proved better than their white audience; I was affected by their modesty and feeling. A disagreeable detail had extended well into Sunday and I did not finish the letter. Yesterday was my most interesting day yet, going about in the matter of my function. I do not know what it is to be: I am satisfied, definitely, by the trend . . . I have met the intelligentsia of this spot: Russ, an editor and teacher of social science; his assistant, John, probably continental refugee, author of books, on social labor problems; another John, Ph.D. Columbia, teacher of social sciences; author of a successful textbook in government. Good fellows, working clerically, without stripes even. Doing a job, though, and making a life of it because they must . . . Tell Tukie there is here at my tent a little black kitten, and near it a dog who fetches coconuts out of the water, one ageless old rooster, a baby kangaroo with forepaws soft as her fingers, and a resplendent ring-necked parrot.

June 7

I am not doing anything today and I have a good place to do it in. I imagine that Americans generally are excited today. I have seen a bulletin announcing the fall of Rome and the invasion of France. There was no detail. It is a big event. I long for swift aggressive prosecution of the war, I together with the other eleven million. And hope earnestly for success in the huge European war. Coming here does make the implications of war vivid. The overwhelming distances are something only travel among them can bring home . . . How the little taken-for-granted things back home seem all-important: a decent cup of coffee, an egg, a bit of butter, sunshine, paved walks, opportunity to buy, a glass of water, a hot shower. Little things, aren't they, and yet, if you do not have them, they are worth fighting wars for . . .

June 8

I am useful today. Strange news, is it not, from me in the Army? I am grateful for respite from shovel and broom, and hence do not mind lingering on. It is uncommonly wet today, and saying that here can make you guess why I mentioned sunshine among the things to return to, worth fighting for . . . Circumstances are dead against anything like creative reading or writing just now. I am terribly jealous of time. All the old scholars, the Chaucers, Sydneys, Miltons, were soldiers somewhere along their career, but how grandly, compared with these innumerable multitudes of men and technical buncombe. I observe there is no dearth of good men. I see many excellent men doing lamentably picayune work. Often there is no other kind of thing that needs doing. There are so many imponderables that the Army must reckon with. It is when you see inferior men in a responsible seat that you grieve to your soul . . .

June 11

I used to write you that Army activities reminded me of a game at which boys play, and in the best Latin sense of the word, I called it puerile. This impression continues here. The shamwork, I mean, and much more I do not care just now to particularize .'. . I see some Aussies, swank and carefree in their English-bred worldly-wisdom. They are hard, weather-stripped, nobody's fools, rakish in their jaunty big hats and pyjama-like pants.

I think the Americans amuse them, for the Americans are not modest . . . Metropolitan men dominate the temper of Army groups, not the country boys. The city is brash, the country timid . . . We are starved for invasion news — distribution of bulletins is very poor.

June 13

There is no constructive challenge in work here at the moment. I hope this will change, but the more I see of the job, the organization, and the men, the more I feel that my hardest task will be to keep peace with myself. This will change if I become serviceably useful, but most men have not that feeling; the situation is greatly against it. Many men simply serve an availability role most of the time: thence the psychological problem . . . A chance to contribute may come; it may not. Even Army "big-shots" often get no chance to score. They can move only in a well-grooved curricle; such is the conduct of Army business . . .

June 15

There are men enough of calibre enough in the place I am working to teach a full-fledged college . . . I have learned a lot about the Army in the past week, regret the necessity for such a blunting, dulling routine as its work comes to, and try to "adjust." What a wealth of fiction and drama this war is going to evoke. New local color, new psychological experiences. And every man of the myriads reacting differently. Although the uniformity the Army prizes saturates mind and soul at last and the men, if they respond ideally, become as like as well-oiled bearings in a wheel . . . Though I go through the motions of assent I shall resist all regimentation of the spirit — this requires constant alertness and prodigious effort. I shall ask you for reading and study materials when I am better settled . . . I wish you would counsel me to patience, for I strain at the reins, and am driven, and cannot go. Like dream phobias and you cannot escape . . . If only all these millions could gird up their loins tonight and all simultaneously assault and press the attack and so have done with it! Invasion news comes through thinly, slowly: it sounds good . . . God bless you, my dear, and give you courage, and patience, and peace   My prayers are always for you.

The Calvin Forum, October, 1944.

2

Letters from the Philippines

I am in the Philippines. You must have prayed for me these late days, for God spared me in danger . . . The coming from New Guinea had been quiet and conditions not uncomfortable. The vexations were the old, now very little ones — disagreeable fatigue details. I lay on deck, sometimes talking, sometimes just lying, impressed again by the magnitude of many things. I have gone about on the sea so much lately I begin to be friendly to the mood of the seafaring Paul of Tarsus, and like the elder Yeats have a new relish for that matchless narrative of the shipwreck. The big things were there as I lay, the sea, and the full vault of a star-studded and moonlit sky, and fore and aft the dark hulks of others in the convoy. Till the orders came to be ready for debarkation. What we saw looked very much like New Guinea and for some time that was all. Then we knew that it was not, and that this was war. Planes, and being fired on, enemy planes therefore, and the big guns of heavy ships booming, and friendly bombs falling on ground pockets. It was a spectacle, too, new to almost all who were there, and they crowded along the rails and on top of the ship's cargo to see the better. When an enemy plane fell into the sea the men applauded by clapping their hands. It was all so new, there were so many vessels, and nothing had come close, not yet. Thus a whole day and a night, and well into another day, we all the while standing by for debarkation. Planes again, sometimes close, and barrages of allied fire. Then it came to us. I was up forward on deck and the gunner there must have seen it in the clouds for he said to his mate, "Point it there." I followed his finger and saw the planes and fell flat, taking cover. The roar of the diving engines was awful. The ves-

[214]

sel shuddered to the thunder of its own gunfire. The bomb hit thirty feet from me. It is best to say it simply as it was: God spared me. I do not yet know the quality of bravery. I have often felt and said that not all the dead are heroes because they die. A man can live on so many levels of significance, and particularly in the Army there is much merely activistic action. I knew a few of the casualties; they had a brazen bluffness about them, living only in the disintegrated and superficial soldier's self. In such a narrow pale it is easy to be bluff and brave. But when much humanity is brought to bear on the deed, be it of dying, when past and future meet in an awful present, it is not easy. We soldiers should be honest, I too. Fear, cold fear, grips the heart; you clutch the steel, the ground, you hug it, naked, helpless. In the dispatches the freighted personal drama of such a shaking event probably reads, "One small vessel damaged by a bomb hit." We who were there do not like to read these dispatches . . . We did what we could. I was busy soon shoveling the charred debris overboard. It chanced that an enormous carton of currency in bills and coin was part of the cargo, and there it lay blackened, burnt, and melted shapeless among the bodies. Money never looked cheaper to me. And was it love of this had caused the tragedy? I longed to be ashore, and came there at last. A man is not the target of the bomber as a vessel is, and although in later days incendiaries, fragmentation, and other bombs found a victim here and there, it was good to be on land. The work had to go on, much loading, lifting, setting up, pulling down, moving, always with a shovel hanging from the hip, always new holes. In that week I did not sleep two hours consecutively at any time, sometimes in four different holes a night, never two nights in the same place, usually unwashed, all clothes dirty. Conditions are rapidly becoming better. I can say I have not yet been miserably sick at heart, not even in the long watches, restless nights, and hard work of that timeless time. I can rest in God's care — not a hair, not a sparrow — do we not know it, He asked? Aye, and we do, we do . . .

November 11

Night has not closed in yet. The evening is a lovely one. I have learned to like the cocoanut groves and the bays. Weather, setting, climate here are just as they were in New Guinea. Strikingly alike in every respect, except one. There are typhoons here. I know because I have gone through them. One night especially

I almost preferred Jap planes to the destructiveness of the wind. The rain comes simultaneously in torrents . . . A person gets used to Pacific warmth. It is not dry or sharp, simply a continuously clinging warmness . . . The Filipinos are a humble, cooperative people. So many are pathetically poor. They need clothes. You see lovely lace patterns torn to tatters on women and children, men in shirts porous with wear. They are clean. Their faces are joyous. They are glad we are here. I have seen some towns again, war-ghosted, of course. And I heard church bells a Sunday or two ago vying with distant artillery fire.

November 12

I woke to the sound of bells again, from which ruined church I do not know. I shall have to do some reconnoitering soon. No chapel has been erected yet and I missed the place of the service this morning although I had wanted to go. There is some interest among the men in "church," especially in these late weeks. But talk and conduct in burrow and foxhole is the same old imitative vulgarity. I have always been sensitive to banalities, saying and repeating the obvious ad nauseam. This goes on continuously. What else is there to say? Ideas were never present, and after two years over here the little stock of merely personal experiences has gone threadbare. Thence the banalities and a kind of overall sullenness of expression. There is this too. Every man wants to be interesting, and this commendable wish leads as among high school girls to featuring news scoops. There are a thousand tempests in a teapot daily. Passionate contentions about the misheard and misread. Moreover there is censorship, which means that what one knows is not to be repeated to anyone. This makes the telling more luscious, and big full-bodied men go around like adolescent girls whispering things into each other's ears. Everywhere people mumble and whisper. Sometimes it almost drives me crazy. There is no talk of books, except by the few, and those tolerated only as eccentric characters. There is no discussion about ideas. The soldiers have only the same ideas on the same subjects. These are the subjects: bitching, that is, critical little pot-shots at military follies of a peripheral kind. When this goes on I sometimes try to get the men to follow out the details to some basic causes. When that gets beyond their depth, you find them turning tail and beginning to defend the Army. Women, not wives, sisters, sweethearts (the men have a kind of dual code) are discussed in terms of mere sex experience. After that, ratings. Why the other fellow gets them, why they don't. And what they are going to do about it. As though it were within a soldier's power to do anything. Next, gossip, the real old haggish kind. Behind the other fellow's back, until he comes in and you go out. Finally home and personal experiences. There is much argument against school and no notion of education except for utility. I see very few who care at all to learn. The young are most interested in learning; the old are certain that "they know." I have given up trying to draw the men into discussions. There is no logic, no capacity to subordinate, coordinate, select the relevant from the irrelevant. What can I do but go about silent as the sphinx? I am glad that I came into the Army with extra-military perspectives. What of those who do not, West Pointers and eighteen-year olds? War brings men to grips with the elemental realities but let no one say the Army does . . .

November 15

For once I wonder how the reports of our campaign read in the newspapers at home. It is always irksome that the battles are won in the newspapers before they are well begun in the field. They who write the beginning of an operation are too ready to point out the implications of its eventual conclusion in their first article . . . I do not write of the vexations of the Army lately only because these have been set into perspective against the larger issues of life and death, but they continue as always. It will require a century of writing to expose all the artificiality and superficiality of what is involved in the word Army. You will not find it in the news reports and in the histories, but you will find it eventually in the literature of the world. For the truth will out, especially when, as now, it is being suppressed. I chafe to speak out. I shall some time, in the interest of democratic institutions. The Air Force is a different thing from the Army, for it is a young organization and the dead weight of conventionalized usages has not poisoned it with dryrot . . . All day it has rained. We woke to it this morning. There is a sense in which we welcome such a day. It is not good flying weather . . .

November 18

There are things I should like to tell you about my work, but cannot. I can say only that I work in military intelligence. I

[217]

feel that my odd case has saturated through to many ranking officers. There is courtesy over against me and some awareness among the responsible of the wrongness of it. I cannot expect the appreciation of this problem that would come from educated men. Army leaders, for the most part, are not that: the school of experience, hard knocks, smartness in the ways of the world are things they understand, and what is more than this they partly fear, and for the most part belittle. They feel embarrassed about my case, however, and there is a will to do something, but in the ossified system no way, at least no easy way. There is some appreciation, though, of the work I do and my mode of getting on with the men. Often lately I can reach beyond the province of my rank and do some work that matters. I know a lot about what has been, what is, and what is to come. Afterwards I shall be able to explain the Pacific campaigns well, for I know how it was ... And if the military seems to be using me accidentally sometimes, I still have God, and self, and you to be right with. It's too hard, too long, we have sacrificed too much to waste this substance in any bitterness or desire to escape the call to duty. In my heavier experiences here a kind of wish, Let others do it, has come up. But not often. I feel best when I do what is before me as well as I can. The rest is God's. I think that is walking confidently by His side. It is the truth of the line, Have no thought of the morrow. And the words, heavenly Father. I think it is a brave business, this Christian living, head on into destiny shaped by Him. Though I do what I can, plan intelligently as possible, am "instinctively thorough about my crevice and burrow." But I do not fear the day and the how, calculating the chances, wondering how will it be. I believe in His purpose and commit myself to its achievement.

November 23

I should not have known that this was Thanksgiving Day if I had not been told. There was no church. We read no proclamation. There was no turkey. The pressure of work is great, but I took time to count my blessings. There are some I cannot include this year, but the main things are all there. The familiar prayer has more poignancy for me because of this past year: "Our daily bread," "Thy will be done," "Deliver us from evil ..."

December 18

Remember the little packet of thread and needles you sent me off with? Well, tonight I took to sewing stripes on. What an ordeal! It was warm and sweaty and the light was poor. I had one neatly sewed on when I saw that it was at an angle, and I cut it off with a razor. Then I pinned both on to keep them in place while sewing and sewed one-half on, and saw that I had it wrong side too. So I chucked the whole thing. It is so symbolic of the whole piddling pettiness. Can you imagine real men pointing to their arm to command respect? "He spoke as one having authority" — that is the real thing. Imagine educators running around in society, their rank on their sleeve: Lo, I am a dean, I a registrar, I am associate professor. Respect me, see my insignia. It is all very superficial, very merely skin-deep. I am proud of my failure in sewing on these stripes. Perhaps I can find a Filipino woman to do it. I must not be ungrateful; I must be worldly-wise. But this is not my element. Is it not a little ironic that I who have been the expressive opponent of the technical am to have the technician's brand on me? There seems to be no military way just now, perhaps never, by which I can be made an officer. The senior officers would like to find or make a way, but cannot. I am able, however, to go beyond the scope of rank in my work. Today again I wrote a kind of feature article for our official but secret publication. At least I am useful.

December 25

There were Christmas greetings in the mail. Soldiers like to be remembered. It says something about those people who care to do it. I spent the afternoon with a former Calvin student. We walked to a small town nearby. The weather was clear, and I saw how fair this island is. The houses are simply made of bamboo tied with abaca, but wonders are done with these materials. As opposed to New Guinea these people are conspiciously clean. Their white is white, the dirt spanked out of it with a paddle. Today they wore their best dress. We saw a cock-fight. The Filipinos like gambling. Even the children play at marbles, using pennies for keeps. We watched a native folk-dance, the boys reticent, the girls coy, supervised by the poised young mother of the entertaining home. This is a Catholic country; the principle of restraint is in the people. The priest dominates, unseen but effective. The people are small, gentle, simple, happy. Their towns are neat. Some had made stars from the scarce paper they had. One read "Victory Christmas." Children had all learned to say Merry Christmas. A teacher invited us in, tried to make our stay pleasant. She told of her teaching, all of which is done in English. We returned to camp for Christmas dinner, and it was a good dinner. Another student made it a point to come in from a neighboring outfit. I have had much occasion to observe many men, and I have found that our group produces the best young people, much the best in big ways and small. There were several alerts tonight. Though none brought planes they kept me from writing you as fully as I wished. Remember these words: "Peace I leave with you, my peace I give unto you. Not as the world giveth, give I unto you. Let not your heart be troubled, neither let it be afraid."

December 31

I visited a neighboring town again yesterday. The shops have attractive names and must have been fascinating once, but now there is nothing at all in them. The women of this island are small, have attractive long hair, walk very erectly, often carrying their bundles on the top of the head, and they spit out of their mouth like a man. You can also smell them. This is not because they are dirty, for they are clean. They love white. This is they themselves. What, you will say, am I doing so close up to them? Well, I have a laundress and I ask her to sit on my bed to figure the bill. I want to be courteous to these tired people and the bed is the only place to sit. The women marry young. The men do not work hard. Many simple ways to improve their circumstances seem never to have occurred to them. Drainage of the town, for instance. The principle of the wheel, for another. And the use of glass. There are no windows, just apertures. In the best houses these are fitted with shutters; but if the shutters were closed the house would be pitch dark. Rich and poor seem to sleep on the bamboo floor, usually on mats. They are a family folk; there are many children. Their honesty has impressed the men. A soldier left 200 pesos in his pants when he gave it out to be laundered by a Filipino woman. He could not go after it, he did not know her or where she lived. Next day laundry and money were returned. My guess is that cloth has come in from the States for the people to make clothes of. For on all the school girls now (the schools are open again) I see gingham, percale, and cheap cotton dresses. In almost all homes there is a sewing machine, rickety sometimes but still going. Civilization here seems to be built around that. The best buildings in the towns are the municipal buildings, the Catholic churches, and the schools. One is impressed by the fact that this is a United States culture laid over a Mongolian race which has been long in the Spanish Catholic tradition of things. It is my impression that the improvements are things brought over from the States through Civil Service and governmental agencies. If you look at the Island as I saw it today from out in the water you see how fair it is. The sky is a deep blue. The heat is not overly oppressive now. Many small garden root crops are grown here. One is called camote. There is also the equivalent of a sweet potato. And the kangkong leaf is eaten. Also the banana, the cocoanut, and cocoanut salad. This salad is an expensive rarity in the States. It is made from the deliciously crisp innermost sprout of the young cocoanut tree, and there is only one such morsel in a tree. It is good, but to my taste not much better than choice celery. I have not seen rice here, but that crop is, of course, the staple in the diet of the Filipino.

This has been a long year, a memorable year. I have seen many novel and some horrible things and gone far over God's earth and feel stronger than ever that there is certainly purpose in the world and that it is God's purpose and that men are the responsible agents. I do not know just what He has in mind for me, just what for you. But there is nothing trivial or unimportant in any of it. It is full of purpose. My prayer on this last day of the year is that God may bless you, and strengthen you, and protect you with the wings of His love.

The Calvin Forum, February, 1945.

3

A Letter from Japan

Two weeks of a soldier-tourist's observations are not enough to justify me in supposing that I know Japan. I am already beginning to feel that the Japanese are complex, and that I shall have to do some studying before I can hope to capture their national character in a description. Nevertheless, I want to set down my first impressions.

I am still a soldier, of course, and really not a tourist at all. What astonishes me most, accordingly, is the completeness of the Japanese co-operation with the Americans, their full acquiescence in the spirit and their flawless compliance with the letter of the Potsdam Declaration and the instrument of surrender.

My guess is that if a poll were taken, it would show that the Yanks in Japan, almost without exception, are pleased with the Japanese and quite captivated by them. You will remember that in our training we were told that they were dirty and yellow and worse, and it was all as simple as that while we fought them from Port Moresby on up beyond the Philippines. Hence we are dazed and taken aback now — so out of touch with reality a soldier becomes — to find these people so interesting. They have values and ways of life which make us stop and consider.

The Japanese are making a deep impression upon us as a remarkable people. I know there are some in the States who were not fighting them in the Pacific and are not now here to assist in the occupation and establishment of control, who fear this swiftly favorable impression that is being made upon us and caution us to beware of the serpent under the flower. The ambassadors in Secretary Hull's office, they will recall, were ingratiating too.

Nonetheless I feel that after some years, when we have an historical sense, we shall all stop to remember how really remarkable all this was, this sudden end of the war in the Pacific, this fast and effective occupation. It is well to remember the simple large facts. Some think these mark the end of the war here as more dramatic than the end of the war in Europe.

The fact is that the Japanese chose to surrender. They had heard from President Truman what the alternatives were, unconditional surrender, yes, but at once with some integrity, or later with complete annihilation. They had been defeated, and decisively, but just as Germany had been defeated decisively with the Allied crossing of the Rhine. Not more so. These facts I have seen publicly announced and may therefore recount. The Japanese had more planes at the end than they had at the beginning of the war. All earmarked as they were for use in *kamikaze* attack, these could have inflicted untold loss upon Allied ships and men. And what was the figure General MacArthur announced lately as the total armed forces to capitulate? Seven million, I believe, seven million men under arms. This strength Japan had. It was not enough for victory: the strategy of Allied progress had been too effective for that. But it could have prolonged the war by many months.

Remember the armies in China and the by-passed thousands in New Britain, New Guinea, the Netherlands Indies, Formosa and the north, and think of the millions committed to the defense of the homeland. True, the defeat was decisive. The by-passed garrisons, the armies never contacted on the field, were useless for Japanese victory; the clean-cut and telling strategy of the combined Allied services was thoroughgoing, the case for Japan hopelessly lost.

Nevertheless this is to the credit of Japan, this proves her more human than Germany (human pity, you remember, was the note the Emperor sounded in his address to the people), that in the face of such defeat she chose to surrender. In this she was reasonable, and reasonable she has remained. She lined up her tanks on the airfields, the easier for us to count them, and labelled and ticketed the planes with the dreadful *kamikaze* sign for our disposal. We came unopposed.

Can you imagine driving into Chicago at high noon without seeing a person on the street, except the police, their arms raised in salute? So we entered Kyoto. They handed us the key to the country on a lacquered plate, and gave it with a smile. I do not know what they were thinking as they did it. But that they did argues for an accomplishment. The reports come in: no deaths, no violence, no riots, no subversive activity, everything according to plan, hardly an incident to keep us alert.

Neither the word, *civilization,* nor its adjective, *civilized,* comprehends all that can be valuable in a people. But the Japanese are civilized. Japan is a civilization; it is full of human achievement as contrasted with natural wealth.

The rigid economy of this human thrift impressed me during the first afternoon of the coming up from Wakayama to Kyoto. The landscape itself hints at it, picturesque in its neatness, as though daily brushed by the hand-brooms so common in the homes. Slovenliness means waste, and there can be no waste in Japan, not so much as a dry leaf or a scrap of paper. Here in this office the charwoman craves the splinters from our rations boxes, and the janitors store the cigarette butts in their pockets with care. This country is densely populated, you know, and only one-fifth of it is arable. Hence the terraced mountain-sides, tier-like steppes from the river plains up to the peaks, each so much precious land snatched from nature. Not by an engineering project, this, but by hand through the centuries. There are waterwheels in the creeks to irrigate the rice, and in the bends of the fast streams there are stakes to prevent erosion of the banks. There are no fences, for fences take room, and no room can be spared from the growing. The villages have a single path; one is enough if you are willing to walk, and the Japanese must walk if they are to eat. Moreover, the towns themselves are set on the least tillable places, back against the bluffs or over the rocky terrain; and the houses are contiguous. You cannot easily overstate this, this rigor and sacrifice, this human inurement to need, this thrift of the people.

We in the States take it out on nature when we feel hemmed in or in want; we learned it from the frontier in a land of plenty; but the Japanese take it out of themselves, and sometimes have only virtue to show for their hunger. All this gives the "spiritual superiority" they proclaimed over Asia in opposition to "western materialism" a meaning we might do well to ponder.

Much in Japan as you see it for the first time seems to come straight out of your fourth reader. Such are the parasols, the kimonos, the kites, the scarecrows, the constant clop-clop of the cleated wooden sandals, the babies bobbing up and down in the hammocks slung from their mothers' backs, the shrines and temples set in hand-groomed gardens. There is, however. a certain greyness, monotony and uniformity in the scene, in the

[224]

invariably tiled roofs, the uniformed students, the dun-colored slacks of the women on the streets.

This uniformity is evident everywhere. The people have been chastened into order and neatness by their natural situation, but I guess that much of the discipline has been imposed also by the saber-rattling police. The police bulk large in the public life; perhaps they have to, as they do also in crowded Europe, there being so many people in so little room. Be the cause what it will, you see the effect. On the safety lanes for the street cars there is no jostling or elbowing, no rushing past one another, no yelling or noise. The people form in lines in the order of their coming, and patiently wait them out. So in the department stores, those leaving remain on the left, even though no one is coming up and the whole stairs is free for the taking. It may be that the word for this is regimentation. Soldiers used to say that a "Jap" was good if he could carry out his own plan, but nonplussed if he had to adjust himself to a new element in the situation. I do not know how true this is.

I think this is true: the Japanese way of life is aesthetic and religious (that is, not secular as ours is). Here for the first time I feel more of the force of what Adams meant when he called ours a business civilization. The Japanese do not live for the making and the talking of money. They live for the living. And because they lack opportunity for new sensations they distill a lot of value from old ones. Daily actions become rites, and the habitual instead of becoming worn by time becomes ever more aesthetic. The tea ceremony is illustrative. The host carefully selects his materials, delicately whips the tea into a froth, and hands the bowl ceremoniously to the guests. The bowl is beautiful and requires daily admiring. When it is handed you, you hold it carefully, as a precious chalice. You take one sip, savor it, take two sips, three and a half. Then you examine the bowl, studying it, taking note of the artist who made it. You praise the host and bowl.

This is aesthetic living woven into the stuff of life and not affected as the last resort of the cynic. You see more of it. You see the art in the home, thrifty but fine. You have read of this, seen it in the prints. They do not waste values in Japan.

You go up street and down alley and wonder sometimes what the people eat, what they wear, and whether it is all for beauty and nothing for use. Precious porcelains, the baked colors of the lovely Satsuma ware, the silk kimonos with their gay-colored obis, the lacquer, the cloisonné, the opal and sapphire, amethyst and jade, the Mikimoto cultured pearls, the tea chests and the cherry wood, the pretty fans, the colored prints in oil and water, all these you see, and even so you have not attended a festival, you have not gone to the shrine, nor visited the gardens, nor been at the Palace.

A captain told me last night that the Japanese habit of bowing was beginning to annoy him. The captain has been annoyed before and will be again. Bowing is as gentle a gesture as any and can be sincere. I wish you might have seen how gracious it was last evening when all the members of a family we called on bade us goodnight. So many people bowing not as a machine but as a symphony under the host's unspoken direction is pleasant to receive and to remember. There had been singing at the home ("Joy to the world, the Lord is come," they in Japanese and we in English) and the host said, "Christianity is peace," and the hostess said "Pray for us." This too in Japan, where the people were dirty, yellow...

I do not know what they are going to eat this winter. Surely what they raise in those buckets of earth and troughs of soil they set on the pavement beside the doors, and the vegetables planted in the firebreaks and in the lots laid waste by the bombs will not be enough. I believe Japan is the first country we are telling to get along on her own (it must be best so, but had France demonstrated so much of human durance so long?). The Japanese suggest they will get along. They will not whimper and they will not beg. Some will die.

These impressions are far from exhaustive. I have not mentioned the geisha girls. I have not told you of the stratified society, of those hopelessly caught in the lower strata who must sell their bodies or carry others in rickshaws at seventy. Beside the limousines of princes and tycoons, you see wretches draying the stuff of the wealthy on heavy carts.

There is no time now to write of the shrines, or the sweet smiles of the singularly obese gods of the East. The shrines are ugly, squat; there is no freedom in them. You see it at a glance. The god is false.

And ours is true. If only we could write that into the instrument of surrender, and have this flawless acquiescence, this perfect compliance, what a victory it would be. The Japanese, the books say, are not adaptable; they are imitative. They cut crazy capers in adjusting themselves to atomic energy, but they appreciate ethical achievement.

The song in that home and in their tongue was: "Joy to the World." Some have turned away from the pot-bellied gods of Buddha. The order has gone out that the Japanese may not look to the east, they must look to us now. I am uneasy, for the Japanese understand ethical achievement. Will they see His star in our West?

The Calvin Forum, December, 1945.

LIST OF HENRY ZYLSTRA'S
PUBLISHED WRITINGS

ADDRESSES

"The Role of Literature in our Time." Address, Teachers Convention, October, 1946.

"Modern Philosophy of Education." Address, Principals Convention, September, 1950.

"Christian Education." Address, Teachers Convention, September, 1951.

"Why Read Novels?" Calvin College Alumni Lecture, April, 1956.

ARTICLES

"A Mid-Nineteenth Century Dutch View of American Life and Letters," *Publications of the Modern Language Association of America*. LVII, No. 4 (December, 1942).

"What Kind of Education?" *The Calvin Forum*, February, 1947.

"Naturalism in Public Education," *The Calvin Forum*, May, 1947.

"The Calvin Library," *The Banner*, August, 1947.

"Calvin College, the Capstone of a System," *The Christian Home and School Magazine*, October, 1947.

"Dutch Comment on the Van Raalte Settlement," *The Calvin Forum*, November, 1947.

"No Concern of Ours," *The Calvin Forum*, October, 1948.

"What is Fiction For?" *The Banner*, December 17, 1948.

"Now and Then," *The Calvin Forum*, January, 1949.

"The Christian and His Fiction," *The Banner*, April 22, 1949.

"Commercial Journalism," *The Banner*, September 9, 1949. (Reproduced in *Covenanter Witness*, November 30, 1949.)

"We Missed an Opportunity," *The Banner*, November 11, 1949.

"Poet and Public," *The Calvin Forum*, December, 1949.

"Notes on Novel Reading," *The Banner*, February 17, 1950.

"The Indefeasible Title of Conquest," *The Banner,* June 30, 1950.

" 'Interests' and Education," *The Reformed Journal,* March, 1951.

"Liberalism and Dogma," *The Reformed Journal,* March, 1951. (Reproduced in *Christian Digest, 1953*).

"The Spirit of '76," Reflections on Calvin's Diamond Jubilee, *The Reformed Journal,* April, 1951.

"Teachers' Salaries," *The Reformed Journal,* May, 1951.

"The Junior College Problem," *The Reformed Journal,* May, 1951.

"Towards a Calvinistic University," *The Reformed Journal,* June, 1951.

"Our University Ideal," *The Reformed Journal,* August, 1951.

"Wordsworth and Hollywood," *The Reformed Journal,* September, 1951.

"Formal Discipline in Our Schools," *The Reformed Journal,* November, 1951.

"Report to Our Readers," *The Reformed Journal,* December, 1951.

"Formal Discipline Reaffirmed," *The Reformed Journal,* January, 1952.

"Eccentric Religion," *The Reformed Journal,* February, 1952.

"A Vital Language," *The Reformed Journal,* March, 1952.

"The Peril of Jargon," *The Reformed Journal,* April, 1952.

"Our Dutch Tradition," *The Reformed Journal,* May, 1952.

"The Contemplative Life," *The Reformed Journal,* August, 1952.

"Calvinism and Art in Our Time," *The Reformed Journal,* September, 1952.

"The Calvin Campaign," *The Reformed Journal* (unsigned), October, 1952.

"Are Junior Colleges the Solution?" *The Reformed Journal,* November, 1952.

"1957," *The Reformed Journal,* December, 1952.

"Junior Colleges Reconsidered," *The Reformed Journal,* February, 1953.

"High School and College," *The Reformed Journal,* March, 1953.

"Eggheads," *The Calvin Forum*, May, 1953.

"Dr. Zylstra's Reply" (to Dr. Hollander's criticism of "Eggheads"). *The Calvin Forum*, October, 1953.

"Teachers Wanted," *The Reformed Journal*, June, 1953.

"The Metrical Versions of the Psalms," *The Reformed Journal*, July, 1953.

"Thoughts for Teachers," *The Reformed Journal*, September, 1954.

"Of Writing Many Books," *The Reformed Journal*, January, 1955.

"Literature and Dogma," *The Reformed Journal*, March, 1955.

"Herman Bavinck," *The Reformed Journal*, September, 1955. Introduction also to *Our Reasonable Faith*, Wm. B. Eerdmans Publishing Co., 1956.

"Hospitality," *The Reformed Journal*, December, 1955.

"Cecil De Boer, the Journalist," *The Reformed Journal*, January, 1956.

"Anti-Liberalism in de huidige Engelse literatuur," *Bezinning*, January, 1957.

BOOK REVIEWS

"A Bad Novel," a review of *Free As the Wind*, by Dacomb Atwood. *The Calvin Forum*, June-July, 1942.

"Prominent Holland-Americans," a review of *Hollanders Who Helped Build America*, by B. H. Vlekke, with an Introduction by Henry Beets. *The Calvin Forum*, August-September, 1942.

"The Royal Dutch Theatre at the Hague," a review of a book by Gerd Aage Gilhoff, *Germanic Review*, XVII, 4 (December, 1942), 299-300.

"Humanism and Christianity," a review of *The Flower of Grass*, by Emile Cammaerts. *The Calvin Forum*, April, 1946.

"Tradition and Literature," a review of *The Classics and the Man of Letters*, by T. S. Eliot. *The Calvin Forum*, January, 1947.

"Plain Talk," a review of *The Art of Plain Talk*, by Rudolph Flesch. *The Calvin Forum*, January, 1947.

"Creative Teaching," a review of *Forever Growing*, by Paul Green. *The Calvin Forum*, January, 1947.

"Patriotic Verse," a review of *My Country*, by Russell W. Davenport. *The Calvin Forum*, March, 1947.

"A Provocative Article," a review of "Calvinism in American Theology Today," in *The Journal of Religion,* XXVII, No. 1 (January, 1947), by Clarence Bouma. *The Calvin Forum,* April, 1947.

"Towards a Responsible Press," a review of *A Free and Responsible Press,* by R. M. Hutchins and others. *The Calvin Forum* (unsigned), May, 1947.

"George Macdonald's Christian Teaching," a review of *George MacDonald: an Anthology,* by C. S. Lewis. *The Calvin Forum,* June-July, 1947.

"For Freedom and for Food," a review of *Landverhuizers,* by P. J. Risseeuw. *The Calvin Forum,* October, 1947.

"The Anatomy of Bewilderment," a review of *The Pawn,* by Bert Landheer. *The Calvin Forum,* November, 1947.

"Classics of Devotion," a review of *Doctor Johnson's Prayers,* edited by Elton Trueblood. *The Calvin Forum,* January, 1948.

"Lovelessness," a review of *Black Bethlehem,* by Lettice Cooper. *The Calvin Forum,* April, 1948.

"Calvin's Works," a review of *Calvin's Commentaries. The Calvin Forum,* May, 1948.

" 'Religious' Fiction," a review of *No Trumpet Before Him,* by Nelia Gardner White. *The Calvin Forum,* June-July, 1948.

"Comfort in Desolation," a review of *Cry the Beloved Country,* by Alan Paton. *The Calvin Forum,* June-July, 1948.

"A Tragedy of Pity," a review of *The Heart of the Matter,* by Graham Greene. *The Calvin Forum,* August-September, 1948.

"Dutch Poetry in Translation," a review of *Coming After,* by Adriaan J. Barnouw. *The Calvin Forum,* October, 1948.

"A Country Report," a review of *The Home Place,* by Wright Morris. *The Calvin Forum,* October, 1948.

"The Criticism of Poetry," a review of *Points of View,* by T. S. Eliot. *The Calvin Forum,* January, 1949.

"A Gift Volume," a review of *A Golden Treasury of Psalms and Prayers for All Faiths,* by Peter Pauper Press. *The Calvin Forum,* June-July, 1949.

"Worship and Work," a review of *The Cloud of Unknowing. The Calvin Forum,* June-July, 1949.

"Dogma and Life," a review of *Creed or Chaos?* by Dorothy Sayers. *The Calvin Forum,* August-September, 1949.

"An Historical Chronicle," a review of *A Land I Will Show Thee* by Marian M. Schoolland. *The Calvin Forum,* August-September, 1949.

"Comedy," a review of *The Lively Pilgrim,* by Bastian Kruithof. *The Calvin Forum,* January, 1951.

"His Gorge Rises," a review of *The T. S. Eliot Myth,* by Rossell Hope Robbins. *The Calvin Forum,* April, 1952.

"Two Novels," a review of *Kingdom Within* and *Too Late the Phalarope. The Reformed Journal,* October, 1953.

"The Religious Situation," a review of *Modern Uncertainty and Christian Faith,* by G. C. Berkouwer. *The Reformed Journal,* January, 1954.

"The Craft of Fiction," a review of *A Writer's Diary,* edited by Leonard Woolf. *The Calvin Forum,* August-September, 1954.

"Liberalist Dogma," a review of Kathleen Nott's *The Emperor's Clothes. The Calvin Forum,* August-September, 1954.

"From Atheism to Christianity," a review of *Surprised by Joy,* by C. S. Lewis. *The Reformed Journal,* March, 1956.

LETTERS

"Letters from New Guinea," *The Calvin Forum,* October, 1944.

"Letters from the Philippines," *The Calvin Forum,* February, 1945.

"A Letter from Japan," *The Calvin Forum,* December, 1945.

PAGEANT

A Tree of Life, a Pageant depicting in word and symbol the history of Calvin College and Seminary on the occasion of her Diamond Jubilee. March, 1951.

BOOKS TRANSLATED FROM THE DUTCH

Christ in His Suffering, by Klaas Schilder. Wm. B. Eerdmans Publishing Co., 1938.

Christ On Trial, by Klaas Schilder. Wm. B. Eerdmans Publishing Co., 1939.

Christ Crucified, by Klaas Schilder. Wm. B. Eerdmans Publishing Co., 1940.

Talks With Gabriel, a novel by Arjen Miedema. Wm. B. Eerdmans Publishing Co., 1950.

The Epistles of Paul to the Churches of Galatia, by Herman N. Ridderbos. Wm. B. Eerdmans Publishing Co., 1956.

Our Reasonable Faith, by Herman Bavinck. Wm. B. Eerdmans Publishing Co., 1956.